Film, Music, Memory

Cinema and Modernity

EDITED BY TOM GUNNING

Film, Music, Memory

Berthold Hoeckner

The University of Chicago Press
Chicago and London

The University of Chicago Press, Chicago 60637
The University of Chicago Press, Ltd., London

Published 2019
Printed in China

28 27 26 25 24 23 22 21 20 19   1 2 3 4 5

ISBN-13: 978-0-226-64961-0 (cloth)
ISBN-13: 978-0-226-64975-7 (paper)
ISBN-13: 978-0-226-64989-4 (e-book)
DOI: https://doi.org/10.7208/chicago/9780226649894.001.0001

Library of Congress Cataloging-in-Publication Data

Names: Hoeckner, Berthold, author.
Title: Film, music, memory / Berthold Hoeckner.
Description: Chicago : University of Chicago Press, 2019. | Includes index.
Identifiers: LCCN 2019018466 | ISBN 9780226649610 (cloth) | ISBN 9780226649757 (paperback) | ISBN 9780226649894 (ebook)
Subjects: LCSH: Motion picture music—History and criticism. | Memory in motion pictures.
Classification: LCC ML2075 .H615 2019 | DDC 781.5/42—dc23
LC record available at https://lccn.loc.gov/2019018466

♾ This paper meets the requirements of ANSI/NISO Z39.48-1992 (Permanence of Paper).

Contents

Foreword

The Same Old Tune, but with a Different Meaning

TOM GUNNING

Berthold Hoeckner's *Film, Music, Memory* offers more than a nuanced and highly original discussion of the way film music shapes our experience of specific movies, although it certainly does that. Hoeckner demonstrates that the visuality of cinema and the acoustic nature of film music create a truly modern representation of human memory. In recent decades a number of fine scholars have offered major revisions to the history and the aesthetics of film music, areas previously neglected by both film historians and musicologists. Hoeckner benefits from these pioneering studies but goes further. He lays the foundation of a truly symbiotic account of the way film music forges an intimate relation to film's visual style and narrative patterns and themes. This is more than simply tracing how musical themes correspond to the moods or actions of narrative films. Hoeckner probes how this intimate fusion of film narrative and music affects us as viewers. We assume that film music underscores (or even manufactures) the emotions of the film story it accompanies. But Hoeckner pursues more subterranean pathways. He shows how film scores not only signify or evoke memories, but lead us as viewers/auditors into acts of recollection—of earlier moments, the reaches of a character's memory, and our own sense of the call of the past.

In this archeology of film listening and viewing, Hoeckner sketches a theory of an optical-acoustic unconscious, a counterpart and partner of the optical unconscious Walter Benjamin found operating in film and photography. As a historian of early cinema, I have often been fascinated by the initial statement Thomas Edison, inventor of the phonograph, issued as he embarked on his research into motion pictures. Edison declared in his patent caveat that his new invention would "do for the eye what the phonograph had done for the ear." And what was that, exactly? Edison didn't elaborate on his statement, but our subsequent experience of his inventions tells us they do a lot more than simply record sounds and moving images. The temporal welding together of sound and image that defines most movies opened not only a new modern aesthetics but, as Benjamin understood, a means of grasping the nature of modern experience. But as often happens in film studies, the investigation of sound has lagged behind visual analysis. Hoeckner helps correct this prejudice. We might say that Hoeckner does for the ear what Benjamin did for the eye.

For all his informed subtlety in the reading of film scores, Hoeckner's true subject, I believe, lies in a profound plumbing of the nature of technological memory, that memory which resides outside human bodies. Already in antiquity, Plato warned about the deleterious effect writing might have on human memory. Memory, he wrote in *Phaedrus*, would no longer be responsible for the preservation of culture and would atrophy. The growth of artificial memory has renewed suspicion that technical cultures of recording may undermine living memory. But, moving beyond that simple dichotomy between living and technical memory, Hoeckner demonstrates that the technological is also the extension of the human, and that especially in the realm of aesthetics it can both help us understand how we think and feel, and shape it in new ways. Memory, in Hoeckner's critical commentaries, never becomes a preexistent subject that music simply helps cinema to portray. Rather, by activating the optical-acoustic unconscious, film music works on us, triggering processes of memory that infuse the moving image.

But if Hoeckner's theory of the imbrication of film music and memory provides new tools for our understanding not only of cinema but of modern memory, it is perhaps his role as critic that is most impressive in this book. Criticism seeks out the specific and unique in individual texts, guided by more general concepts and theories. The value of Hoeckner's general concepts is demonstrated by the insights they generate into individual films. His case studies, ranging from Hollywood classics such as *Letter from an Unknown Woman*, *Penny Serenade*, and *I Remember Mama* to more recent titles like *Little Voice*, *Sleepless in Seattle*, and *The Purple Rose of Cairo*, uncover unexpected layers of complexity in their seemingly seamless summoning of emotions and memory. I have often been amazed at Hoeckner's ability to uncover layers of association in films I had basically dismissed. Yet his critical analysis is less about establishing the value of a film than showing how the processes of popular storytelling weave together the deepest layers of our mental and emotional lives. Hoeckner shows that *We Bought a Zoo* can be as revealing about how memory works as an art house classic like Chris Marker's *La Jetée*.

This a work that both evokes our fond memories of movies and demands concentrated attention to the means by which such memories are created through the intertwining of music and story, time and image. Hoeckner takes us on quite a journey, and makes sure we hear tunes that will keep us going on our way.

Introduction

Film has shaped modern culture in part by changing its cultures of memory. This book demonstrates that this change has rested in no small measure on the mnemonic powers of music. We remember music, but music also remembers: events and people, ideas and emotions, traditions and identities. With the advent of cinema, music became involved in a new technology of audiovisual memory, placing cultural knowledge in individual and collective memory. This new technology is part of what Bernard Stiegler has called "tertiary memory," which results from all forms of recording.[1] With the capacity to reproduce temporal objects in sound recording and film, technology advanced a novel mode of exteriorizing memory. Compared to acts of remembrance tied to the human body and subject to its limitations, cinema could store the past and reproject it in ways that contributed to new forms of cultural consciousness. Throughout this book, I will demonstrate how film music shaped these forms not only through memory in film but also through memory of film.

Venturing into the domain of cultural history, I follow a trend in the scholarship on film sound that James Buhler, invoking Francesco Casetti, has recently compared to the disciplinary evolution of film studies from traditional ontological and methodological approaches toward a "field paradigm" concerned with "novel interpretation over systematic theory."[2] To be sure, systematic approaches continue to provide an ever more nuanced understanding of film music's role in the soundtrack, in cinematic narration, and in the audiovisual experience of the spectator.[3] While recent research in the field has made forays into new areas, ranging from gender studies to media archeology, historical research on the production and reception of film sound has never abated.[4] My book is not only indebted to this scholarship—its ideas, its terminology, its detail—but shares its longstanding interest in films that do historical work as aesthetic objects that warrant and reward close reading.

My main focus is *representations of memory* in American and European cinema. While most films invoke memory in some form—a flashback episode, a plot affected by the past, a story told in retrospect—many are explicitly about memory: an amnesic character, a traumatic event, a surge of nostalgia.[5] As the history of cinema unfolded, moreover, films began to remember their own history through quotations, remakes, and stories about earlier modes of filmmaking. While many cultural forms are recursive, these moments of medium self-consciousness are telling expressions of how cinema has imagined its role in the formation of cultural memory. Music has long been integral to cultures of remembrance—for example, when resounding in rituals of public commemoration or when serving as a private memento. But once music became an essential element of cinema, it facilitated storytelling through recurring themes and helped to conjure up other worlds; in doing so, film music also entered cultural memory as the sound of bygone eras. While some cultural historians have regarded representation as a social construction of reality, cinematic representations of music-induced memory have created this reality in multiple layers and as such are part of what Susan Radstone and Katharine Hodgkin have called "regimes of memory."[6] For example, the music that triggers the flashback of a character in a movie may later trigger a spectator's flashback to the film itself, along with the circumstances of its viewing. The soundtrack of *Forrest Gump* (1994), whose eponymous hero recounts American history from the 1950s to the 1980s, was intimately familiar to audience members who had grown up during this period, but its music is also now remembered by younger viewers, added, by way of the film, to the soundtrack of their lives.

Storage, Retrieval, Affect

My book does not follow or fashion a historical trajectory. Instead, it offers a repertory of phenomena and concepts that demonstrate how music contributes to cinematic representations of memory in ways that are historically specific yet seem to resurface in changing historical contexts. Its seven chapters are grouped into three parts, which parse music's role in enduring dimensions of memory: storage, retrieval, and affect.

Part 1 focuses on matters of storage that emerge at the intersection of mental and material processes: mnemonic techniques internal to the human body and technologies of an external recording apparatus. The slippage between the two is a frequent topic in films where the creation of memories is central to the plot. Chapter 1, "Record Recollections," traces the transition from preserving autobiographical memories in the musician's body to storing them on shellac and vinyl. George Stevens's *Penny Serenade* (1941) is exemplary in that it showcased the fusion of photograph and phonograph into a new apparatus—the phono-photograph—that could conserve the past visually in musical recordings as memory objects. Chapter 2, "Tertiary Rememories," addresses the fears about the socioeconomic consequences of memory technology, as literalized in Omar Naïm's *The Final Cut* (2004)—a futuristic film about a brain implant that saves all sensory input as a video file, to be edited after a person's death for a "rememory service." This process problematizes Stiegler's idea of how the "retentional finitude" of human bodies may be overcome in a transductive symbiosis with technology. If exteriorized memory holds out the promise that cinema is life, it falls to music's temporality to fulfill that promise.

The three chapters of part 2 revolve around music's role in cinematic modes of retrieval. Chapter 3, "Double Projections," theorizes a phenomenon that proliferated when the use of preexisting music for film accompaniment during the silent era distracted viewers, who complained that excerpts from well-known operas called up specific scenes on their mental screen. Although the clash of internal and external projections was initially experienced as disruptive, it spawned a new mode of audiovisual intertextuality, eventually including the recall of film within film by means of music. Catering to a growing constituency of cinephiles and audiophiles, these intertexts take on an important function in the high modernist cinema of Alexander Kluge and Jean-Luc Godard, whose extended montages often draw on well-known music to involve viewers in what I call critical interferences and formal synchronicities between memory image and screened image. Turning to related practices in vernacular modernism, chapter 4, "Auratic Replays," deals with films such as Woody Allen's *The Purple Rose of Cairo* (1985) and Nora Ephron's *Sleepless in Seattle* (1993), whose main protagonists are habitual spectators who watch their favorite movies repeatedly, giving rise to their reenactment, with music sometimes conjuring up memorable scenes to be replayed "in real life." Chapter 5, "Panoramic Flashbacks," considers the popular notion of the quasi-cinematic recall of one's entire life from the perspective of death: seen as embedded flashbacks or as frame-tale narrations, or both, as in Max Ophül's 1948 *Letter from an Unknown Woman*. Here, music enters the soundtrack of modern life as a souvenir of an encounter, a sign of an obsession, a source of an emotion.

The focus on cinematic accounts of affect in part 3 extends the book's forays into larger social concerns, where music functions as a cue to replaying traumatic memories or is deployed as a means to secure affective attachments. Chapter 6, "Freudian Fixations," draws new connections between the parallel histories of psychoanalysis and film in the figure of the musician, who—not unlike a shell-shocked soldier—exemplifies how traumatic events became fixed within a victim's mind and can be treated by reliving them in a cathartic cure. Portraits of the (often female) performer as a medium for retaining and transmitting childhood trauma abound, for example, the pianist in Compton Bennett's *The Seventh Veil* (1945) and the singer in Mark Herman's *Little Voice* (1998). These case studies testify not only to the persistence of psychoanalysis in the cinematic imagination, but also to the enduring appeal of Freudian models to explain the workings of memory in media technology and culture. In contrast to these stories about trauma, filmic recollections of positive, often nostalgic, childhood memories have contributed vital aesthetic glue to the social fabric in the aftermath of war and violence. Chapter 7, "Affective Attachments," studies two flashback narrations, each told by a daughter reminiscing about a parent who became formative in the creation of trust—economic trust and racial trust, respectively. In George

Stevens's *I Remember Mama* (1948), a mother manages the budget of an immigrant family in early twentieth-century San Francisco, fostering trust in the banking system; in Robert Mulligan's *To Kill a Mockingbird* (1962), an empathetic Southern lawyer defends an innocent black man in the 1930s, trying to instill trust in the legal system. In both films, music underwrites the affective attachment between child and parent as an antecedent to generalized trust, and also fosters viewers' trust in the truthfulness of the cinematic memoir.

The Optical-Acoustic Unconscious

Trust in cinematic recollection—as sustained by music—calls for an overarching conception of the relation between film, music, and memory. I develop such a conception from a passage found in a short essay about Proust discovered in Walter Benjamin's *Nachlass*:

> Concerning the *mémoire involuntaire*: not only do its images appear without being called up; rather, they are images we have never seen before we remember them. . . . Yet these images, developed in the darkroom of the lived moment, are the most important we shall ever see. One might say that our most profound moments have been equipped—like those cigarette packs—with a little image, a photograph of ourselves. And that "whole life" which, as they say, passes through the minds of people who are dying or confronting life-threatening danger is composed of such little images. They flash by in as rapid a sequence as the booklets of our childhood, precursors of the cinematograph, in which we admired a boxer, a swimmer, or a tennis player.[7]

Here Benjamin broaches the central concern of my book—albeit by focusing on vision and not (yet) on sound. He posits an affinity between *mémoire involuntaire* and photography because they share the mechanism of a recording apparatus: a sensory stimulus—like Proust's famous madeleine—calls up earlier events automatically and with unfailing precision. As such, photography can make us privy to something we have never seen—something once developed "in the darkroom of the lived moment."

This astounding formulation points to a phenomenon Benjamin called the *optical unconscious*. Miriam Hansen has shown how this phenomenon was introduced in his "Little History of Photography" (1931), which asserted that the discovery of the optical unconscious through photography was akin to the discovery of the instinctual unconscious through psychoanalysis.[8] For Benjamin, photography and film could reveal something that would otherwise not be visible due to the limits of our perceptual apparatus. A camera can arrest the still image of a jumping body in midair; a projector can render movement in slow motion; a close-up can show a detail impossible to discern with the naked eye. Two facets of the optical unconscious are critical: first, "it broadly refers to the idea that the apparatus is able to capture, store, and release aspects of reality previously inaccessible to the unarmed human eye," and second, it "refers to the psychic projection and involuntary memory triggered in the beholder as it assumes something encrypted in the image that nobody was aware of at the time of exposure."[9] Both facets are embedded in the above passage, which regards involuntary memory as a quasi-photographic mechanism for the recording, storage, and replay of experiences that remain unconscious at the instant of exposure, but may become conscious at a later moment of replay. Benjamin added a new aspect to the optical unconscious in the third version of his seminal essay "The Work of Art in the Age of Its Technological Reproducibility." Just as Freud's *The Psychopathology of Everyday Life* (1901) had "isolated and made analyzable things which had previously floated unnoticed on the broad stream of perception," so had cinema given us "a similar deepening of apperception throughout the entire spectrum of optical—and now also auditory—impressions."[10] In adding the auditory dimension, Benjamin was likely responding to Theodor W. Adorno, who had leveled a lengthy critique at the second version of his essay. But Benjamin did not develop this domain in any detail.

The idea for my book originated with the insight that the optical unconscious and what Robert Ryder has described as an acoustic unconscious can be combined toward what I call the *optical-acoustic unconscious*.[11] In a nutshell, I propose that the addition of sound has enabled film to capture, store, and release aspects of reality previously inaccessible to our audiovisual sensorium. Music, especially, can make us conscious of something in the cinematic experience that—to vary Benjamin's formulation—we seem to have never experienced before we remember. Invariably, sound and music contribute to our perception of the image: the sound of crickets in a landscape at dusk, the singing of workers marching in protest, or elegiac strings expressing the sorrows of an abandoned lover. Combined, auditory and visual stimuli enter into a perceptual unit—a phenomenon that Michel Chion described so elegantly with the neologism "synchresis," a portmanteau of synchronism and synthesis.[12] Sound, whether part of the world depicted or added as a form of commentary, *alters* the image by making viewers conscious of something they might otherwise not notice. The sound of crickets may provide a sense of humidity in the air; singing may transmit the energy of the workers; the elegy may give voice to heartbreak.

What is more, sound and music can *store* images and serve as a cue for *retrieving* them. The crickets may bring back the landscape, the singing conjure up the workers, the elegy recall the feeling of loss. In this sense, the optical-acoustic unconscious points to a medium at work within a medium: sound—and especially music—can function as a recording and playback device for "images we have never seen before we remember." Here the optical-acoustic unconscious taps into the similarity between memory and imagination, considered by the psychologist Hugo Münsterberg to be concomitant aspects of cinema as early as 1916. For music does not just recall images—in doing so, it appears to generate them, suggesting that the past is not merely recreated (or reprojected) but also newly created (or projected). If psychoanalytical conceptions of film have generally assumed the need to hide the cinematic apparatus, filmic representations of audiovisual memory often draw attention to its mode of production.[13] In this regard, the optical-acoustic unconscious connects to James Lastra's notion (originating with Rick Altman) of "representational technology" as something historically contingent, that is, as grounded in what Mary Ann Doane has called the medium's changing "material heterogeneity."[14]

Dancing Shadows

A recent example may illustrate how the optical-acoustic unconscious links representational technologies with representational forms and practices and as such serves as a primer for the more elaborate case studies in subsequent chapters. The scene in question is from *We Bought a Zoo* (2011), a family movie directed by Cameron Crowe and based on the 2008 memoir of the same title by Benjamin Mee. The film tells the somewhat corny story of Ben (Matt Damon), who, recently widowed, seeks a new beginning for himself and his two children by moving to the countryside and buying a house that comes with an animal park in dire need of renovation. Ben struggles both to reopen the zoo, with the help of its manager, Kelly (Scarlett Johansson), and to get through to his troubled teenage son, whose distress is triggered by the decline of the zoo's aging tiger. It is only after his son accepts the tiger's impending death that Ben is able to do the work of mourning his wife.

Crowe conveys Ben's own acceptance in two poignant scenes, fifteen minutes apart, during the second half of the film. The first follows his unsuccessful attempt to feed the tiger. That night, Ben sits at the kitchen table with his Macbook. The camera cuts to the screen, where it shows him opening an iPhoto album with a snapshot of his wife. Softly, one hears the beginning of "Sinking Friendships" from the 2010 album *Go* by Jónsi Birgisson (the guitarist and vocalist for the Icelandic post-rock band Sigur Rós), who contributed several songs as well as shorter theme music to the film's soundtrack. As the volume increases ever so slightly, Ben makes the photo of his wife full-screen, then moves the cursor to the advance arrow in the upper right hand corner; there are forty-one pictures in the album. Shot and reverse-shot follow—Ben looking at his wife and her "looking back." Then a shot of the cursor, still hovering over

Figure 0.1 Four pics (out of 41) from the iPhoto album Ben keeps as a memory of his wife.

the arrow, undecided. Then a close-up of Ben's uneasy face. Frustrated, he takes off his reading glasses and closes the laptop. The music stops.

The second scene comes after Ben and his son reconcile over the tiger's imminent death. Once again, Ben sits down with his laptop, this time on the kitchen floor, and now he runs the iPhoto slideshow. An extraordinary two-and-a-half-minute sequence follows, singled out by reviewers as the film's most memorable moment. With "Sinking Friendships" now dominating the soundtrack at full volume, the sequence combines two 75-second segments, from the beginning and the ending of the song, seamlessly cutting from the last line of the first iteration of the pre-chorus ("Wishes overdue are well saved in locks / Wishes overdue . . .") to the second iteration of the chorus ("No one knows you, till it's over / You know no one true, till it's over"). What makes this elision so effective is how it allows the music to align with the two segments of the visual sequence. In the first, we see Ben watching the slideshow with photos of his wife and children (see figure 0.1).

These pics, from a black-and-white wedding portrait to photos of

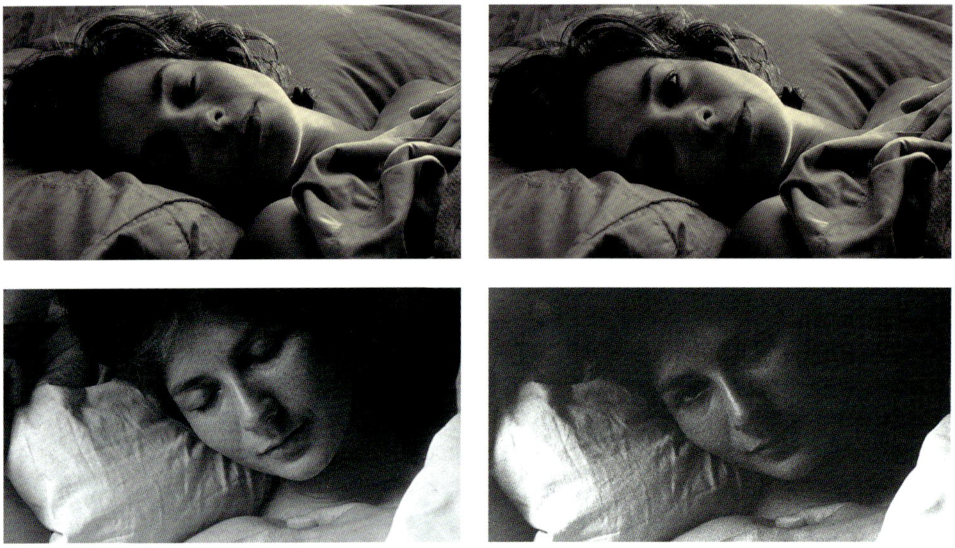

Figure 0.2
From photo to film: Ben's wife comes alive, opening her eyes (*top*), quoting a similar sequence from *La Jetée* (*bottom*).

young children, are family memories—random snapshots of life captured with all its contingencies: a Polaroid of Ben's wife taken in winter, a photo of her left on a table during the holiday season. All are photos of photos. Preserved in iPhoto, they attest to a change of materiality and platform, while exhibiting new modes of production and reception. This self-conscious nesting of media technologies—a film showing a digital image of a photographic print—points to a future anterior that Roland Barthes saw in all photography, namely the sense that a person depicted is subject to future death, just as the moment of capture belongs inexorably to the past. This sense emerges when Ben watches the slideshow, welling up as his memories flood back, while music and lyrics give voice to his catharsis: "We're swimming in the blue . . . My eyes are soaked all way through . . . I'm singing a sad tune / Is this song to you?" But the pre-chorus suggests that there is more to be done, that the "wishes overdue . . . well saved in locks" must be unlocked, fully.

And now, just as the music seems to take a deep breath before launching into the chorus, something astonishing happens with a black-and-white photo of Ben's wife lying on her bed: she opens her eyes and starts breathing (see figure 0.2). This startling shot is a quotation of an iconic moment in Chris Marker's *La Jetée* (1962), an influential science-fiction film about time travel notorious for being narrated in voiceover with only black-and-white still photographs—except once, when a sleeping woman, shown on her bed in eleven slowly dissolving stills, suddenly opens her eyes to look at the camera for a few seconds as if called to life by the only instance of seemingly synchronized source sound: chirping birds.[15]

Crowe's quotation of Marker seems made for the optical-acoustic unconscious. *La Jetée* tells the story of a man who, as a boy, had seen a man die on a jetty of Orly Airport while running toward a woman, her face being the only thing he remembers from the time before the nuclear war that broke out soon after. Now living underground as a captive in a post-apocalyptic world, he is used by scientists experimenting with time travel for survival. They send him back to the past because, unlike other prisoners, he possesses a strong, if vague, memory image, of the moment on the jetty, that might enable him to stay for a while. Traveling back in time, he falls in love with a woman; returning to the present, he finds out he is to be killed by the scientists. When people from the future contact him to help him escape to the future, he asks them instead to return him to the world of his childhood, where he hopes to meet the woman who might await him. And so he finds himself at the jetty on the day in his childhood, assuming that the boy he once was will be there as well. Looking for the woman's face at the end of the pier, he notices a scientist from the underground camp and suddenly realizes that the man he saw killed is himself.

La Jetée dramatizes the predicament of multiple temporalities in photography—akin to what Deleuze called "sheets of the past," which are present in the time image. For Barthes the nature of the medium was a matter of life and death: "By attesting that the object has been real, the photograph surreptitiously induces belief that it is alive . . . but by shifting this reality to the past ('this-has-been'), the photograph suggests that it is already dead."[16] Marker's story of time travel anticipated Barthes's sense of the future anterior: the boy's vague recollection of the woman's face is inseparable from his memory of the man's death. *La Jetée* stages this moment in terms of the optical unconscious: the "little image, a photograph of ourselves" is "developed in the darkroom of the lived moment." The boy has never properly seen this image before remembering it. As the narrating voiceover suggests at the beginning of the film, "Nothing tells memories from ordinary moments. Only afterwards do they claim remembrance on account of their scars. That face which was to be a unique image of peacetime to carry with him for the whole wartime: he often wondered if he had ever seen it."

La Jetée further explores the possibility of multiple temporalities in an allusion to the famous redwood scene of *Vertigo*, where Scotty and Madeleine marvel at a cross-section of a thousand-year-old tree whose growth rings are the record of different times, all tangible in the present. The *Vertigo* reference carries over into Terry Gilliam's *12 Monkeys* (1995), which reworks the austere modernism of Marker's film into a Hollywood-style thriller. Shortly before the ending, the time-traveling man (Bruce Willis) and the woman (Madeleine Stowe) visit a movie theater during a screening of Hitchcock's *The Birds*—a film the man insists he saw as a child. Fleeing their pursuers, the woman transforms herself into a blonde (like *Vertigo*'s Judy changing back into Madeleine) and the man into the mustache- and wig-wearing person he suddenly remembers having seen

Figure 0.3 From memory image to moving image: after seeing his wife in a photo open her eyes and start breathing, Ben looks at a snapshot of her and their children, which turns, when the drums join the song's chorus, into live action (*above*). The scene appears to take place in the kitchen, before his very eyes, being reflected in the lenses of his spectacles (*right*).

as a boy being shot at the airport. The moment of recognition in the foyer of the theater is underscored by Bernard Herrmann's Wagnerian cue "Scene d'amour" from *Vertigo*, as if wafting over from the auditorium.[17] Inasmuch as Trevor Duncan's Mancini-like score sutured the frozen frames of *La Jetée*, its limpid "lite"-ness was also a distant echo of Herrmann's Tristanesque fervor, which culminated with Scottie's desire to remake Judy in order to revive Madeleine.

Music links these layers of the cinematic intertexts by lending life to the lovers' utopian return to the past, as if they could resist the inevitability of death. In *La Jetée*, the escape from the present culminates in a single instance of presence. Crowe's iPhoto sequence seizes upon this one moment of live action because it releases the melancholy photographic stills into the moving pictures of cathartic mourning. Just as the crescendo of bird sounds seems to give voice to he man's desire to awaken the woman, the buildup of Jónsi's vocals playing behind the slide show appears to

unlock Ben's "overdue wish" to replay the past. The arrival of the chorus coincides with his wife opening her eyes, matched by a close-up of his, teary and blinking, as he faces snapshots of his family frolicking outside on a summer day. Then something even more striking happens: when the drums join the chorus, their powerful beats free her from the photographic capture of the very moment where, with her hands already in midair, she was about to jump up from the ground (figure 0.3). Looking up from the computer screen, Ben now sees his wife take that jump and run around with their children in the kitchen—until the song dies down.

This is a moment where music transforms the optical unconscious into the optical-acoustic unconscious. Jónsi's song short-circuits the deadly logic of photography's future anterior. Unleashing the full force of the chorus, the onset of the drums sets into motion the lively leaps and the frisky sounds of the family that had been frozen into snapshots. Music thus shatters the shackles of "the photograph's immobility," which Barthes saw as the source of a "perverse confusion" between "the Real and the Live."[18] At the song's climax, live action cuts through the neo-Lacanian opposition between the mortifying gaze and the vivifying voice.[19] Unfolding in the here and now, music unties the time suspended in the photograph.

Hansen notes that Benjamin wavered between two extremes of repetition, negative and positive: "one, Nietzsche's eternal return congealed in the law of the commodity . . . ; the other, dialectically embedded in the first, repetition as the striving for a past happiness that Proust pursued to the point of asphyxiation—a repetition that Deleuze has taught us to read as the *production* of that past in the very movement of repetition."[20] Both *La Jetée* and *We Bought a Zoo* are caught in this oscillation, but from opposite ends. If Marker framed his story with inescapable death at the confluence of past and present, Crowe seizes on the possibility of coming back to life at this very juncture. The man's memory of his own undoing on the jetty is undone by Ben's wife returning from the realm of shadows to dance before his eyes—a spectacle reflected in the lenses of his spectacles. Both times, sound and music turn photographic stills and snapshots into live action, now flashing by "in as rapid a sequence as the booklets of our childhood, precursors of the cinematograph." Without the chirping birds and music's "temporalizing power," the time-traveling lover and mourning husband would not have remembered.[21] By playing a song behind a slideshow Ben activates a feature built into Apple's application, reaching deep into the archeology of audiovisual media to such representational technologies as early twentieth-century illustrated song, whose slides were vivified by a singer. Then and now, the optical-acoustic unconscious intuits how music seems to possess a magic force that makes us see and remember otherwise, for it breathes life into the memory image, making it move.

Storage

CHAPTER ONE

Record Recollections

> Records have turned out to be special modes of storing history. On certain records by Mingus, Coltrane, or Billie Holiday, Sun Ra's *Heliocentric Worlds*, in some piano concertos by Mozart, in many early pieces of rock, later with Dylan, Hendrix, and on many other records are stored certain feelings I had while listening in such a precise way that I am not satisfied to call this simply "memories." . . . Those records recorded something when playing; they did not just play back. The record, pick-up, speakers, and receiving ear together with streams of feelings appear to have created a recording device that stores these streams of feelings. . . . I mean that records function as storage devices for bodily and perceptual states which register the difference between my present and former lives.[1]

A playback device as a recording apparatus integrated with the human body? The cultural historian Klaus Theweleit may have taken his inspiration from the 1880 essay "Memory and Phonography" by Jean-Marie Guyau, who compared how the vibrations of one's voice are inscribed on a metal plate to corresponding processes in the brain:

> It is quite probable that in analogous ways, invisible lines are incessantly carved into the brain cells, which provide a channel for nerve streams. If, after some time, the stream encounters a channel it has already passed through, it will once again proceed along the same path. The cells vibrate in the same way they vibrated the first time; psychologically, these similar vibrations correspond to an emotion or a thought analogous to the forgotten emotion or thought. . . . If the phonographic disk had self-consciousness, it could point out while replaying a song that it remembers this particular song. And what appears to us as the effect of a rather simple mechanism would, quite probably, strike the disk as a miraculous ability: memory.[2]

Much has changed since the days Theweleit listened to vinyl. There are still speakers (often headphones) and ears; there are still streams of emotions and "bodily and perceptual states." But what is largely missing in this age of Pandora and Spotify is the recording as a physical object.

In his study of the phonograph and popular memory in America, William Howland Kenney notes that, regardless of musical style, recordings have functioned as "mnemonic devices."[3] He describes a remarkable survey conducted in 1921 by Thomas A. Edison Inc. that asked Americans in forty-three states to list their favorite recorded tunes, as well as songs they would wish to see added to the catalog. Respondents not only "preferred 'old music well-rendered,' music that 'takes us back to Grandfather days,' tunes that brought 'memories of home,' old tunes that 'take us back to the days of childhood'"; they also reported that replaying recordings was a way of remembering deceased family members.[4] The survey had been created to corroborate findings by psychologists at the Carnegie Institute of Technology, who had devised a study using 135 Edison records, classified into categories ranging from basic or complex emotions ("joy," "wistfulness") to more elaborate rubrics, such as "Stimulate and Enrich Your Imagination" or "Tender Memory."[5] Autobiographical memories proved to be most important, for records could even bring departed loved ones back to life.

When the record became a plot device in cinema, it not only exemplified music's mnemonic powers in general but showcased the record's special ability to record and store the past. A paradigmatic case is the recording of "Melancholy Baby" as used in Fritz Lang's *Scarlet Street* (1945). The film tells the story of Chris (Edward G. Robinson), an unhappily married man with artistic aspirations who is infatuated with a younger woman, Kitty (Joan Bennett). "Melancholy Baby" plays as Kitty's lover, Johnny (Dan Duryea), reads the love letter Chris has written her, and when the needle gets stuck in the groove on the line "I'm in love with you," we sense that something is amiss. Chris rents a swank apartment for Kitty, sets up a studio there, and—after Johnny sells two of his paintings, attracting the attention of a prominent dealer—is pleased when Kitty claims his pictures as her own. One night, Chris enters the apartment. Again, the record is playing and sticks on "in love," and he observes from the hallway as Johnny resets the needle and kisses Kitty. Chris retreats to a bar, haunted by their voices and the sound of the faulty record, and when Kitty, in the following scene, laughs at his proposal that they marry, he kills her with an ice pick. Johnny is charged with the murder, tried, and sentenced to death. After Johnny is executed, Chris returns to his apartment, where the song and voices replaying in his head intensify. That we see no flashback, only Chris's face, tormented by guilt, suggests that Lang was confident viewers had "recorded" the earlier scenes and would now play them back before their inner eyes, as Chris apparently is doing.

In the two films discussed below, musical recordings take on even more explicit roles as plot elements that register the impact of cinema on audiovisual memory. These records store the memories of characters and viewers alike by adding a visual dimension of the recording apparatus described by Theweleit. As a material object, a record may partake in the psychophysical process of memory formation. This process involves the matrix from a recording session in Giuseppe Tornatore's *The Legend of 1900* (1998) and the faulty groove of a 78 in George Stevens's *Penny Serenade* (1941). In both films, a very specific record becomes a musical playback/recording device that illustrates the striking merger of human body and mechanical apparatus and thus epitomizes the momentous shift in the culture of memory brought about by cinema.

Musician as Memory Machine

Tornatore adapted *The Legend of 1900* (*La leggenda del pianista sull'oceano*) from Alessandro Baricco's single-player drama *Novecento: un monologo*.[6] The film tells the story of a fictional pianist (Tim Roth), who is named Novecento ("1900") because he was found that year as an infant on the ocean liner SS *Virginian* by a member of the engine crew. After his adoptive parent dies in an accident, the newly orphaned Novecento grows up to play the piano in the ship's orchestra. As word of his prodigious talent spreads, he is offered a lucrative recording contract, but he cannot bring himself to set foot on land. When the *Virginian*, having served as a hospital and cargo ship during World War II, is finally scuttled and sunk offshore, Novecento goes down with the vessel.

The story is told in a series of flashbacks by Max (Pruitt Taylor Vince), a trumpet player who befriended Novecento during the roaring twenties, when the ship was a hub for the rich and famous, journeying to and from Europe, as well as for the poor and hopeful, emigrating to America. A member of the orchestra, Max witnessed Novecento's extraordinary musical skills firsthand, including his spectacular win against the famous ragtime and jazz pianist Jelly Roll Morton, who had come aboard to challenge him to a piano duel. He watched Novecento walk away from a lucrative deal after a recording session on board, and he saw him fall in love with a girl traveling to America but fail to follow her onto land. The film begins shortly after World War II, when a broke Max tries to sell his trumpet at a music shop in New York. Before parting with his instrument, however, he plays a melody, which catches the attention of the shop owner, who recognizes the tune from a broken record matrix found hidden in a recently acquired piano. As Max recounts Novecento's story, flashbacks alternate with attempts to find and rescue his friend from the *Virginian*, being stripped in the nearby harbor before its final journey. Managing to get on board one last time, he plays the matrix on a portable gramophone. The music lures Novecento out of hiding but fails to bring him to land.

The story of the matrix is an allegory of audiovisual memory at the dawn of the age of mechanical reproduction. As the *Virginian* passes the Statue of Liberty during the opening credit sequence, passengers look ahead to the Manhattan skyline emerging from the mist:

> The one who sees America first—there's one on every ship; and don't be thinking it's an accident, or some optical illusion—it's destiny. Those are people who always have that precise instant stamped on their life.[7]

As Max speaks these words, in voiceover, the camera zooms in on a young man's face and his left eye until we see the skyline in his iris (figure 1.1). The shot reflects—literally—the nature of the cinematic apparatus, whose quasi-photographic imprint is, to recall Benjamin, "developed in the darkroom of the lived moment," making us see "images we have never seen before we remember."[8] Tornatore's film extends the idea to the figure of a machinelike musician, whose photographic memory is essentially phonographic.

One night, the eight-year-old Novecento creates a sensation when he is found at the ballroom piano playing an ethereally beautiful piece, entitled "A Mozart Re-Incarnated" in Ennio Morricone's splendid soundtrack. The mythology of musical prodigies rests in part on their superior memory—the ability to listen to music and replay it at once. Tornatore introduces his wunderkind with the metaphor of the sensory imprint. Drawn to the music resounding from the first-class ballroom, the boy looks at the dancers through the semifrosted glass of the ballroom doors while the orchestra's pianist (as the script has it) "creates a sound Novecento appears to have recognized."[9] A reverse-shot of his eyes

Figure 1.1 First encounter with "America": the skyline of Manhattan first seen by an immigrant (*top*) is "stamped" on his eye (*bottom*).

Figure 1.2 Novecento's first encounter with music. Novecento, as a child, sees a pianist (*top*) and later, as a pianist, "sees" the world in the ocean (*bottom*).

conveys the nexus of photographic and phonographic memory that can reproduce anything he has heard (figure 1.2).

Novecento's command of diverse styles is shown in a sequence that cuts from him playing a riveting ragtime that sends first-class passengers into a crazed dance, to a Chopinesque etude, à la op. 25, no. 2, that mesmerizes steerage-class travelers on the lower deck. There he continues with a slow blues followed by a zesty tarantella, a genre he easily picks up from an Italian passenger beating the rhythm and simulating a melody. Novecento is not just a musical genius but a motion picture accompanist *avant la lettre*. In a 1920 manual for film pianists and organists, Edith Lang and George West note that a "*good memory* is a valuable help to the player," who should not simply "try to memorize certain compositions as a whole" but "especially furnish his storehouse of remembered music with stock phrases and motives, adapted to different moods, so that he can always draw from this library in his head."[10] Since all music can be film music, *Legend* became an opportunity for Morricone to display his extraordinary craft as a film composer—not just his consummate knowledge of art music and popular music, but his encyclopedic memory of film music itself (as we will see shortly). When Max later asks his friend what goes through his mind when hitting the keys, a shot of his eyes superimposed over the ocean suggests that Novecento may be looking at the sea but is watching what is projected on his mental screen. "He traveled," Max explains, "and each time he ended up someplace different."[11] If music makes Novecento see, what he sees makes him play.

Tornatore develops Novecento's film-musical talents in a number of scenes that reveal cinema's roots in precinematic culture. Responding to Max's question "Where do you get it . . . the music?" Novecento improvises four different piano pieces to characterize four different people in the ballroom: theatrical octaves for an aristocratic woman dancing with her young lover; a wistful nocturne for a man haunted by melancholic memories; a titillating tango for "a prostitute . . . thinking about becoming a nun"; and a meandering misterioso for a stowaway hiding in the first-class salon. "He knew how to read people," notes Max, "the signs people carry on them, places, sounds, scents, their land, their story, everything written on them. He would read and, with infinite care, he would catalogue, organize, and make order in that immense map that he was drawing in his mind."[12] Morricone may have cherished the opportunity to have his fictional alter ego shift from the dramatic to the lyrical or from illustration to expression, only to end with a perfectly synchronized pantomime of the stowaway scurrying through the room amid hastily alternating chords and pausing for moments of furtive inspection to a slyly descending chromatic melody. These ad-hoc characterizations are an object lesson in early film accompaniment, where the pianist would play the picture by drawing not only on the practices of program-music but also on the stock gestures of nineteenth-century musical theater.[13]

Novecento's parodies of early film music add to his ambivalence toward the emerging culture of mechanical reproduction, playing out in his piano duel with Jelly Roll Morton, who pioneered the publication of notated jazz pieces. When Morton performs three of them, Novecento counters each, first mocking "Big Fat Ham" with a deliberately childish variant of "Silent Night" and then, moved to tears by Morton's famous tango "The Crave," replaying the tune note-for-note but "faster and in a more passionate way."[14] Finally, Novecento parries Morton's famously difficult "The Finger Breaker" with a *perpetuum mobile* piece played so fast that he can light a cigarette from the burning hot strings—an act of superhuman virtuosity that brings down the house. Yet he is not just a machine, but also a musician with a soul. This is why Tornatore pairs the public spectacle of the piano duel with the intimate recording session of the mysterious matrix, showing Novecento's true aesthetic convictions (see figure 1.3).[15] Here's the description from the screenplay:

Novecento starts improvising at the keyboard while staring ahead as he does habitually.

Suddenly, from one of the portholes, he sees a girl among the many passengers on the ship's deck; she is wiping her face after rinsing herself at one of the water basins. The girl approaches the porthole. She looks at herself in the glass and tidies up her hair. But, because of a strange effect of the light on the glass, she doesn't notice that someone is playing a piano and looking at her insistently on the other side of the window.

There is something magical in the way that girl is examining her eyes and stroking her skinny yet luminous face. Novecento is struck. He keeps looking at her, but without the absent-minded expression as when he is lost in his imaginary journeys. He looks at her as if he is meeting someone that he knows already without remembering who this person is. Gradually the bouncy and well-paced music that he is playing turns into a mysterious and seductive melody, like that face from which he cannot turn his eyes away.

Max and the others don't understand the reason for this transformation, but they are charmed and keep following his hands with astonishment, as if they are wondering where that divine music is coming from. They ignore that Novecento is reading those notes in the eyes of the unknown girl that he is now following as she brings herself to the parapet and, showing only her profile, looks at the horizon. She looks far away with the passion of someone who really knows how to look at the sea, with that ill-concealed trepidation of a daydreamer; this [daydreaming] is exactly what Novecento is doing now, without even realizing it; for the first time he is bringing music out of a feeling that he has never known before.

It is only when this female figure, so full of hope, is about to move that Max notices her, and that Novecento is looking at her. And it is when she is out of sight away from the porthole that Novecento concludes his performance. But he remains immobile, lost in the contemplation of that face which now seems to be forever impressed in his imagination.

The other three clap, moved by the intensity of that melody.[16]

The scene dramatizes the stakes of creating music in the age of technological reproducibility and its impact on audiovisual memory. Note how Novecento's improvisation opens with a rhapsodizing introduction whose toccata-like passagework becomes an instrumental recitative in search of a theme. Just as he discovers the girl, he finds a nocturne-like melody (not unlike Chopin's well-known op. 9, no. 2), which he harmonizes like a pop ballad—a signature of Morricone's style (see figure 1.4). Inspired by the girl, the melody expands with a second iteration that leads to an expressive climax, before drifting away in a short coda.

Noting that "sound film was latent in photography," Walter Benjamin concludes the second section of his artwork essay with a passage he deemed so important that it is italicized variously in the three versions of the essay. I quote it here from the first version because it invokes explicitly the "interpenetration" between reproductions of visual art and the art of film:

The technological reproduction of sound was tackled at the end of the last century. With that, technological reproduction had not only reached a standard that permitted it to turn all traditional works of art into its objects, subjecting their effects to profound changes, but had also captured a place of its own among the artistic processes. Nothing is so illuminating for the study of this standard as the recognition of how its two differing functions—reproduction of the work of art and the art of film—interpenetrate one another.[17]

As a portrait of the girl, Novecento's improvised melody captures the here and now of a unique moment, while its acoustic vibrations cut into the matrix to preserve that moment for a there and then. The interplay between the visual and the auditory broaches the old and the new: as Novecento paints the girl into music, her head is framed by the porthole,

Figure 1.3a "Recorded with Love." During a recording session in steerage with an engineer whose mustache and glasses suggest a fictive cameo of Walter Benjamin (*top*), Novecento sees a girl outside and improvises a melody (*middle*) that becomes a musical portrait of her (*bottom*).

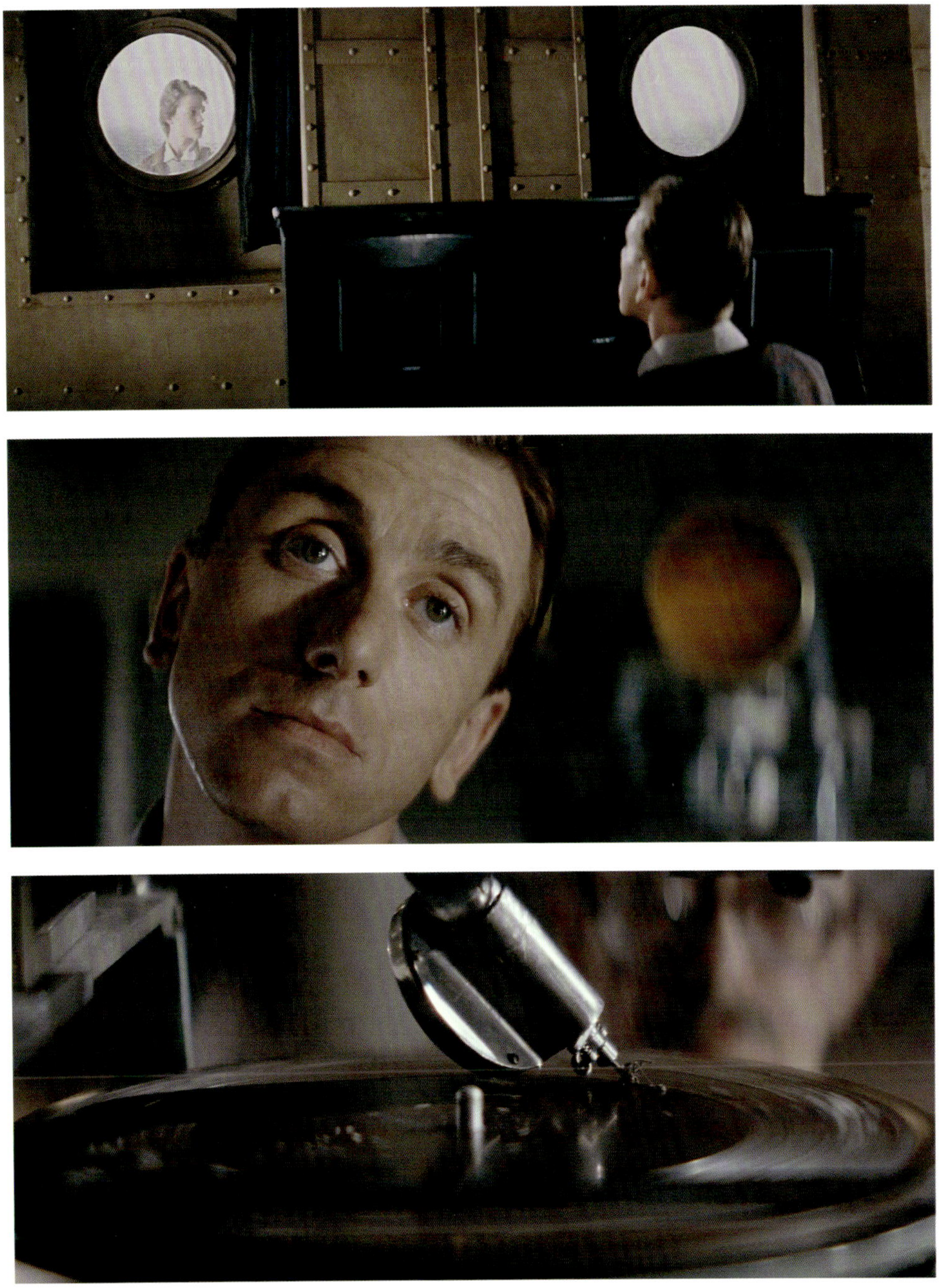

Figure 1.3b The musical portrait of the girl is also a record of Novecento seeing her through the two porthole eyes (*top*), while his musical vision is picked up by the recording horn (*middle*) and written onto a matrix (*bottom*).

Figure 1.4 Novecento's musical portrait, first statement of melody (transcription).

creating the effect of intimate portrait paintings common in the nineteenth century. Shot and reverse-shot suggest how visual and auditory recording devices—ears and eyes—work together or, in Benjamin's formulation, "interpenetrate one another": when his music is played back from the matrix, Novecento keeps looking for the girl in the portholes. How could his melody sound without her? Taken aback by the producer's promise to "print millions of copies," Novecento snatches the matrix and walks off: "My music is not going anywhere without me." His music is the girl, and the girl is his music. Ending Novecento's artistic innocence, the recording session marks his fall from the graces of auratic art. At stake is the very irreproducibility Benjamin described as "unique existence in a particular place . . . that bears the mark of the history to which the work has been subject."[18]

Tornatore plays a little insider's game to illuminate Novecento's predicament. The recording engineer—with his mustache, round glasses, and curly hair—looks suspiciously like Benjamin, a caricature of the very critic who diagnosed the "withering of aura" in the age of technological reproducibility, here serving as the operator of the recording equipment. Confronted with the consequences of modernity, Novecento holds on to the inviolable bond between art and aura. Yet the recording session also enacts the live accompaniment for silent film, where the pianist responds to the screen in real time from the same viewpoint as the audience. When Novecento's musical portrait of the girl migrates into the underscore, the singular performance circulates as a phantasmagoric commodity, recalling this moment for us. Once his music, to use the evocative phrase coined by Robynn Stilwell and James Buhler, crosses the "fantastical gap" from source to score, it enters the realm of the reproducible soundtrack.[19]

Morricone makes this point by playing, like the director, a sort of insider's game. Novecento's nocturne alludes to the musical portrait of a woman created by Stefan Radetzky, the shell-shocked combat pilot, piano virtuoso, and fictional composer of the "Warsaw Concerto" in the 1941 RKO war drama *Dangerous Moonlight* (released as *Suicide Squadron* in the United States), for which British composer Richard Addinsell wrote the score. Stefan meets Carol, an American reporter and his future wife, for the first time in Warsaw during a German air raid in a half-bombed-out building, where he is working on the concerto. Looking at Carol, he suddenly receives an inspiration for its second theme (figure 1.5).[20] The film opens with Stefan, amnesiac after surviving what was presumed to be a suicide mission, banging out random, dissonant chords on the piano, while Carol hums "her" theme to help him recover his memory. The concerto takes Stefan back to that night in Warsaw, and the story unfolds until his near-fatal crash brings him back to the present. The

Figure 1.5 Carol inspires the second theme of Stefan's "Warsaw Concerto" in *Dangerous Moonlight*; it is the theme's reprise in the solo version of the concerto (measures 158–61) to which Ennio Morricone alludes in *The Legend of 1900*.

Figure 1.6 Novecento breaks the record to prevent the music from circulating his first encounter with the girl.

film ends with Stefan playing the second theme and recognizing Carol by recalling their first encounter.

By alluding to the second theme from the "Warsaw Concerto," Morricone references its role of "recording" love at first sight. Yet in the context of the recording session, Novecento's melody also exemplifies music's new function in the age of film as external—tertiary—memory. Although Novecento rejects recording technology, he still makes an unsuccessful attempt to give the matrix to the girl, after which he breaks the record and throws it away (figure 1.6). The music that stays with him on the ship becomes a symbol of romantic interiority and a sign of his monadic existence, floating, unmoored, away from the outside world.

This is why Max fails to lure Novecento to shore. When he plays the matrix on a portable record player in various locations on the stripped vessel, the tinny sound created by the wobbling turntable changes into Novecento's original performance, now resounding from the underscore. The transition from contingent source to transcendent score illuminates the "logic of the trace" that Miriam Hansen locates in the "indexical dimension of aura's relation to the past . . . whose ghostly apparition projects into the present and (to invoke Roland Barthes) 'wounds' the beholder."[21] She cites Benjamin's reflections on the double portrait of the photographer Dauthendey and his fiancée—who later slashed her veins after the birth of their sixth child—to illustrate the "complex temporality in which the past moment encrypted in the photograph speaks to the later beholder of the photographed subject's future":

> No matter how artful the photographer, no matter how carefully posed his subject, the beholder feels an irresistible urge to search such a picture for the tiny spark of contingency, of the here and now, with which reality has (so to speak) seared the character of the image, to find the inconspicuous spot where in the thusness of that long-forgotten moment the future nests so eloquently that we, looking back, may rediscover it.

The "spark of contingency," Hansen explains, could not be revealed by "circumstantial knowledge" about the young woman's later suicide. Instead, the "futurity that has seared the photographic image in the chance moment of exposure" discloses itself to the viewer who scans the image to detect it in her "gaze into the off, past the camera and past her fiancée, absorbed in an 'ominous distance.'"[22] Similarly, Barthes identifies such sparks of contingency in a photograph's *punctum*—any inconspicuous detail that makes the beholder "shudder" by uncovering the catastrophe of time defeated.[23]

What would be that spark of contingency in Novecento's musical portrait of the girl? Where is the "futurity that has seared" the *phonographic record* "in the chance moment of exposure"? Consider how Novecento's impromptu music is both a portrait of the girl and a portrait of the pianist creating that portrait. Most conspicuous in their chance encounter is the beginning of the melody, which marks the moment Novecento notices her in the window. Yet it is the inconspicuous onset of the coda whose sudden quickening of pace in the accompaniment heralds her departure even before she disappears from his sight. To adapt Hansen's formulation, the coda reveals the "complex temporality in which the past moment encrypted in the *recording* speaks to the later beholder of the *recorded* subject's future." In this sense, the coda is the "spark that leaps across time" and thereby gives voice to the "futurity that has seared" the phonographic record, telling us that the girl will leave the ship while Novecento will stay behind with his music. Although he musters the courage to approach her before she disembarks in New York, he fails to give her the matrix wrapped as a gift before they are separated by other passengers pushing her toward the exit. Here the melody of her portrait enters the orchestral underscore, with the coda ending the very instant she sets foot on land. As score detaches itself from score, the soundtrack not only detaches itself from the original scene of recording but also replays Novecento's separation from the girl during that scene.

With his telltale name, Novecento becomes a liminal figure of music, not just lost between land and sea, but also linking two centuries and their shifting modes of mediating memory. By throwing away the matrix, he holds on to the uniqueness of the auratic moment preserved in his own body. Yet the matrix survives, hidden by Max in the grand piano that is later salvaged from the ship's ballroom and ends up in the music store. Its discovery ensures that the legend of Novecento can be told after all. In this sense, the matrix also gives voice to the "futurity that has seared" the cinematic record of our encounter with Novecento, so that it may enter the soundtrack of *our* lives. As something—some *thing*—that can be discarded and recovered, the matrix epitomizes how, in the age of technological reproducibility, the contingency of a recorded memory may become the very condition of its transcendence.

Things to Remember

Several years ago I was searching on Amazon for a DVD of *Maytime* (1937), the most successful of the eight MGM musicals starring Jeanette MacDonald and Nelson Eddy. One review—written when the VHS version was issued a few years earlier—caught my eye, and I reproduce it here, in full and as written:

> My grandmother took me to the Bristol Theatre when i was just a kid for a revival of all these great Jeanette & Nelson films. (in the 50's) I loved them all but "Maytime" was my favorite. I remember feeling really sad and being perplexed with my grandmother crying at the end of the movie. I thought it was sad too but,,,,,. Then years later after my grandmother passed away i saw it again and saw what she saw in this film. It was pure beauty, love, romance, tragidy and reunion of the spirit. I have this film now and each time i watch it i think of that special time with my grandmother. This film will always have that meaning for me and the song "Sweethearts" has always been my favorite song. This might sound mushy to some people but i'm glad i have those wonderful memories of my grandmother thanks to this wonderful film. Just one small piece of advise. Have the tissues ready at the end.[24]

Having grown up during the 1950s and 1960s, the reviewer worked in the entertainment industry and built himself a home movie theater with a gold curtain ("Something that theatres can't be bothered with anymore").[25] This attitude not only testifies to what the cultural historian Svetlana Boym terms "restorative nostalgia"—the desire to return to the past in some form; it also exemplifies the broader relationship between cinema and cultural memory, which Annette Kuhn researched in the 1990s, focusing in part on the shrinking number of fan clubs dedicated to Jeanette MacDonald and Nelson Eddy.[26] If the reviewer's grandmother could have been a member of such a fan club, his own memory of her relies on records, VHS tapes, and DVDs, now increasingly replaced by streaming services. Indeed, Kuhn analyzes her interviews with members of MacDonald & Eddy fan clubs as a nested doubling of represented remembrance in films and actual remembrance of films.

Maytime is special in this regard, for it is a story about musical memory. Its frame-tale narrative is told by Marcia Mornay (MacDonald), a famous soprano who has retired to a small New England town. She had launched her career at the court of Louis Napoleon and fell in love with the poor baritone Paul Allison (Eddy), also an expatriate, from Virginia. But their romance is doomed; Marcia has already pledged to marry her forbidding mentor, Nicolai Nazaroff (John Barrymore). Consistent with the "too-late" trope of melodrama, she and Paul are granted only a single day to declare their love. Their escape to a May Day fair becomes a utopian moment, sealed by the song "Will You Remember"—the only number

Figure 1.7
Maytime: dying in old age, Marcia leaves her body to reunite with Paul, singing "Will You Remember" as on the Mayday they fell in love many years ago.

kept from Sigmund Romberg's 1917 Broadway version of *Maytime* and one that earned MacDonald a gold record. Having embarked on a successful career in Europe, Marcia returns to the United States for a production of *Czaritza* (a fictional opera based on themes from Tchaikovsky's Fifth Symphony), for which Paul is hired as a costar. Nicolai notices the chemistry between them and confronts Marcia after opening night. He grants her request to release her from their marriage but kills Paul in his apartment just as Marcia arrives. Paul dies in her arms. The film ends with Marcia passing away at Maytime, trees blooming around her. A vision of Paul approaches, singing "Will You Remember," and the ghost of Marcia's young self leaves her body to join him in a reprise of the song (figure 1.7).

According to Kuhn, this layering of past and presents is emblematic of fan reception: "Just as one's youthful self does not die as one ages, so the enduring fan's devotion survives the death of its object." To illustrate this sense of "transcendence," she quotes a touching passage one of her informants, Dorris Braithwaite, wrote for the newsletter of the Nelson Eddy Appreciation Society: "Now Nelson is gone and so is my husband. But I play records and videos and they are both with me again and I feel just as young and in love as I was all those years ago."[27] As the spectral image of the young Marcia is summoned by Paul's song, the ending of *Maytime* aligns with the ownership of records and videos that serve as aide-mémoire in projecting this fantastic return of the past. The materiality of those objects matters: it is symptomatic of the larger shift in the culture of memory through the advent of recording technology.

Let me retrace that shift. In the summer for 2010, I used interlibrary loan to order the sheet music of "Will You Remember," published by Schirmer in 1938. While playing at the keyboard through the cardboard-bound copy that arrived from the public library in Aurora, Illinois, I noticed something marginal: a tear on the side of the first page and the tape with which the corner had been fixed (figure 1.8). The damage and the repair called to mind a passage from Bill Brown's essay "Thing Theory":

Figure 1.8a Copy of "Will You Remember" from the Aurora (IL) Public Library. Wear and tear evince the music's thingness.

Figure 1.8b
A second voice is notated on a handwritten insert (*top, showing the ending*), but that second voice had already been notated in the score with pencil (*bottom*).

We begin to confront the thingness of objects when they stop working for us: when the drill breaks, when the car stalls, when the windows get filthy, when their flow within the circuits of production and distribution, consumption and exhibition, has been arrested, however momentarily. The story of objects asserting themselves as things, then, is the story of a changed relation to the human subject and thus the story of how the thing really names less an object than a particular subject-object relation.[28]

While my fingers could feel the wear and tear of the score when turning the pages, the high-resolution image here makes their thingness patent. A scan works like a close-up, which the early film theorist Jean Epstein treasured as cinema's *photogénie*, its animistic capacity for "summoning objects out of the shadows of indifference into the light of dramatic concern."[29] My concern, to be sure, was historical: the copy held by the public library in a medium-sized city of the Midwest had not be checked out for years and now emerged with the help of imaging technology from the shadows of indifference to make visible that which would otherwise remain unnoticed by the historian of culture.

At first sight, mending the worn score merely averts any disruption in the circuit of production and consumption. But folded into the score was also a bifolio of music paper, on which the second voice from the duet sung by MacDonald and Eddy was written out by hand. If fans wanted to act out a scene from *Maytime*—a common practice, according to Braithwaite—they would have needed a second singer. Since that second voice was essential to the reenactment, someone had made an effort to pencil it into the score. For Allan Megill, such markings should not be treated by a historian as a *source* "intended . . . to stand as an account of events" but as a *trace*—that is, as something "remaining from the past that was not made with the intention of revealing the past to us, but [which] simply emerged as part of normal life."[30] Yet those penciled noteheads were not just a trace of past performances; they also appeared like shadows, a visible echo of bygone voices that remain forever unheard.

As a trace, the Aurora copy of "Will You Remember" is not a memory object like the MacDonald and Eddy memorabilia—such as photographs signed "Best Wishes, Nelson Eddy"—that I found at the time on eBay. The score's thingness, as disclosed in the digital close-up, connects with Benjamin's notion of the optical unconscious that understands the new sensory experience of photography as a form of memory. Marveling at how Karl Blossfeldt's stunning magnifications could reveal tiny details of plants, Benjamin noted in his "Little History of Photography" that the medium's "devices of slow motion and enlargement" could uncover "physiognomic aspects, image worlds, which dwell in the smallest things."[31] The unintended index that "sears" the technologically mediated image works like the involuntary memory triggered by sensory experience. Here Benjamin draws not only on Proust but also on Henri Bergson's conception of the relation between sensory perception and thought. In *Matter and Memory* Bergson had proposed an opposition between habitual memory, located in the sensorimotor mechanisms of the body, and pure recollection, which "records, in the form of memory-images, all the events of our daily life."[32] To illustrate their difference, Bergson devised the image of a memory cone (figure 1.9): "For, that a recollection should reappear in consciousness, it is necessary that it should descend from the heights of pure memory down to the precise point where *action* is taking place. In other words, it is from the present that comes the appeal to which memory responds, and it is from the sensori-motor elements of present action that a memory borrows the warmth which gives it life."[33]

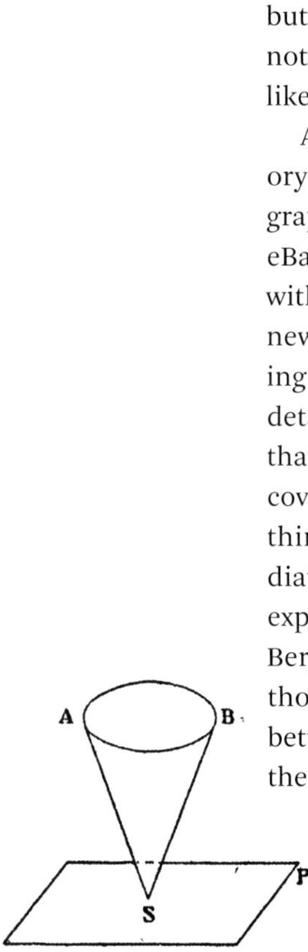

Fig. 4.

Figure 1.9 Bergson's memory cone.

This difference between "one memory that repeats and the other which imagines" anticipates a distinction psychologists draw today between implicit memory (which includes the procedural memory that allows us to ride a bike, put on a dress, even play the piano or conduct a choir) and explicit memory (which includes the episodic memory through which we actively remember autobiographical events). As these two forms of memory draw on different neural networks—the hippocampus, for example, is essential to the formation of episodic memory—

mémoire-souvenir aligns itself with objecthood, *mémoire-habitude* with thingness. The materiality of things helps to recruit bodily memory, while the meaning of objects requires mental abstraction. As Brown puts it, "Things lie beyond the grid of intelligibility the way mere things lie outside the grid of museal exhibition, outside the order of objects."[34]

This is where music enters. Music may not only draw things into the symbolic order of objects, but may also resist doing so by asserting its own sonic materiality, which may not rise to the level of consciousness until it is recorded and played back. Might there be an acoustic unconscious that enters into an optical-acoustic unconscious? Let us consider now how music has been seen to participate in the production of memory, not just by attaching associations to a piece of music performed from sheet music, but by leaving an audible trace in physical matter—a record—thereby giving rise to new forms of visual recollection.

Phono-Photograph

If Novecento was loath to have his musical portrait of the girl mechanically reproduced, many respondents to Edison's 1921 survey requested certain songs because they recalled specific memories. Once vinyl records became part of mass culture, they became memory objects themselves. How so can be gleaned from George Stevens's 1941 *Penny Serenade*, a heartrending story about a middle-class marriage that is, as the promotional tagline had it, "united by love and tested by tragedy." The film is less about music than about music's cinematic deployment to tell that story in a series of flashbacks. In the first scene, Julie Adams (Irene Dunne) is getting ready to leave her husband, Roger (Cary Grant), but something holds her back: an album of 78s, which a friend of the couple, Applejack, has pulled off a shelf. We see "The Story of a Happy Marriage" printed on the front cover as he takes one record out and puts it on the gramophone. Julie asks him to stop. But after he leaves she flips through the album, which has memorabilia attached to individual sleeves: a pair of knitted baby socks, the cover of a magazine about Japan, a wedding invitation (figure 1.10). Julie returns to the gramophone to start the music again.

The sequence that follows is astonishing (see below figure 1.11). Julie is lost in thought: the song takes her back in time. Suddenly, the needle gets stuck in a groove, returning her to the present. As Julie resets the needle, an overhead shot shows the gramophone from above and the spinning record turns into an iris showing her with a magazine in hand sitting opposite the figure of the listening dog that was the trademark of the Victor Talking Machine Company. Two gramophones in the foreground reveal that we are in a record store. Once again the needle gets stuck, drawing the attention of Roger Adams walking by the storefront.

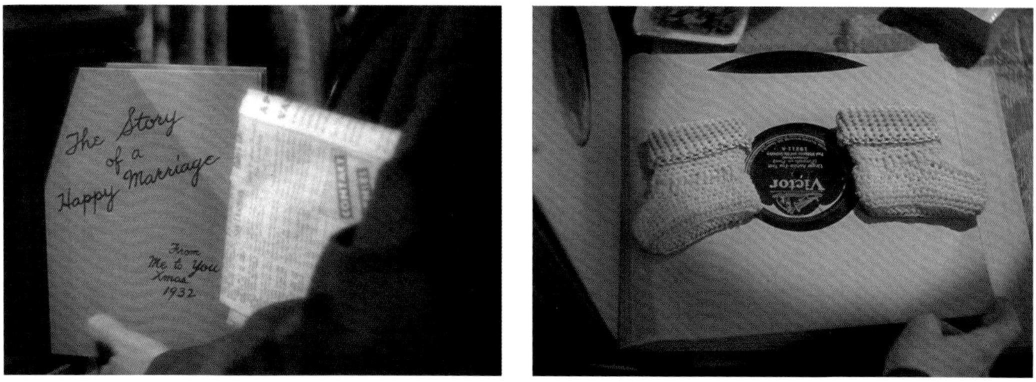

Figure 1.10
"The Story of a Happy Marriage": an album of records instead of photographs, with mementos attached.

Figure 1.11
(*facing*)
The phono-photograph in *Penny Serenade*. Julie listens to the record, and when the needle gets stuck, she resets it (*top*). The record turns into an iris that takes her back to 1929 (*middle*), when Roger saw her in the record store resetting the needle on that same record (*bottom*).

He looks inside and sees how Julie rushes to the gramophone to reset the needle. Their eyes meet.

If the flashback narration was a cinematic convention, *Penny Serenade* offers a striking variant in that the story is told through an album of 78s. Each record that Julie puts on takes her back to an episode in her marriage. In the age of shellac and vinyl, the association between music and autobiographical memory changed significantly: no longer dependent on live performance, recordings provided many more opportunities for personalized consumption. Today we are used to music's complete portability through listening devices that offer instant playback, but this development that was long in the making. Vinyl recordings did not eliminate sheet music, which one could sample by having them performed in the store by musicians—a practice shown in an early scene from Florenz Ziegfeld's *Glorifying the American Girl* (1929). We can see a piano in the back of the record store where Julie works. Given the thematic use of songs in early cinema, it comes as no surprise that the first 78 in the couple's marriage album is "You Were Meant for Me" by Nacio Herb Brown (music) and Arthur Freed (lyrics). Introduced in *The Broadway Melody of 1929*—the first sound film to win an Academy Award for Best Picture—the song places the beginning of *Penny Serenade* at around 1929, surely tapping into the memories of audiences familiar with the song's origin.

The opening scene of *Penny Serenade* illustrates how phonographic records changed the culture of memory. With recordings, a song became locked into a unique rendition that always sounded the same—differences in playback equipment or environment notwithstanding. Yet if recordings created a more uniform memory of a song across audiences, individual records could, as material objects, still bear the mark of uniqueness, and bestow it back onto the song.[35] The record of "You Were Meant for Me," bears such a mark, the skip at the end of line "I was meant for you," where the needle gets stuck:

You were meant for me
I was meant for you [*for you, for you, for you, for you*] . . .

Victor

You're like a plaintive melody
That never lets me free.
I'm content the angels must have sent you
And they meant you just for me.

Stevens carefully aligned the music with the action. When Roger Adams walks by the storefront, the music is just part of the urban soundscape. But the repeated "for you" stops him in his tracks and makes him look into the store. When Julie resets the needle, their eyes meet just as the song resumes with the line, "You're like a plaintive melody." The camera lingers on Julie as she lowers her eyes, perhaps a little embarrassed, but then looks up again. For those who knew the song, the suggestiveness of the words might have appeared like a striking coincidence, for Julie's resetting of the needle elides four somewhat superfluously florid lines from the lyrics—"Nature fashioned you / And when she was done / You were all those good things / Rolled into one." And so, when the song continues with its "plaintive melody / That never lets me free," it seems the tune has indeed *captured* Roger, who, having resumed walking, stops and turns around. He enters the store to the corny couplet "I'm content the angels must have sent you / And they meant you just for me." Roger purchases the record—and the rest is history.

The faulty groove points to the phonograph's privilege, ever more palpable in the digital age: to provide a material record of an acoustic phenomenon. While sheet music offered a mere prescription for performance, analog recordings could store sound in a body that retained some of its physical properties. In Brown's terms, the defective 78 refigures its relation to its owners by making the song unique and special, as if it were meant just for them. This promise is part and parcel of the popular music emerging from Tin Pan Alley in the early twentieth century. It involves what Adorno, in his 1941 essay "On Popular Music," famously called "pseudo-individualization," by which he means "endowing cultural mass production with the halo of free choice" and making listeners "forget that what they listen to is already listened to for them."[36] In *Penny Serenade* the ownership of a song is tied to ownership of a record—a specific record. The broken exemplar, playing at a particular time in a particular place, reinforces the song's message. The repeated "for you" puts a particularizing spin on the meaning of "meant"—and indeed is the reason for the couple's first encounter. The idea that two people are meant for each other is the basic tenet of romantic love, whose metaphysical promise is given a material premise in the record. As I will show in chapter 4, Annie, Meg Ryan's character from *Sleepless in Seattle*, is deeply invested in interpreting such phenomena as signs of magic. In *Penny Serenade*, this serendipity is expressed in the first two lines of the verse, which Stevens may have omitted because they were inherent in the scene: "Life was a song, you came along."

The 78s from the Adams family album show how Theweleit's recording apparatus became characteristic of sound film. If the records summon memories as described by respondents to Edison's survey, the film goes a step further: it supplies the actual pictures. When the rotating record transforms into an iris that opens onto the past, we witness the fusion of phonograph and photograph. Adorno once made the striking observation that, in German, "the term 'plate' [*Platte*] is used without any modification and with the same meaning in both photography and phonography," noting that records could become "virtual photographs of their owners."[37] Raising the curtain on the story of Julie and Roger, the record-iris shows the merger of photograph and phonograph into the single medium of sound film in 1929—the very year RCA acquired Victor, then the leading producer of phonographs and phonograph records. The record-turned-lens that reveals Julie sitting in the music store next to the company's trademark dog suggests that recordings, as soundtracks, could not only record consumer's personal memories but also replay them before their inner eye.

The fusion of talking machine and viewing machine ushered in the new age of audiovisual media that would forever change audiovisual memory. If music had long known how to evoke images, the silver screen offered a novel venue for the "theater of the mind" that had been so central to radio.[38] The flashbacks of *Penny Serenade* did more than combine "audio dissolve" and "video dissolve," which allowed film musicals to transition from time-bound narrative into timeless song and dance or even to take place "*within* the spectator."[39] In resetting the needle, Julie thus retraces a major step in media history. Looking at her pensive face, viewers first wonder what she sees before being treated to the content of the reel that the music projects on her mental screen. By getting stuck, the needle tells audiences that the record is the same on the other side of the dissolve. As with Novecento's matrix, the materiality of the memory matters, no longer as a liability threatening destruction of the auratic memory, but as an asset in its preservation. Playing the record one more time saves the marriage, as Julie is unable to break up the collection: "I can't seem to divide them; they belong to both of us." If the story's happy ending fulfills the song's premise—"You're like a plaintive melody / That never lets me free"—it does so not just because this is "their song" but also because the needle gets stuck in the damaged groove of "their record."

As *Penny Serenade* represents and registers the new audiovisual mnemonic of cinema, it points to the new analytic of the optical-acoustic unconscious, involving not only camera and projector, but also phonograph and gramophone. Looking back from the digital age, where playlists are randomized to trigger involuntary memories that take us back to different times of our lives, the optical-acoustic unconscious models how the movie palace became a darkroom of the lived moment. As sound film

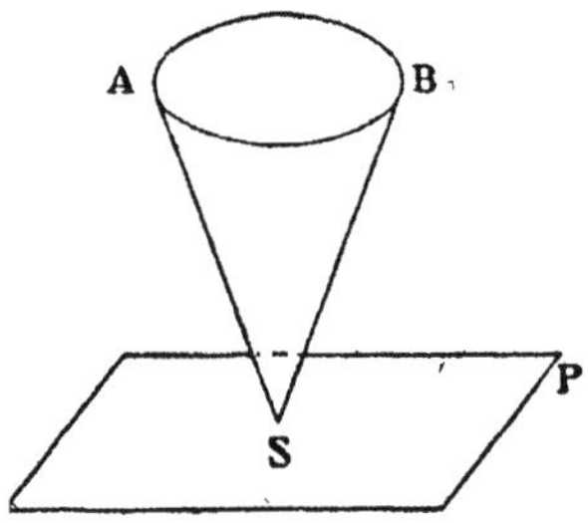

FIG. 4.

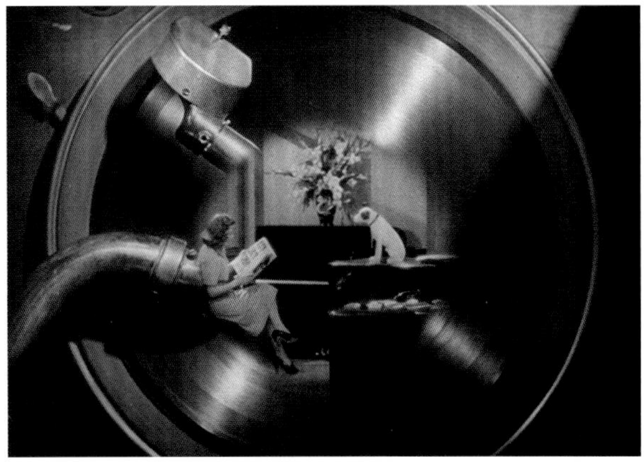

Figure 1.12 Bergson's memory cone and the record-iris from *Penny Serenade*.

recognized the evocative power of music to record visual memories, the phono-photograph became the new *mémoire involuntaire* where musical madeleines made of shellac could not only tell but also show.

Once music was mechanically reproduced, it begins to operate the shutter on the inner eye. Bergson's memory cone morphs into the phono-photograph (figure 1.12). The cone's tip becomes the needle that cuts through the plane—or plate—of the present and turns into a lens, zooming in on the past to show us not only our recorded recollections, but also how the material memories of audiovisual media matter.

CHAPTER TWO

Tertiary Rememories

The Final Cut (2004), directed by Omar Naïm, is a sci-fi drama that revolves around a brain implant, called Zoe, capable of recording every sensory impression in a person's life. Not unlike Michel Gondry's *Eternal Sunshine of the Spotless Mind*, released the same year, *The Final Cut* hones in on the personal and societal dilemmas caused by technical manipulations of human memory. The story centers on the "cutter," Alan Hakman (Robin Williams), who reviews the Zoe footage with a special machine (nicknamed Guillotine) and selects from a myriad images the most pleasant episodes for special "rememory" services, attended by family and friends (figure 2.1). When Hakman is asked to do the rememory of Charles Bannister—the deceased attorney of the implant maker, EYE-Tech—Fletcher, a former colleague and friend who has meanwhile become an anti-Zoe activist, pressures him to hand over Bannister's video in order to disclose his abuse of his daughter and thereby help bring down the rememory industry.

The plot line about the rememory enterprise intersects with a second one, about Hakman's own childhood trauma. The precredit prologue shows the ten-year-old Hakman visiting another town with his parents, where he explores an abandoned factory with a local boy, Louis Hunt, who accidentally falls from a beam. Seeing Hunt in a puddle of blood, Hakman, thinking he is dead, runs away. After spotting the adult Hunt in Bannister's video, Hakman breaks into the EYE-Tech plant to search for Hunt's file, only to discover that he himself carries an implant. In a special procedure, Hakman accesses his own device to verify that Hunt did not die as a child—the "blood," it turns out, was spilled paint (see figure 2.2 below). Having violated the "cutter's code"—a cutter must not have an implant—Hakman gets a special tattoo to disable its recording capability. Nonetheless, after the disk of Bannister's implant has been destroyed, Fletcher realizes that Hakman's implant recorded a full viewing of the attorney's life, including evidence that might be used against EYE-Tech. He kills Hakman to obtain his implant.

The Final Cut registers deep-seated anxieties about the social consequences of memory technology. It belongs to a group of late twentieth-century movies about prosthetic memory, such as Paul Verhoeven's *Total Recall* (1990) and Kathryn Bigelow's *Strange Days* (1995). Though lesser known and less acclaimed, Naïm's film offers an unusual, yet pertinent, example of the proliferation of what Bernard Stiegler, in the third volume of *Technics and Time: Cinematic Time and the Question of Malaise*,

Figure 2.1
The cutter at his "Guillotine" (*top*), with which he selects from the totality of images captured by the Zoe implant (*bottom*).

has called "tertiary memory"—a memory "resulting from all forms of recording."[1] Stiegler, to recall, argues that the development of devices for the recording and reproduction of temporal objects initiated a new epoch in the evolution of technology, driven by a process of exteriorization in which memory, originally intrinsic to human beings, became inextricably tied to external instruments and devices. The twentieth century, he notes, became "the century of the industrialization, the conservation and the transmission—that is, the selection—of memory," so that the "production of industrial temporal objects (phonograms, films, radio and television programs, etc.)" has led to "the fact that millions, hundreds of millions of consciousnesses are every day the consciousnesses, at the same time, of the same temporal objects."[2] As a result, "cinema weaves itself into our time," such that "life is *always* cinema" and "we go to the cinema in order to find life again."[3]

It is this audacious claim that I will consider in relation to *The Final Cut*, suggesting that Naïm's film rehearses central tenets of Stiegler's theory and that both should be viewed as interlocking symptoms of a larger cultural concern with the implications of technologically produced memory.

Figure 2.2 Human versus technological recollection: young Hakman remembers that Louis Hunt died (*top*) but later, in his implant video, discovers he was alive—his head moves and there is no pooled blood (*bottom*).

Put differently, the cinematic obsession with the interplay of organic and mechanical devices that can record lived experience has not just come to permeate cultural practice, but as such has also penetrated theories of culture. Not surprisingly, filmmaker and critical theorist use similar examples that appear to validate underlying phenomena—above all the idea that human consciousness is bound to the existence and experience of temporal objects. Inasmuch as *The Final Cut* is an implicit representation of Stiegler's postulates, Stiegler himself takes explicit recourse to cinematic practice to shore up his diagnosis about tertiary memory, notably in his trenchant analysis of a scene from Fellini's *Intervista* (1987), which he put forward as exemplary for the way cinema, as life, copes with death—a scene that I will revisit with an ear toward music. Amid the interactions between recording technology and the phenomenology of time, my interest in music's impact on audiovisual memory turns from episodic memory—music as a cue to past events—to the condition of remembering as a temporal act. The storage of memories is not just spatial and associative, but bound to the experience of duration, of a past unfolding in the present.

Retentional Finitude and Tertiary Memory

Within its mildly futuristic setting, *The Final Cut* imagines a new technical response to what Stiegler describes as "retentional finitude." Since human memory is limited by our physiological capacities and is obliterated by death, the Zoe implant preserves a mechanical record of lived experience. Hence, it is touted by EYE-Tech as organic: the implant itself grows with the brain and its nerve endings. While such a symbiosis between machine and the body is the stuff of science fiction, Stiegler sees a similar dynamic at work in the *transductive* (that is, mutually constitutive) relation between humans and technology—an idea he adopts from the philosopher of science Gilbert Simondon. For Stiegler, this relation is evident in our perception and understanding of time.

Naïm's film dramatizes this technological exteriorization of memory with the Zoe implant as the most recent development of tertiary retention. To stem the loss of personal recollection with the death of the biological body, the implant preserves the individual experience that forms epigenetic memory and becomes what Stiegler calls *epiphylogenetic* memory—technics "inscribed in the non-living body."[4] Planted into the brain, the recording device takes on the appearance of a living organism, but the mechanical record cannot live on its own after death. Although the implant is a prosthetic device that remedies the originary lack of retentional finitude, it comes with a lack of its own. As the record of sensory data is converted into memories for the survivors, its human host, now dead, has no control over what is selected. The creation of episodic memory is the task of the cutter. Even as the implant generates a video with a status line that shows a digital chronometer next to the name of the bearer, this video is not life-cinema in Stiegler's sense because it is missing consciousness—specifically *time* consciousness.

In *On the Phenomenology of the Consciousness of Internal Time*, Edmund Husserl tried to account for the unity of a temporal object given in discrete moments. He did so by shifting attention from the object itself to the way consciousness constitutes the object when fusing individual instances into a living present. Instead of thinking about time as the succession of present moments turning into past moments, Husserl proposed that consciousness possesses a "width," which creates a temporal field with a temporal fringe. When hearing a melody, we do not hear a sequence of single tones but perceive the melody as a unified object, as follows: the perception of each passing tone is retained in consciousness (retention) while anticipating the perception of the next tone (protention). Husserl thought of retention as primary memory, which must be distinguished from recollection as secondary memory: retention involves perception; recollection involves cognition. Recalling a previously heard melody—replaying, as it were, in our head—is only *like* the original perception of the melody. Since re-membering is re-presentation—an act of imagination—Husserl claimed that the difference between perception and recollection is absolute.[5]

Stiegler contests Husserl's categorical distinction between primary and secondary memory by pointing out that recollection is always already at work during perception. Since recording technology—a form of tertiary memory—made exact reproduction possible, the very existence of identical temporal objects has shown us that perception is never pure. The fact that we never hear, and hence remember, the same recording in quite the same way reveals that recollection itself is inherently selective and ineluctably bound up with forgetting. Stiegler's description of this process is telling: "In all remembering of past temporal objects there is a necessary process of *dérushage*, of montage, a play of special effects, of slowing down, accelerating, etc.—and even freezing of the image: this is the time of reflection that Husserl analyses precisely as such, a moment of the analysis of memory, of recollection's decomposition."[6] The choice of cinematic terms is deliberate: *dérushage* is the rough cut for a first viewing, already influenced by the techniques of montage, special effects, and so forth. For Stiegler, life is cinematic because these techniques are being applied when we view the world. Cinema appears to work the way consciousness works, because consciousness works like cinema. He describes consciousness as "this post-production center, this control room assembling the montage, the staging, the *realization*, and the direction, of the flow of primary, secondary, and tertiary retentions of which the *unconscious*, full of protentional possibilities (including the speculative) would be the producer."[7]

In *The Final Cut*, the cinematic metaphor of a producing unconscious and a postproducing consciousness plays out differently in the two plot strands. In the film's opening flashback, Hakman watches himself, as in an observer memory seen from an outside perspective, while the implant video he sees later is like a field memory that assumes a point of view within the field of action (see figure 2.2). Hakman is haunted by the image of Hunt in a pool of blood, but the implant record, which shows no blood and sees Hunt's head turned toward Hakman, proves that image to be inaccurate. His recollection of the accident is not only selective but also imaginative. In response to the traumatic event, Hakman experiences dissociation—a detachment from physical reality. This kind of selective staging of perception is of course his job as a cutter. Yet while his rememory movies are deliberate montages of tertiary retentions, he has no control over his own "edited" recollections of childhood trauma.

Stiegler's metaphor of a producing unconscious and a postproducing consciousness grounds his conception of time consciousness in forgetting. Its foil is the inability to forget:

> Imagine hypothetically that I have an infinite memory and that I can remember what happened yesterday. I thus remember every second and fraction of a

second exactly identically. When I come to the end of the day, I remember that at that moment I am remembering the entire day, which I begin to do again in remembering myself anew, each second exactly and identically, etc. There is no longer any difference, because there has been no selection: time has not *passed*.[8]

Total recall eliminates time consciousness, creating the specter of a temporal *mise-en-abîme*—a hall of memory, akin to a hall of mirrors—that swallows up the past. Since perfect recollection leads to absolute knowledge, omniscience results in an eternal present where time ceases to exist. This omniscience effect explains why, in *The Final Cut*, there is an ethical code that prohibits a cutter from having an implant: recording the complete record of other implants is the first step of technics toward infinite retentionality" that is, "in fact, God's memory."[9] As the tagline on the DVD cover put it: "In the end, he sees everything."

If infinite retention threatens to abolish time, Hakman's job is to make time pass. As master of the rememory ceremony, he must navigate both rivers of the underworld, Mnemosyne and Lethe: remember *and* forget. This is why the rememory movie requires dismembering the Zoe record. In a recent analysis of *The Final Cut*, Garrett Stewart has noted that "we revert to a condition of total storage that requires, as at the beginning of cinema, the incision of the cut—or, in other words, deletion and recombination—in order to make narrative."[10] True to the name of his profession, Hakman cuts the video up with a machine, whose control wheels simulate working with actual film stock. Whereas the acquisition of sensory data occurs mechanically, the creation of memory requires a human touch. At first, this division into automatic and manual labor seems to align with Husserl's absolute difference between perception and recollection. Yet the cutter mediates between the unedited daily rushes and the final version and thereby partakes in the transition from epigenetic memory to epiphylogenetic memory. In Stiegler's words, "The being's experience, registered in the tool (in the object), becomes transmissible and cumulative: thus arises the possibility of a heritage."[11] If tertiary memory is, as Mark Hansen put it, an "experience that has been recorded and is available to consciousness without ever having been lived by consciousness," then a cutter's job is to make that recorded experience available to consciousness, so that it can be relived by the survivors.[12] Hence the cut is always an edit that severs and sutures, dismembers and remembers.

This double function becomes manifest in montage. The rememory service is the cinematic montage—a new form of "temporal ecstasy, whose primary effect is a profound transformation of the conditions of reification and event-ization."[13] For Stiegler, event-ization means "selection": it is memory at work but based on such new temporal experiences as those of real-time, direct, or live transmission. Made possible by technology, these new temporal experiences break down the difference between presentation and re-presentation. The recording of the Zoe implant is locked by default into a first-person point-of-view, such that the raw video presents the immediacy of lived experience. Selecting moments from this video and assembling them into a feature-length movie that re-presents life becomes a process of reflexive remembrance akin to the creative freedom of the filmmaker, who can speed up or slow down "as if in a montage, a cinemato-graphy of recollection."[14] In overcoming retentional finitude, the *dérushage*-like use of Zoe technology in the rememory movie exemplifies Stiegler's conception of time consciousness: "montage is what (re)constitutes the Living Present, always already dying"; "montage is obvious in re-memorization, and what Husserl identifies as the 'remarkable' phenomenon of recollection, in which 'the past of the duration is given to me, given precisely as the "re-givenness" of the duration.'"[15]

Music and the Presence of the Past

Here music matters: it closes the gap between presentation and representation. When Hakman accesses his implant to replay Hunt's accident, the suspenseful moment he crosses the beam is scored with the music from the original flashback. In broaching the difference between perception and recollection, music connects the story and its telling. When a client previews the movie for his late brother's rememory, he is pleased that Hakman's choice of music "suits his life somehow."[16] Amid the many functions of film music, one basic feature is often taken for granted: music provides a sense of *time passing in the present*. This matters in light of Stiegler's critique of Husserl, who was haunted by his absolute distinction between perception and recollection: "If the way in which recollection makes the past present fundamentally differs from the presence of the past in retention, how can a representation be true to its object? Such fidelity could only be that of *an adequate correspondence between a present 'now' and a past 'now.'*"[17] This correspondence is sustained by music, which appears to endow the cinematic montage of the past with that sense of now. If a cinematic montage shows the selecting hand of memory at work, music makes that hand disappear—and often seems to disappear itself by becoming unheard as underscoring. Yet music not only joins the discontinuous images into a continuous present, but also promises to store that continuity as a slice of lived time.

That music brings temporal continuity to cinema bolsters Stiegler's claim that life is always cinema because of two coincidences: "the phono-photographic coincidence of past and reality," and "the coincidence between the film's flow and that of the film spectator's consciousness." Since Husserl failed to consider the possibility of recording temporal objects, Stiegler hypothesizes "an *essentially* cinemato-graphic structure for consciousness in general, as if it had 'always had cinema without realizing it.'"[18] Ben Roberts has reformulated this more pointedly: "The temporal flux of cinema coincides with consciousness . . . because consciousness is itself to be understood on the basis of a temporal flux."[19] Music reinforces that basic flux: unfolding in time, it grounds the experience of watching the past in the living present, and it makes tangible the idea that cinema shares with life the structure of temporal objects. Thus music adds a crucial dimension to the "phonographic revelation" brought about by tertiary memory.[20] If tertiary memory reveals that perception is selective because it is shaped by recollection, the addition of music to a cinematic sequence shows that the act of remembrance is, in turn, always tied into the temporal structure of perception. Music brings to cinematic consciousness the sense that time was and remains real; it provides a palpable experience of a time that was passing once and is passing now. Through music, past and present converge in the flow of time.

Not surprisingly, music for longer memory montages tends to have a strong sense of flow—for example, in Terrence Malick's *The Tree of Life* (2011), where an extensive flashback montage of childhood memories is scored with the second tone poem from Smetana's *má vlast*, depicting the course of Bohemia's famous river Vltava. However generic, the music Hakman selects for the rememory movie about his client's deceased brother shares some of its features, notably the undulating figuration. Brian Tyler, who wrote the score for Naïm's film, begins with a gently oscillating minor third (A-C) at midtempo in the piano, which serves as foil for a simple melody, padded by soft strings. A middle section drifts back and forth between F-major and G-major chords, which invoke a Lydian mode and thereby create a feeling of fluctuating stasis, occasionally deflected toward a doleful A-minor chord. Called "Rememory" on the commercial soundtrack (issued by Varèse Sarabande), the cue is feel-good music with only the smallest tinge of poignancy—its serene glow outshines any feeling of loss, conflict, or suffering. Propelled by the music's placid movement, the rememory montage becomes a vehicle for memories *worth* remembering. Everything else has been cut from the record: when the client has left, Hakman returns to the Guillotine to delete a stark scene of domestic violence that did not make it into the final cut.

Such erasures suggest that the "tertiarization" of life in the industrialized production of memory has a moral dimension. Who is to decide what to cut and what to keep? Amid a growing ambivalence about manufacturing remembrance, Hakman, true to his name, produces hackwork: "literary, artistic, or professional work done on order usually according to formula and in conformity with commercial standards."[21] The business model of EYE-Tech capitalizes on the tradition of the expurgated obituary: *De mortuis nihil nisi bonum* (Of the dead, nothing unless good). For a cutter, the edit is not only an aesthetic choice but an ethical act, and Naïm draws attention to the precarious role technology plays in this dubious venture. In a scene not used for the theatrical release of *The Final Cut*, one of Hakman's colleagues reminisces about a time when implants recorded only "peak moments," when the picture was in black and white, and when there was no sound. More recent video has, in her opinion, become "too real" and thus feels "too much like life" (the scene is called, tellingly, "Moving Pictures"). The view that earlier recordings were technologically less perfect but aesthetically more satisfying registers unease about a general evolution toward greater realism in the cinema. Flawless fidelity shifts the moral choice back from the tool onto its user—arguably the crux of all technology.

While Stiegler stresses the originary link between organic interiority and mechanical exteriority, Naïm's film belabors the tension between the precision of technical reproduction and the imperfections of human representation. Since the total record of the Zoe implant includes reprehensible actions, even crimes, Hakman serves not only as editing consciousness but as evaluating conscience. After reviewing a life through the eyes of the deceased, the cutter creates a rememory movie that administers both forgetting and forgiveness. Anti-implant activists protest against the human overreach inherent in this double act: "It is not our place to see through other people's eyes. That is for God and God alone." Hakman responds to the accusation that he makes lies out of people's lives by presenting himself as a monitor with a higher moral mission, who justifies showing what survivors want to remember by erasing what should be forgotten. Confronted by Fletcher, he remarks that the technology sells because it fulfills "a human need." The ethical foundation of the argument seems weak, but it is buttressed by the venerable conjunction of technology and magic: Hakman associates himself with the ancient practice of the "sin eater," who, after putting bread and salt on a corpse's chest and coins upon the eyes, "would eat the bread and salt and take the coins as payment, thus absorbing the sins of the deceased, cleansing their soul and allowing them safe passage into the afterlife."[22]

If Naïm's script borders here on the kooky, its religious overtones resonate with such starkly dystopian blockbusters as *The Matrix* (1999), where a few remaining disciples of "the real" try to upend an Orwellian world of industrialized simulation. Although *The Final Cut* stays clear of overtly Manichean battles, it delights (like *The Matrix*) in the capacities of the cinematic medium to explore new powers of simulation. At the same time, Naïm's film remains committed to an underlying humanism that undercuts its critique of commercially administered amnesia with the successful resolution of Hakman's childhood trauma. Haunted by involuntary—but incomplete and inaccurate—flashbacks of Hunt's fall, Hakman eventually recovers the traumatic blackout by accessing his own implant, which shows that Hunt did not in fact fall to his death. While

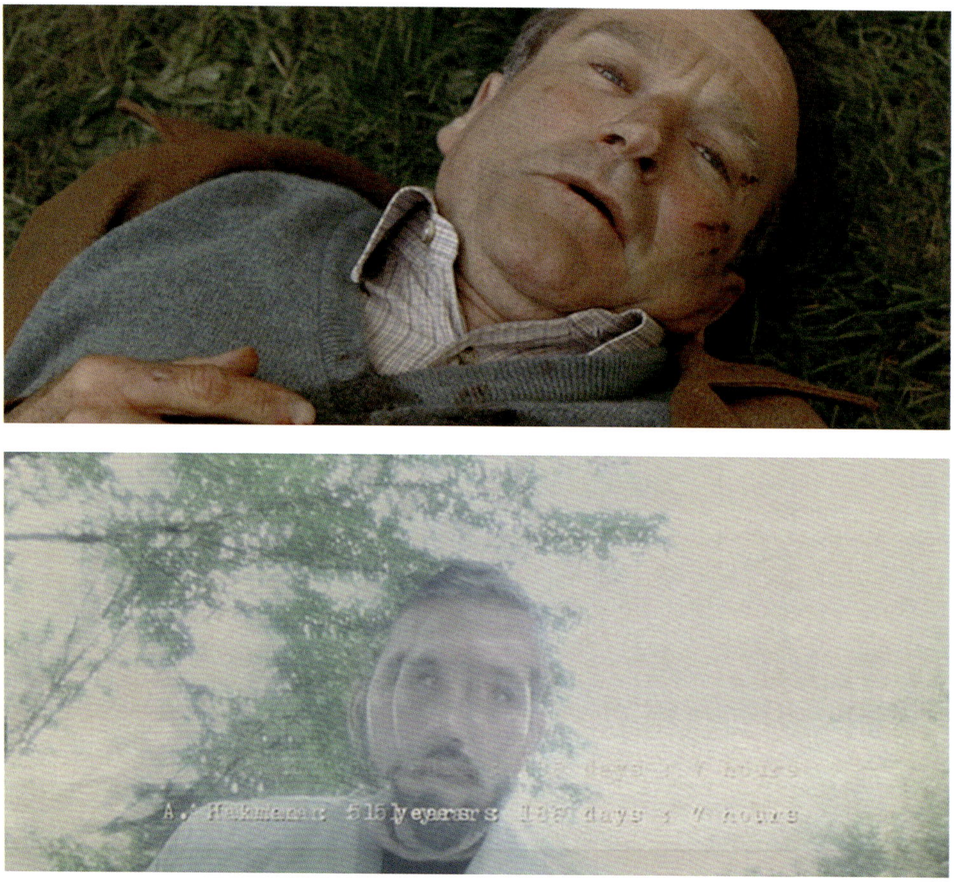

Figure 2.3 Hakman dies, looking at Fletcher (*top*), but with his senses failing, the implant no longer properly records his sensory impressions (*bottom*).

Fletcher seeks to unmask the hypocrisy of the rememory culture, Hakman sees its potential for personal redemption. When Hakman seeks closure by placing on Hunt's gravestone a necklace that he had kept as a material memento of the accident, Fletcher's men kill him to secure his implant for Bannister's posthumous persecution.

The story ends here, but in a final scene, Fletcher, sitting at the very Guillotine he has come to despise, reviews video from Hakman's implant. In this quasi-epilogue, the film returns to the ethical conundrums of tertiary memory. In an astounding transition from the penultimate scene, Hakman, mortally wounded, realizes that he is dying. Here the screen switches from a shot of him lying on the ground—Fletcher's point of view—to a first-person point-of-view shot of Hakman looking up at him (see figure 2.3). The latter shot appears to be footage from Hakman's implant with its distinct video quality, including status line and visual artifacts, the deterioration of the image signaling the device's failure due to his impending death. As we switch back to Fletcher's point of view, Hakman raises his hand to look at his bloodied palm, then another cut to the video from Hakman's implant shows the hand rising before his

Figure 2.4 Fletcher watches a rememory montage created in the dying Hakman's mind showing him as a child.

eyes. Crucially, the video is silent: whereas his heavy breathing remains audible from Fletcher's point of view, Hakman sees Fletcher moving his lips with no sound, suggesting that under the physical duress of his dying body, the implant no longer captures audio.

Now something strange happens. As if to fill this sonic void, music enters—not in the first shot (Hakman looking at Fletcher), but in the second (Hakman looking at his hand). The music continues during the cut back to Fletcher's POV, showing Hakman breathing his last, and through the shot of young Hakman looking into the mirror at age ten, the year of the accident—a shot we saw earlier when Hakman accessed his implant to solve the mystery of Hunt's survival. But suddenly video and music end with a jarring screech that sounds as if someone had pushed the stop button on a mechanical playback device—and a split second later, Fletcher's head moves in front of the frozen frame as if he had been watching implant footage of his former friend (figure 2.4).

Since when has Fletcher been watching? The abrupt ending of Hakman's video is perplexing, but the music provides a clue as to what is happening. It sounded briefly when Hakman accessed his own implant and saw himself as a kid looking into the mirror. This is rememory music—a ruminative piano floating above a string pad—another one of Hakman's favorite musical selections, which he has used twice as the score for unusual clips presented to his girlfriend Delia. On the soundtrack, those cues are called "Inversion" and "Dreams," and for good reasons. "Inversion" serves as the score for a whimsical rememory clip Hakman composed from shots of a man, W. Davis, looking into the mirror at ages eighty-two, seventy-two, fifty-five, forty-four, twenty-one, thirteen, and nine (figure 2.5). "Dreams" accompanies a wondrous clip from implants that have, as Hakman explains, "a defect" and "cannot differentiate between what the eye sees and what the mind sees"; as a result, these implants record "dreams, daydreams, hallucinations," such as watching colorful fish in tropical waters from inside a car with a radio playing.

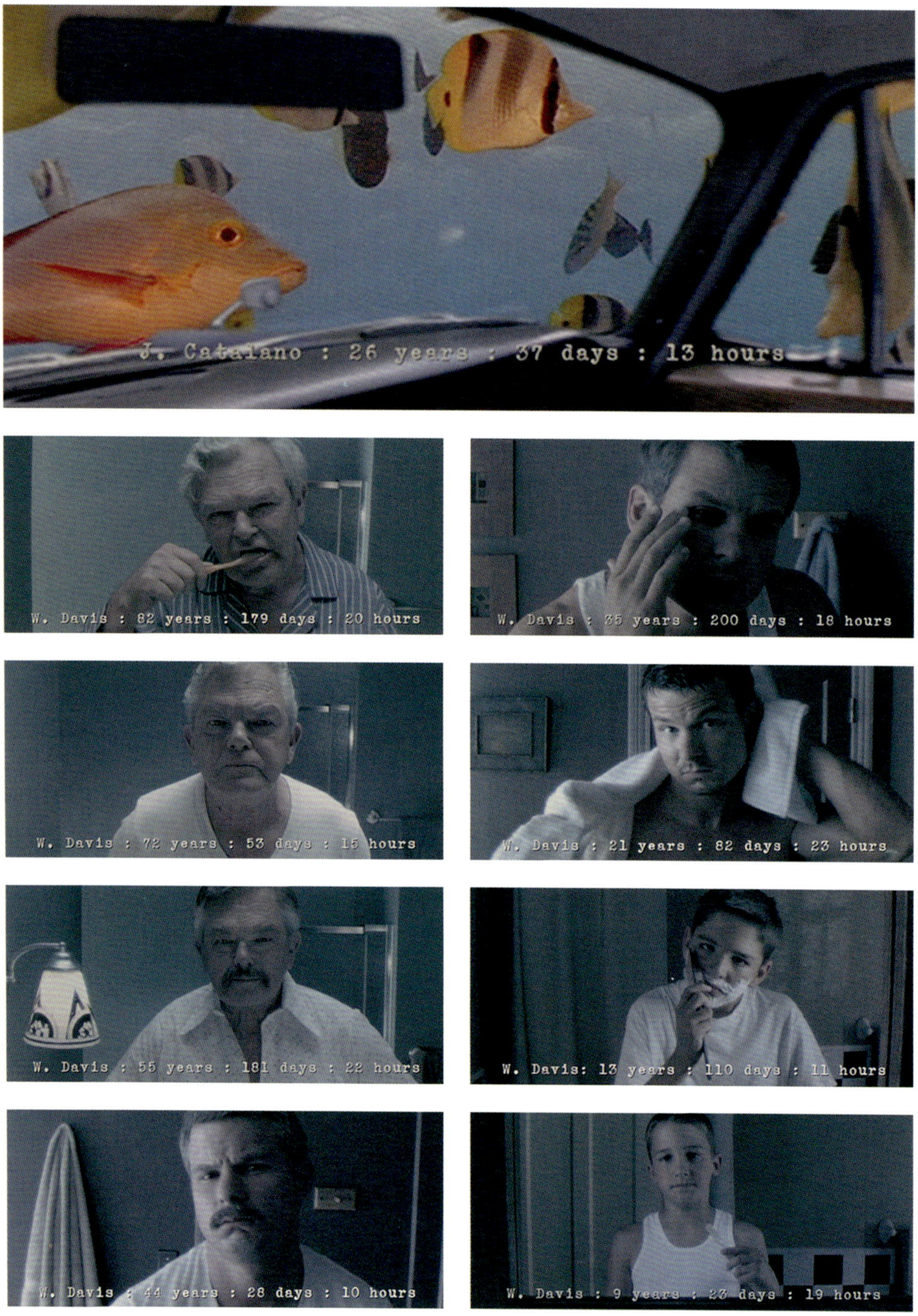

Figure 2.5 Images from a defective implant, recording what the mind is imagining (*top*), and Hakman's experimental montage of a man "aging backwards" (*bottom*).

Since memory is a close cousin of imagination, Hakman uses the same music for fancy dreams and fantastic recollections.

This explains why that music enters when Hakman is dying and why it ends so abruptly. As his body breaks down, the malfunctioning implant no longer captures impressions from Hakman's failing senses but records what he remembers before passing out.[23] What Fletcher can see and hear, with us looking over his shoulder, seems to dramatize Stiegler's notion of consciousness as a "post-production center" for "assembling the montage, the staging, the *realization*, and the direction, of the flow of primary, secondary, and tertiary retentions of which the *unconscious*, full of protentional possibilities (including the speculative) would be the producer."[24] Accordingly, Hakman's visual perception of his hand would be a primary retention; the memory image of himself as a boy, a secondary retention; and the recording of these by the implant, a tertiary retention. Indeed, if all three kinds of retentions are "produced" by Hakman's unconscious, his cinematic consciousness would then be responsible for their actual montage, including the choice of appropriate rememory music.

Here the music imparts what Hakman knew all along: that it can smooth the slippage between memory and imagination. Stiegler explains that "postproduction occurs when the 'rushes' and the montage are out of sync: this is the phenomenon of the dream."[25] This temporal dissociation is apparent when the implant captures Hakman's consciousness at the very moment he is losing it. Before his senses go silent, however, the music cues the childhood memory. Indeed, what Fletcher pulls up on his screen appears to be the beginning of a panoramic flashback montage such as people have reported in moments of mortal danger or imminent death—a powerful cinematic trope to which I will return in chapter 5. Triggered by a release of chemicals in the brain to soften the impact of a fall from great heights or to offset the panic of drowning, it is the experience where (in Benjamin's words) "a whole life flashes by in a rapid sequence."[26] His death approaching, Hakman starts to create his last rememory movie: the final cut of his own life.

Cinematic Reflections on the Future Anterior

But this is not the ending of *The Final Cut*. If Fletcher hits the pause button on Hakman's own rememory, it is to make way for another kind of rememory in which Naïm wraps up *his* film in a final sequence. Here Fletcher becomes the filmmaker's proxy, bringing out his directorial consciousness as well as his authorial conscience. The sequence begins with Fletcher reviewing Hakman's life at the Guillotine, which displays on its three screens three different moments, eventually showing Bannister's video, as once seen by Hakman (see figure 2.6). This is a remarkable shot.

Figure 2.6 Incipient total recall as a temporal *mise en abîme*: Bannister's implant video is nested into Hakman's implant video, showing the time stamps of both.

When the status line of Hakman's implant video appears below that of Bannister's implant video, the different time stamps testify to the incipient *mise en abîme* of tertiary memory. The nested frames create what Deleuze might have described as layered sheets of the past, now made present in a striking visual palimpsest. The shot reveals how an implant worn by a cutter, who has viewed thousands of implant videos and whose own implant will later be viewed by another cutter, would lead to an exponential increase in the stored memories that might be controlled by a single cutter. Looming large is the possibility of a godlike total recall that would afford mastery over time. Having access to any moment in any person's life—not unlike an omniscient narrator or a film director—such an über-cutter could make a selection from these moments to tell a story and thereby create time anew.

The suppressed gaps of child abuse in Bannister's record channel an Orwellian fear of total surveillance that goes hand in hand with simulating a sanitized brave new world. But once Fletcher has found them, the camera pans to another monitor of the Guillotine, which shows a clip of Hakman congratulating him on his birthday—remember: they were once colleagues and friends. Naïm's decision to score these two seemingly unrelated moments of Hakman's life with a reprise of the "Rememory" music suggests how they could be part of a rememory montage, not unlike the one Hakman showed to his client in the first scene. Now firmly nondiegetic, however, the music points to Naïm's own postproducing consciousness—the director's final cut. If Hakman and Naïm are both memory makers, the "Rememory" cue clinches Stiegler's claim that life is cinema because of the two coincidences already mentioned above, but now quoted in full:

—on the one hand, the phono-photographic coincidence of past and reality ("there is a double conjoint position: of reality and of the past," which induces this "reality effect"—believability—in which the spectator is located, in advance, by the technique itself);

—on the other, the coincidence between the film's flow and that of the film spectator's consciousness, linked by the phonographic flux, initiates the mechanics of a complete adoption of the film's time with that of the spectator's consciousness—which, since it is itself a flux, is captured and "channeled" by the flow of images. This movement, infused with every spectator's desire for stories, liberates the movements of consciousness typical of cinematic *emotion*.[27]

Film music *connects* these two coincidences because music allows the disparate temporalities in film, past and present, to converge. Theories of film music have long held that music endows the shadows on-screen with life. Music animates. As such, it not only creates a "reality effect" but also contributes, vitally, to the phonographic flux that "initiates" the coincidence between the flow of film time and of spectator time. Music thus helps to "liberate" spectatorial consciousness so that it can experience cinematic emotion.

In *The Final Cut*, this emotion emerges at the end of the final scene, when Fletcher not only reviews an episode from his friendship with Hakman but looks straight into his friend's eyes—one of those moments when the Zoe implant captured its bearer looking into a mirror. Naïm fashions this final face-to-face meeting through a series of shots and reverse-shots, where increasing close-ups of Fletcher alternate with full-screen video of Hakman getting dressed in front of his bathroom mirror (figure 2.7). Looking directly into his friend's eyes, Fletcher wells up: "It's for the greater good, Alan. Your life will mean something. I promise." This ending is an unusual variant of the shot/reverse-shot technique—developed, as James Chandler has shown, by Frank Capra in the 1930s—where face-to-face encounters catalyze "sentiment as reflected feeling" that springs from an act of sympathy.[28] What psychologists call perspective-taking—adopting another person's point of view—may lead to a change of heart and behavior. If moral sentiments are, in Chandler's words, "feelings registered through a virtual point of view," then the closing scene of *The Final Cut* takes that virtuality to another level.[29] Indeed, the two men, looking into the screen (Fletcher) and out from the screen (Hakman), are not only facing each other but facing us, the viewers. What are we to feel?

Since Hakman is alive only on video, his mirror image elicits what Barthes described when looking at a photograph of his mother as a child—the experience of an future anterior: "*she is going to die*."[30] For Stiegler, Barthes's claim that every photograph is the "catastrophe" of death having already occurred puts death at stake in "the dramatic outcome of every narrative, every play, every cinemato-graphic emotion."[31] Although

Figure 2.7
A final encounter, shot and reverse-shot across time: Hakman "looking" at Fletcher (*top*) "looking back" at Hakman (*bottom*).

the experience of a future anterior is not made apparent in every film, there are films—often films about film or films within films—that stage it as a moment of medium self-consciousness. Stiegler's exemplary case is an extraordinary sequence from *Intervista* (1987), a late instance of Fellini's sprawling forays into the surrealist metafilm-documentary hybrid, in which a Japanese-television crew comes to interview the director (who is filming an adaptation of Franz Kafka's *Amerika* in the Cinecittà studios) about the early days in the movie industry. In a famous scene, the aging Marcello Mastroianni—best known for his role as a film director going through a creative crisis in Fellini's 1963 classic *8½*—shows up on the set, dressed for a commercial in the costume of Mandrake the Magician (hero of a midcentury syndicated newspaper comic strip). Fellini and his crew then accompany Mastroianni on a visit to the villa of Anita Ekberg, outside of Rome. She greets her guests with the pomp of a retired diva, draped in a huge cloth, exposing her shoulders in a way that recalls the strapless black dress she wore nearly three decades earlier in her most famous role, opposite Mastroianni, as the American bombshell Silvia in *La dolce vita* (1960), the last of Fellini's so-called Roman Trilogy. During the visit, they end up watching a montage of segments from *La dolce vita*, including the iconic scene in which the character of the gorgeous Anita lures the character of the handsome Marcello into the Trevi Fountain in Rome. For Stiegler, the catastrophe of Anita's future anterior is twofold: when watching the earlier film she does not merely realize that "as image, she is dead *and* she is going to die," but, as the images move before her eyes, she also becomes aware of time passing at present—"I am going to die; I am dying." The consciousness of time passing thus places her "in a time that leads toward the absence of time: non-passing, infinite memory that will no longer be special, where everything will be retained forever in its instant: '*The Instant of my Death*.'"[32]

The inserted montage from *La dolce vita* is nothing less than a rememory. It is conjured up on a white sheet by Mastroianni, channeling the precipitous hypnotic technique commanded by Mandrake in the comic strip (figure 2.8): "My order is immediate," he exclaims, wielding his wand. "Make the good old times come back!"—the Italian subtly invoking a rhyme between past and present: "Il mio ordine è immediato: fai tornare i bei tempi del passato." Calling out "Music" (in English), Marcello then disappears with Anita behind the sheet for a dance of shadows, and the two dissolve via an ingenious "fade on action" into the on-screen couple (figure 2.9).

The music alternates between a muted variant of Nino Rota's "La bella malinconica" from *La dolce vita* and a ghostly, nineteen-second version

Figure 2.8 Preparing a rememory session in *Intervista*: with a flash of light, Marcello Mastroianni, as Mandrake the Magician, conjures a screen.

Figure 2.9
An ingenious "fade on action": Anita Ekberg and Marcello Mastroianni dance *behind* the makeshift screen in *Intervista* (*top*) to become Silvia and Marcello Rubini dancing on-screen in *La dolce vita* (*bottom*).

of Nicola Piovani's *Intervista* theme that serves as a ritornello (see table 2.1). Stiegler has no ears for the music, even though it is critical for the scene's effect. The montage is projected, with a bluish tint, as a silent film with musical accompaniment but no sound, which extends to the complete lack of ambient noise in Anita's house. Thus when Marcello speaks from behind the screen, his voice seems at first to emanate directly from the picture:

MARCELLO: "But who are you? . . . Are you a goddess? The mother? The deep sea? . . . The house? . . . Are you Eve, the first woman on Earth?" How many questions I would still want to ask you, Anita . . . For instance, don't you have a drop of grappa? . . .

ANITA: Fuck off, Marcellino!

MARCELLO: Don't make me laugh! . . . I will lose my mustache!

ANITA: I will get you some. I need some too![33]

We are fooled at first because Marcello's first two lines reword those spoken by his character in *La dolce vita*. The projected dance sequence also reorders two segments from the original dance scene, then cutting to clips from the Trevi Fountain scene that originally appeared later in the film. Half-remembered and half-imagined, the montage stirs past perceptions into a fantastic rememory, underscored by melodies that hover in the no man's land between then and now.

TABLE 2.1. "Anita e Marcello": Alternation of themes from *La dolce vita* and *Intervista*

La dolce vita (Rota), a variant of "La bella malinconica" (length: 2:03)	
Bridge (piano)	Marcello moves behind the sheet to dance with Anita; dissolve to . . .
Theme (combo)	. . . them dancing in *La dolce vita*
Bridge (piano, drums)	In the kitchen, Anita and Marcello watch from behind the screen
Theme (combo)	Marcello speaks; cut back to kitchen
Bridge (piano)	Cut to projection of *La dolce vita* seen from living room
Ritornello dell'Intervista (Piovani) (0:19)	
Theme (piano)	Anita in the kitchen, gets some grappa; Marcello observes her
La dolce vita (Rota) (0:21)	
Theme (piano)	Anita and Marcello watch; cut to Trevi Fountain scene from *La dolce vita*
Ritornello dell'Intervista (Piovani) (0:19)	
Theme (piano)	Trevi Fountain scene, cont.
La dolce vita (Rota) (0:24)	
Theme (piano)	Trevi Fountain scene, cont.
Ritornello dell'Intervista (Piovani) (0:19)	
Theme (piano)	Trevi Fountain scene cont. Cut to Marcello and Anita watching. Anita wipes away a tear; Marcello stops projection

Are these shadows on the screen more alive, less close to death? Wearing heavy makeup and eccentric costumes, Ekberg and Mastroianni at present appear like play figures whose closely miked voices sound as if dubbed from a beyond. The music, above all, gives the magic flashback its liminal quality. Even as the clarinet plays Rota's tune with a warmth that draws the spectator toward the dancing couple, the arrangement is slower and more intimate than the edgy original. Similarly, shadowing

Figure 2.10
Anita and Marcello watch *La dolce vita* (*top*), with the light of the screen projected on their faces like the "ray of sunshine" shown in the last frame of *Intervista* (*bottom*).

the piano with the vibraphone then binds the recurring refrains of the *Intervista* and *La dolce vita* themes into timbral twins, whose eerie sustain makes the images, especially those from the Trevi Fountain scene, recede into a phantasmal distance. Yet the most uncanny aspect is not the remembered footage itself, but how it is embedded into a present that already appears like a memory. When Marcello watches Anita return from the kitchen with two shot glasses of liquor, a minimal touch of slow motion matches the otherworldly color of the *Intervista* theme. For Fellini's marvelous alter ego, the true phantom is Anita today, watching herself while the flickering light from past pictures is reflected on her face (figure 2.10). When the wizard sees her wipe away a tear, he suddenly ends the magic—poof—and the sheet-screen goes up in smoke.

Left with no trace but a lingering haze, we are to realize that the spectacle was dreamt as much as remembered. Fellini employs a conjuror to give away what is always his game: that the images on-screen are the theater of the mind, and that memory must amalgamate with imagination. As Fellini once said about his oeuvre, he always directed the same film "using the same materials . . . from varying points of view."[34] We sense this shifting perspective when the flashback emerges from the dancing couple, whose present movement continues seamlessly into the past. Fittingly, Piovani's cue does not start out with Rota's melody, but begins *in medias res* with the bridge, as if Mandrake–Mastroianni had merely switched on an ongoing tune. When the music alternates between melodies from then and now, its melancholic flow, like the tinted screen, fuses cinematic present and cinematic past into apparitions of the future anterior.

The explosive noise that ends the show and snaps back to the reality of the living room is not unlike the screech we hear when Fletcher stops Hakman's incipient end-of-life montage. Though Naïm is not an *auteur*, like Fellini, both filmmakers are caught between the human desire for rememorization and the critical impulse against its commercial exploitation. In *Intervista*, the folding of one tertiary memory into another forces the catastrophe of the future anterior when, for Stiegler, "the actor's body is conflated with the character's."[35] Time passing is a human tragedy to which music gives voice: what is left from the sweet vitality of the *La dolce vita* and *Intervista* themes is a plaintive echo of music that once animated dancing bodies, now being reanimated from a poignant point of audition that seems inevitably closer to death. As is so often the case, Fellini's nostalgia is punctured by satire, making it more melancholic. His memory montages are made not by a sin eater but by a puppet master who puts on a carnivalesque parade of saints *and* sinners.[36] Never a pure parodist, Fellini's tricks are double-edged: he frames the flashback to *La dolce vita* with Brechtian devices of theatrical disillusionment but cuts off the clip to deepen the sense of sadness in Ekberg's encounter with her former self. Having brought her back to life, Marcello kisses her hand, and she tenderly strikes his vest. Yet this is not a tribute to them but to her. After he takes a bow, we cut back to Anita, who smiles and cries. Cinema is rarely this poignant: a real diva torn between her glorious resurrection on-screen and the catastrophe of her future demise.

Nowhere is Fellini's ambivalence more tangible than in the double ending of *Intervista*. During a pan over deserted sets outside, the melody of Rota's "I clowns" (from Fellini's 1970 film of that name) dies away in a wistful arrangement for solo sax. But as we cut inside, into the empty Studio 5 of Cinecittà, Fellini's voiceover remarks that while his film is done, a former producer had accused him of ending his movies "without the faintest hope, or ray of sunshine." And so, after the lights in the studio dim, a member of the crew steps into the remaining spotlight with a traditional clapper board announcing a first take). The primal action of this moment is obvious: we are back at the beginning of (cinematic) creation, where light bonds life to, or bans life from, celluloid. And so, as the closing credits begin to roll over the frozen frame, the *Intervista* theme returns in its original vivacity. Fellini, to invoke Stiegler, was less interested in the desire for stories than in stories of desire.[37]

The Final Cut, by comparison, caters more to the desire for cathartic closure. Yet the prospect of undoing the rememory business is undone when Fletcher reconciles with his friend through the recorded footage he seeks to destroy. Hakman's fate seems to allude to that of Gene Hackman's character Harry Caul, the main protagonist of Francis Coppola's *The Conversation* (1974), who despairs over his fatal trust in recording technology and who ends up in a panic over total surveillance, ripping open the walls of his apartment in search of bugs. Whether or not the allusion (Hackman versus Hakman) was intended, Naïm's choice of music tries to redeem his hero. *The Conversation* closes with a forlorn Harry Caul, haunted by flashbacks, playing his saxophone as if to stem his paranoia, but the rememory track that accompanies the final review of Hakman's life turns Fletcher himself into a sin eater of sorts. While Fellini retained from Neorealism the idea that morality need not be tied to sentiment, Naïm remains beholden to a Hollywood mainstream, where sentiment paves the road to morality. If *Intervista* indulges in metacinematic irony, the media critique in *The Final Cut* wants to be taken seriously. Exposing the pitfalls of public commemoration, Naïm's sententious ending is prescient but powerless. Today social-media platforms have punctured the protective wall between private and public spheres, allowing algorithms to perform regular rememory rituals for its users by scoring snapshots from their personal timeline with their favorite music.

Tertiary memory imparts the troubling truth that a mediated timeline is a temporal object turning on us. Stiegler writes about the nested nature of this experience:

> *La dolce vita* is no longer simply a fiction for someone viewing *Intervista*: it has become its past, such that watching Anita watching herself perform the scene in *La dolce vita*, the viewer sees himself or herself passing by. This is true even if *La dolce vita* is not part of the viewer's past in the same way it is in Anita's, Mastroianni's, and Fellini's past; all three have actually lived what the spectator sees "in the cinema." *Intervista*, as a temporal object, is temporal in making the temporal object *La dolce vita*, lived by characters in *Intervista* just as by its current viewers—each in a particular role—re-appear.
>
> Consequently, the viewer (of *Intervista*) [is] faced with the impossibility of distinguishing between reality and fiction, between perception and imagination, while (each in his or her particular role) *all* must also say to themselves, "*We* are passing by there."[38]

These are the larger stakes in the claim that life is always cinema: when watching our recorded selves, the experience of dying enters into the experience of living. The tertiary memory of temporal objects does this for us and to us: we see actors alive and aging on-screen just as we see ourselves alive and aging when looking into the mirror every day. In this regard, the moments of rememory in *The Final Cut* and *Intervista* align with the latter's title: the inter-view is a face-to-face encounter made possible when cinema changes its screen into a mirror. This may be why Fellini, the old sorcerer, collapses the creation of light at the beginning of cinema into the light of creation with the flash issuing from Marcello–Mandrake's magic wand, calling upon music to *fai tornare i bei tempi del passato*.

2

Retrieval

CHAPTER THREE

Double Projections

Some years ago, I took a friend to see Wagner's *Die Walküre*—a first for him. At the beginning of the third act, just as the "Ride of the Valkyries" launched into its series of brilliantly orchestrated climaxes, he leaned over and said, "I'm really having a hard time getting those helicopters out of my head." What he was referring to, of course, is one of the most notorious scenes in postwar American cinema: the attack by a US helicopter squadron on a Vietnamese village in Francis Coppola's 1979 film *Apocalypse Now*. In it, Lieutenant Colonel William Kilgore engages in psychological warfare by blasting Wagner's "Ride" from the gunships. Called forth by the music, my friend's memory of the scene impinged on watching what was going on onstage.

I call this phenomenon *double projection*.

Simply defined, double projection is the simultaneous perception of two different images: one projected onto an external screen, the other onto an internal screen. What my friend saw on the operatic stage counts as external projection; what he saw in his head was an internal projection—a memory. The sense of a concurrent projection of past and present images is an aspect of how audiovisual memory was impacted by the invention of mechanically reproduced multimedia. When compilers of early film scores plundered the large stock of operatic scenes for music that could suit specific dramatic situations, they felt compelled to point out that such borrowings carried the risk of double projection. George Beynon warned, in 1921, that "the very fact that opera music has a definite association causes it to become a dangerous thing with which to play." He added a vivid account of what could go wrong:

> If a tense dramatic situation must receive a fitting accompaniment, it would be the height of folly to use the death music from "Carmen." The minds of the patrons would revert at once to the scene outside the bullring. They would see again the blade driven into Carmen's bosom, while her lover falls despairingly across her outstretched body. In the meantime, the Hero on the screen sits bound in the chair, straining to break the ropes that bind him, in order that he can rush to the Maiden that is being spirited away by the wily Villain. Imagine the contradiction of the two ideas, and the incongruity of the attempt to blend them into one.[1]

Carmen is killed before the inner eye, while a completely different scene unfolds before the outer eye in the movie theater. These kinds of "contradictions" were common enough to prompt the film composer and conductor Victor Herbert to report in 1916 how music lovers complained that "their pleasure in picture presentations was to a large extent spoiled by the patchwork character of the accompanying music. When the orchestra played, they heard bits of 'Faust,' or 'Tannhäuser,' or 'Carmen,' or 'Traviata,' the hearing of the music flashed pictures from those operas on the minds of the spectators, and attention was distracted from the characters in the story."[2] To be sure, not all early filmgoers were opera buffs. But once movies treated old pieces to new visual covers, the musically educated members of the audience were the first to register a sea change in the formation of musical knowledge.

Film music is akin to what Gilles Deleuze and Félix Guattari have described as the territorializing force of the refrain (*ritournelle*): "a prism, a crystal of space-time. It acts upon that which surrounds it, sound or light, extracting from it various vibrations, or decompositions, projections, or transformations."[3] The phenomenon in which sound and image are joined *across modalities* is known among psychologists as associative or conjunctive memory, which results from contextual encoding.[4] Michel Chion's "synchresis" imagines this process as a form of projection:

> Transformed by the image it influences, sound ultimately reprojects onto the image the product of their mutual influences. We find eloquent testimony to this reciprocity in the case of horrible or upsetting sounds. The image projects onto them a meaning they do not have at all by themselves.[5]

Image projects onto sound; sound *re*projects onto the image. Here film music performs the "catalytic function" of the refrain: "not only to increase the speed of the exchanges and reactions in that which surrounds it, but also to assure indirect interactions between elements devoid of so-called natural affinity."[6] The cinematic refrain not only reprojects meanings created in synchresis, but also takes on, whenever repeated, new images for later reprojection.

Initially, the resulting double projections were not always welcome. Since the cue-sheet boom of the silent era was built on preexisting music that came with "definite" associations, viewers steeped in classical repertory were plagued with unwanted recollections. As Rick Altman has pointed out, critics claimed that when they recognized the music from a particular opera, "their knowledge of that opera interferes with their concentration on the film at hand."[7] Similar language was used in the two-volume *Allgemeines Handbuch der Film-Musik*, co-authored in 1927 by Hans Erdmann, Ludwig Brav, and Giuseppe Becce.[8] The theoretical volume, which came with the extensive catalog of music classified for use in the cinema, explicitly "prohibited" the use of familiar operas and well-known concert music because "very specific associations are tied to these works that would detract from the effects of the film."[9] Tucked away in a footnote early on, Erdmann made an observation most pertinent to this chapter: once music and the action of scenes from well-known operas have become "inseparable" for the "spectator-listener" (*Zuschauhörer*)—a "cumulative effect also possible with film"—"phenomena of association or interference occur when the usual connection between hearing and seeing has become loose or is lost."[10]

Yet these phenomena could also became productive. The internal image projected by familiar music could in fact enrich the cinematic experience, changing unwanted associations into wanted allusions. Consider how Martin Miller Marks chose to accompany a scene in a recent release of Ernst Lubitsch's 1925 adaptation of Oscar Wilde's *Lady Windermere's Fan*.[11] Early on, Lady Windermere is contemplating what an intertitle describes as the "grave problem" of seating the guests for her birthday party, including someone with the telltale name of Lord Darlington. When Lord Darlington arrives to see her (and not her husband, as he assures her), Marks launches into the Duettino "Là ci darem la mano" from Mozart's *Don Giovanni* to accentuate how "the ever suave Darlington comes up to his would-be 'Lady' and takes her by the hand."[12] The music intimates the lord's dubious intentions and the eventual failure of his seduction. I witnessed how early film audiences might have felt when I played the film scene after taking one of my courses to a performance of Mozart's opera: students immediately recognized how Marks had played the picture like early movie-house pianists well-versed in the operatic repertory.

Nowadays the order is typically reversed, with my friend "seeing" the helicopter attack from *Apocalypse Now* while watching *Die Walküre*. Once cinema came to compete with existing forms of cultural entertainment, such as opera, the tables turned. This does not mean that the visuals first seen with music in the movie theater inevitably create the most lasting impression. A corollary of double projections is the palimpsest, images stacked in the order of experience, where firstness competes with salience in viewers' memory. An overpowering cinematic moment may lock in a specific audiovisual association, overriding the recollection of a riveting operatic performance. When movies began to circulate as products of mass culture, chances increased that the first and most arresting audiovisual encounter would be in the cinema, and that cinematic images projected by music would contend with each other. Before long, these associations and interferences became the foundation of new forms of intertextuality.

Recent practices of remix and mash-up have a broad appeal for audiences who take pleasure in decoding the intertextual references that began to proliferate with the rise of audiovisual media. This chapter will focus on two European directors, Alexander Kluge and Jean-Luc Godard, who deployed double projection as part of their modernist aesthetics, where critical interference (the clash between internal and on-screen images) and formal synchronicity (two images appearing in close proximity through juxtaposition or simultaneously through superimposition) carry a political message. While Kluge has shown a greater affinity with accidental allusion that conjures images from the viewer's archive, Godard continues to relish intentional reference summoned from his prodigious command over the archive of cinematic history. If both directors epitomize a generation of the cinemathèque where literacy and learnedness encompass cinephile and audiophile, they have not just marshaled music's mnemonic powers of reprojection to unsettle and enlighten; sometimes their music also escapes those powers and, by leaving those images behind, becomes buoyant.

Critical Interference

The director and writer Alexander Kluge, whom Peter C. Lutze has called "the last modernist," has long advocated for the greater involvement of viewers in cinematic experience.[13] Following Brecht's idea of epic theater, Kluge sought to empower audiences by changing them from passive recipients into active participants. Since film is realized—to use an oft-quoted formulation by Kluge—"in the spectator's head, not on screen," it must be "porous, weak, brittle" on-screen, allowing viewers to become "active" and develop a "penetrating imagination."[14] Kluge based his notion of a "utopian cinema" on an "imaginative faculty" he believed has existed in our minds for millennia and whose "streams of images, of so-called associations, have moved through the human mind, prompted to some extent by an anti-realistic attitude, by the protest against an unbearable reality."[15] Since the invention of cinematic technology merely added "reproducible counter-images" to the images in the human mind, the "productive forces of cinema can only be developed together with the perceptual powers of the viewer."[16]

Kluge's "principle of cinema" (a gloss on Ernst Bloch's *The Principle of Hope*) is a critique of the false consciousness propagated through illusionist film, whose phantasmagoric wholes are preimagined for passive consumption. His cinema of fragmentation interweaves fictional and documentary modes to break spectatorial habits and engage viewers' fantasies so that they can discover a connection (*Zusammenhang*) between "particles of reality" from the most diverse historical and cultural contexts. For such films as *The Patriot* (1979), *The Power of Emotion* (1983), and *The Assault of the Present on the Rest of Time* (1985), Kluge adopted montage techniques from both silent cinema and Soviet films of the 1920s and 1930s. Miriam Hansen has noted how Kluge's montages seek to "reconstruct an associational mode of experience in constellations akin to writing," thereby creating "an *interference* of discourses which attempts to provoke a more active participation on the part of the spectator."[17] Because cinema must learn from the spectator (and not vice versa), the film unfolding in the head of the spectator "figures the political priority of the spectator's experience as the basis of production."[18]

Interference had come a long way, from distracting early audiences to a didactics of critical distanciation that might foster an "oppositional public sphere."[19]

Although Kluge seeks to free viewers from the dictates of illusionist film, he has exercised a strong directorial control over the creative process, alerting them to the cinematic apparatus. In *The Power of Emotion*, he combines old footage of Verdi's *Aida* with audio from different parts of the opera. The ensuing double projection—music conjuring a scene not matched on-screen—suggests that cinema merely offers "counter-images" to the cinema of the mind. Although Kluge has aimed at deconstructing authorship, his directorial presence remains palpable, not only in his jarring juxtaposition of disparate materials but in his subtly ironic commentary, which nudges viewers into making specific connections and drawing new conclusions. Despite his improvised shooting—working without a script in impromptu settings—Kluge's finished films leave little room for the serendipitous nature of accidental interference. His musical selections for *The Patriot*, cataloged and scrutinized by Caryl Flinn and Roger Hillman, demonstrate the extent to which these apparent accidents are predicated on the deep cultural knowledge they purport to strip away.[20] Often the associations inherent in these selections—like the "Ode to Joy" from Beethoven's Ninth Symphony—are not only predictable but overdetermined.

Perhaps Kluge's most provocative musical interferences occurs at the beginning of *The Patriot*. The film seeks to excavate an alternative history of Germany by pairing two unusual protagonists: history teacher Gabi Teichert, searching for new ways of teaching her subject in the 1970s, and the "knee" of Private Wieland, who was killed in the battle at Stalingrad. Digging in the ground, Teichert literalizes the metaphor of history as an archeology that unearths hidden layers from the past, while Wieland's talking knee (ventriloquized in Kluge's voiceover) becomes the mouthpiece for a history from below that establishes discursive links between pieces of debris buried under the surface of official history. Going beyond a Germany defined by nationalism and national socialism as a country of perpetrators, Teichert is introduced in the opening as "a patriot" who "takes an interest in *all* the dead of the Reich."[21] Kluge quotes Curtis Bernhardt's *Die letzte Kompagnie* (1930), which deals with the heroic death of twelve soldiers and their captain who delay the advance of Napoleon's army into Prussia in 1806.[22] If the degraded footage of the fallen soldiers enhances the sense of their historicity, we hear the music Hanns Eisler had used for the opening credits and final monologue of Alain Resnais's 1955 Holocaust documentary *Nuit et brouillard* (*Night and Fog*)—a connection already alluded to in the similar design of title screens (figure 3.1).

The musical quotation is vexing, yet it builds on the palimpsestic nature of Eisler's score, itself based partly on preexisting music that carried

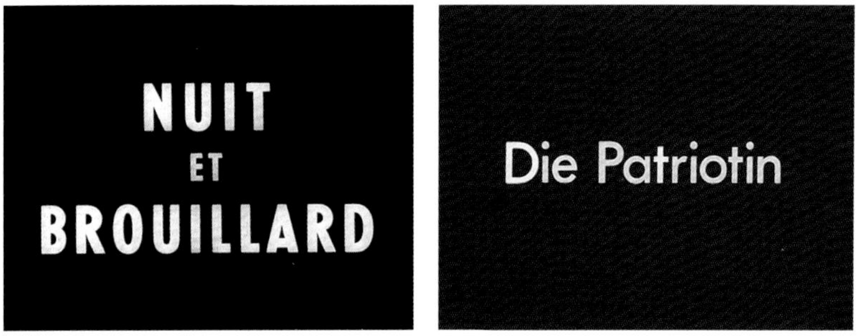

Figure 3.1 Title screens for Resnais's *Night and Fog* and Kluge's *The Patriot.*

an association with German war victims. *Night and Fog* was the first successful Holocaust documentary, an influential film whose blunt showing of horrifying images from the death camps impressed itself deeply on postwar audiences and the cinematic establishment alike. Asked which film had been the most effective in dealing with peace and war, François Truffaut called it "the greatest film ever made."[23] In thirty-two minutes, Resnais combined a chilling visual testimony of systematic genocide with an explanatory commentary written by the poet Jean Cayrol—himself a Holocaust survivor. The film's most conspicuous device is the juxtaposition of black-and-white archival films and photographs with present-day color footage of the death camps. If the latter shows deserted sites in a state of decay—with the camera roaming over the grounds and buildings in search of the unimaginable—the archival material tells, in gruesome detail, a stringent story that leads from the early persecution of the Jews to their mass extermination. When working on the score for *Night and Fog*, Eisler drew on music he had composed in the autumn of 1954 for the staging of Johannes R. Becher's *Winterschlacht* by Brecht's Berliner Ensemble.[24] At the height of the war, Becher had written the first version of the tragedy (then entitled "Battle of Moscow") in his Tashkent exile as a response to Hitler's costly but unsuccessful campaign to take the Soviet capital during the winter of 1941–1942.

Eisler surprised the ensemble with his approach to the final scene of *Winterschlacht*, which depicts the retreat of the defeated German army. Brecht found it "strange" that Eisler deleted all text from the scene and, instead of expressing "wild triumph akin to what Beethoven would have used to depict victory," wrote closing music for strings whose sense of grief the composer explained by noting, "They are Germans, that is sad."[25] This music has already been part of the prelude to *Winterschlacht*, which accompanied a view of scattered soldiers from the destroyed army, as seen in the poster for the premiere. In the concluding melodramatic epilogue, in which a soldier of the Red Army emphatically asks the audience to commemorate as well the defeated Germans for their contribution to the victory of freedom, Eisler recapitulates the first seventeen measures of the prelude, capped with a rousing four-measure flourish played by three trumpets. When working on *Night and Fog*, Eisler chose the first

Figure 3.2 Hanns Eisler's *Winterschlacht* prelude, with changes for *Night and Fog*.

twenty-nine measures of the *Winterschlacht* prelude to score the film's opening credits (*générique*), changing the three-quarter-note anacrusis into three accented half notes and adding a subdued single trumpet entry in measures 14–15 (see figure 3.2).[26]

Frequently working on demand, Eisler had no qualms about recycling music from his own archive. If the prelude's melody, harmonized over a chromatically descending bass line, had functioned as a lament before, why not redeploy it? In autumn of 1956, Eisler took no fewer than five numbers from the manuscript score of *Night and Fog* and inserted them into the stage music for the production of Brecht's play *The Days of the Commune*, which dramatizes the failed attempt of Paris workers to organize a socialist government in the spring of 1871. Six years later, what had been the fifth number of *Night and Fog*, and the second number in *The Days of the Commune*, became part of the music Eisler put together for a production of Friedrich Schiller's *Wilhelm Tell*, simply by inserting the relevant pages from the autograph into the new project. Bits and pieces from the film score also turned up, in 1957 alone, in the Soviet revolutionary play *Sturm*, in Brecht's cantata *The Carpet-Weavers of Kujan-Bulak*, and in a newly composed number Eisler had added to his 1947 score for Brecht's *Life of Galileo*.[27]

Eisler's reuse of the *Winterschlacht* prelude for *Night and Fog* was highly evocative. Resnais later recalled that the composer explained "how to avoid a musical pleonasm," using the score instead "to create something like 'a second level of perception,' something additional with an opposite meaning."[28] In setting the tone for both Becher's drama and Resnais's documentary, the music suggested that a lament for the victims of the Holocaust could also give voice to the sorrow felt for the casualties of war. Amid the uniqueness of the Holocaust, Eisler understood the unfathomable nature of genocide more broadly, aligning himself with Cayrol's concluding words, which challenge "those of us who pretend all this happened only once, at a certain time and in a certain place." Eisler would soon make his more catholic view of human tragedy and suffering more explicit. If Becher had viewed *Winterschlacht* as an attempt to create a German Hamlet, the composer reworked the music of the prelude in a song entitled "Horatio's Monologue," based on words spoken at the end of Shakespeare's drama.[29] Having agreed in the summer of 1954 to contribute to the staging of *Winterschlacht*, Eisler spent early September in Vienna, writing stage music for a production of *Hamlet* at the La Scala Theater. While setting Horatio's lines was not part of his assignment, the way they addressed the nature of human calamity in an epilogue-like fashion may well have been on his mind when he used them for a song in 1956:

And let me speak to the yet unknowing world
How these things came about: so shall you hear
Of carnal, bloody, and unnatural acts;
Of accidental judgments, casual slaughters;
Of deaths put on by cunning and forc'd cause;
And, in this upshot, purposes mistook
Fall'n on th' inventors' heads: all this can I
Truly deliver.[30]

Opening *The Patriot* with music known from *Night and Fog* was so provocative because its prelude had become overdetermined by also accompanying those "bloody and unnatural acts" shown at the end of Resnais's film. Kluge knew that its shocking images of severed heads and emaciated corpses had been etched, indelibly, into public memory. Now these images interfered with those of dead soldiers from *Die letzte Kompagnie*, strewn across a nineteenth-century battlefield covered with fog and shrouded by the darkness of night.[31] But only those familiar with the music for *Winterschlacht* could know that Kluge alluded to *Night and Fog* by using a recording of the prelude for Becher's play. Kluge made his musical quotation hard to detect. Precisely at that moment where one might expect the trumpet entry from the film music, in measures 14–15, he cuts from the Napoleonic war to a brief clip of anti-aircraft artillery firing in 1943, before breaking off abruptly after the second beat of measure 17 with the intertitle "The Knee," which introduces the body part of Corporal Wieland, who died in Stalingrad. The result is a vexing palimpsest of historical layers:

1806 or Napoleonic Wars	*Die Letzte Kompagnie*
Battle of Moscow	*Winterschlacht*
Holocaust	*Nuit et brouillard*
Stalingrad	*Die Patriotin*

Did the double projection inherent in Kluge's montage—dead soldiers on the external screen clashing with Holocaust victims on viewers' internal screen—count as a critical interference or serve a revisionist agenda? Kluge's opening gambit was, according to Eric Rentschler, not only "troubling" because it "collapses Jewish concentration camp victims and German war dead into one"; it was also "disturbing" because *The Patriot* "withholds even a single image of Jewish suffering in a prolonged work of mourning, suggesting that we can talk of World War II without mentioning Auschwitz."[32] Thomas Elsaesser even asked whether Kluge might be considered "a revanchist, a conservative nationalist masquerading as a concerned liberal and even left-winger."[33] Elsaesser diagnoses the absence of the Holocaust in the New German Cinema of the 1970s as an in-between step in the process of mourning, between repression and working through, calling this step "presence as parapraxis." Since Freud's notion of *Fehlleistung* literally means "performed failure," Elsaesser distinguishes between "'parapraxis as mourning work' ('performed failure') and 'mourning work as parapraxis' ('failed performance')."[34] The latter applies to occasions Germans failed to commemorate, and a pertinent example is the request by the German government to ban *Nuit et brouillard* from being shown at the 1956 Cannes Film Festival by arguing that "the average spectator would not be able to distinguish between the criminals of the Nazi regime and the people of today's Germany."[35] Performed failure, by contrast, occurs in films of the New German Cinema, in which "stylistic peculiarities such as repetition or abrupt montage, as well as rhetorical strategies of reversal and irony all point to a 'politics of performative misalignments,' whose effect is an ongoing return and repetition around something, which, perhaps only now and certainly only with hindsight, can be read and deciphered differently: as a 'mourning work-in-progress.'"[36] Performed failures allow film to create an oppositional public sphere that responds to the failed performances in the public sphere.

Kluge's quotation of Eisler's music would be such a performed failure. Double projection becomes critically productive by revealing similarities between internal and external images without removing their essential disparity. The battlefield sequence from the opening of *The Patriot* exemplifies what Elsaesser calls "presence-in-absence" in the New German Cinema (figure 3.3): Eisler's prelude effectively makes present the absence of the Holocaust—not only from the external screen, but potentially from the musical reference itself, as the music stems from

Figure 3.3 "Presence-in-absence" as "critical interference" at the beginning of *Die Patriotin*: the external projection of fictive dead soldiers from the Napoleonic wars (*top left*, a still from *Die letzte Kompagnie*) clashes with images of real bodies from the ending of *Night and Fog* (*top right*), reprojected internally by the prelude from *Winterschlacht* (*bottom*).

Winterschlacht. Not only is it incomplete but it reprojects the images from Resnais's documentary merely internally, within viewers' heads, prompting the question of what the dead soldiers on-screen have in common with and how they differ from the victims of genocide.

This presence-in-absence is even more pronounced when Kluge reprises a much longer portion of the *Winterschlacht* prelude later in *The Patriot*, during a chapter called "Alpine Waterways," which showcases the Third Reich's ambitious but unrealized project of building a system of canals across the Alps to link the North Sea with the Adriatic Sea.[37] The chapter's montage is framed by visually and thematically similar shots: it begins with footage of an Alpine lake with floating ice, followed by a dramatic overhead still shot of mountain climbers at the summit of a snow-covered peak. This pair is matched at the end of the montage by a shot showing the mountains from the original drawing of the waterway project and ending with a picture of mountain climbers negotiating a ridge with their equipment—untamed nature versus nature mastered. In between Kluge pairs footage of German youth working with footage of forced laborers (figure 3.4). Then he shows the photo of an unnamed member of the notorious Organization Todt (which used forced labor for civil and military engineering projects during the Third Reich), which held that "everything is just a question of organization."[38]

How does this montage perform failure? The formal parallels between the deployment of German youth and the use of forced laborers illustrate superior organization, but when the camera dwells on the drawing of

Figure 3.4 The second *Winterschlacht* prelude montage in *The Patriot* uses similarities of shape to showcase untamed and tamed nature, with shots of floating ice and a snow-covered mountain (*top*), and two forms of organized labor: Hitler youth and forced laborers (*bottom*).

the Alpine waterways, conspicuously absent are images of what Hillman calls the "most obscene example of organizational capacity imaginable, the superrationality of Auschwitz."[39] As before, however, the music from *Winterschlacht* by way of *Night and Fog* becomes Kluge's parapraxis as mourning work-in-progress: we may see on-screen the sublime image of reaching a summit, but images of the negative sublime are called up by music internally, performing failure through critical interference.

Formal Synchronicity

If music can project images before one's inner eye, remembered images may also turn up on-screen, in juxtaposition, in rapid alternation, or through superimposition. As Daniel Morgan has shown, superimposition was once championed by the "pure cinema" movement in 1920s France as "a way of thinking in and with cinema," and it often represented dreams, the unconscious, or ghosts in narrative films. Although superimposition has largely gone out of fashion, Morgan detects an "afterlife" within Godard's films, notably in the monumental *Histoire(s) du cinéma*, an eight-part video project created in 1988–1989. Composed almost entirely with visual and auditory quotations from a vast array of films, *Histoire(s)* is an essay on the "interrelation (actual and potential) between the history of cinema and the history of the twentieth century" and "an account of the powers of a medium," but also "a sustained defense of superimposition as an aesthetic and analytic technique."[40] One particularly dense sequence from Part 1A of *Histoire(s)*, entitled "Toutes les histoires," has become iconic because of this provocative claim in Godard's voiceover: "And if George Stevens hadn't been the first to use the first sixteen-millimeter color film at Auschwitz and Ravensbrück, Elizabeth Taylor's air of happiness would never have found a place in the sun." Here is Morgan's description of what follows:

> As Godard mentions the names of the camps, he cuts briefly to a black screen, then to color footage Stevens took of corpses at Ravensbrück as a war photographer for the army. The name of Elizabeth Taylor triggers another cut: over the documentary footage, Godard begins intercutting and superimposing a clip from Stevens's *A Place in the Sun*, showing Taylor cradling the head of Montgomery Clift in her lap and caressing his hair. After several moments, Godard cuts from Clift looking up to a shot of a corpse, mouth open and staring up, a color image that seems filmed off a television screen. He says, "Thirty-nine, forty-four: martyrdom and resurrection of the documentary," a time period that goes from the beginning of the war to (presumably) the liberation of France. Godard then returns to *A Place in the Sun*, as Taylor stands up from the rock where she and Clift have been lying; he superimposes over the clip a detail from Giotto's *Noli me tangere* rotated 90 degrees so that Mary Magdalene now reaches down from the top of the frame while the hand of Christ is visible at the bottom. Taylor bends down to kiss Clift, then rises back up; in so doing, her figure mimics the gesture of the Magdalene, and she assumes a pose such that it is now *her* hand that moves to touch the hand of Christ. Adapting lines from Georges Bernanos, Godard says, "O, how marvelous to be able to watch what one can't see. O sweet miracle of our blind eyes!"[41]

Godard's comment about Stevens sparked a controversy that pitted his belief in the power of cinematic images to access historical reality against Claude Lanzmann's "negative aesthetic" (exemplified in *Shoah*), which aimed at safeguarding such reality, specifically in the case of the Holocaust, through the radical rejection of the photograph as an index of real events.[42] Against Resnais's use in *Night and Fog* of archival footage (partly created by the Nazis), Lanzmann sought to undermine—even destroy—any trust in cinematic representation, requiring viewers to look elsewhere for evidence of historical reality. In *Shoah*, this task falls to survivors who return to sites of atrocities to recount what happened, requiring the viewer to imagine an unfathomable past amid the paucity of the present. Yet in *Histoire(s)* Godard takes the opposite approach, one that follows (not unlike Brecht) the didactic impulse of "teaching an audience how to discern the history within the images, how to read the way history enters into and is mediated by cinema."[43] He does so in intricate montages that embrace the abundance of the historical record by referencing the full spectrum of cultural artifacts—including music.

Nowhere, perhaps, does Godard position himself vis-à-vis Lanzmann as directly as in the harrowing images and clips interspersed in a sequence several minutes earlier, which include an execution, a dead mother next to her small child, a pile of corpses from a concentration camp, and footage of an emaciated inmate struggling with a guard in a ditch. The last, especially, is so disturbing because Godard adds to this battle of life and death a sound effect resembling the choking of a dog. The silent footage, slowed down as if the jumping frames were to highlight the futility of the fight, also overlaps with an archival sound clip announcing fallen soldiers, including a Legionnaire, Bizet Carlona, whose name sounds accompanied by a detail from Van Gogh's *Wheatfield with Crows*. When the roll call for the dead ends, music enters: the opening movement, entitled "Fantasie," of Paul Hindemith's Sonata for Viola and Piano, op. 11 (1919), together with the word *jamais* ("never") superimposed on the struggle, printed "JA MAIS" to suggest a combination of German and French—*ja aber* ("yes but")—which immediately undercuts the French-only meaning (figure 3.5).

"Fantasie" opens with a beautiful lyrical melody winding down to a sonorous D3 on the lowest string, which lends the viola its uniquely mournful timbre. But during the first measure Godard fades in a noisy passage from the frenzied Quadrille from act 4 of *Carmen* to suggest, perhaps, how the random name of the fallen soldier—Bizet—might automatically call up some of the most popular pieces by its most famous namesake. The result is a *sonic* double projection of sorts. It fades a bit after the viola's arrival at D3 on the downbeat of measure three, which coincides with a cut to a clip from the Polish film *Pasazerka* (1963), showing a woman walking along the fence of Auschwitz, carrying flowers—the same woman seen as a uniformed guard standing in front of the fence before the archival footage of the futile fight. The film was based on the 1959 radio play *Passenger from Cabin Number 45*, by concentration camp survivor Zofia Posmysz, about a woman, Liza, who, while traveling on a ship after the war, recognizes someone who looks like a former inmate at Auschwitz, where Liza used to be a guard. Thus Godard frames the inserted clip of the struggle between guard and victim *as a memory*. While the screen goes black again, flashing the title of *Pasazerka* twice and the name of the director Andrzej Munk, the sonata almost fades out at the end of the fourth measure, remaining barely audible amid the Quadrille and Godard's voiceover: "The spirit of Flaherty and Epstein took over. It's Daumier and Rembrandt with his dreadful black and white." We see footage of concentration camp inmates pushing a cart, shown in slow-motion to highlight the strain of the labor, while Godard's voice and Hindemith's music give way to an old recording of "Addio Lugano

"Legionaire Bizet Carlona?
Killed by the enemy."

bella," whose text was written by the anarchist Pietro Gori after being expelled from the city. Why does Godard use the hauntingly beautiful opening from Hindemith's "Fantasie" amid such disquieting images, joining them in the viewer's memory going forward?

Invoking George Stevens minutes later, Godard echoes an essay about William Wyler by André Bazin, who suggested that American directors who served in the war—including Capra and Stevens—tried to confront its horrors by engaging in an "ethic of realism." If Wyler's gripping drama *The Best Years of Our Lives* (1946) featured an actor who had lost both arms, Bazin quoted the director as saying, "I know that George Stevens has not been the same since he saw corpses at Dachau. We were forced to realize that Hollywood has rarely reflected the world and the time in which people live."[44] During World War II, Stevens had the horrific task of heading a film unit in the US Army, shooting footage of D-Day as well as concentration camps (later used at the Nuremberg trials). Godard's montage implies that Stevens's postwar films responded to a crisis of cinematic

Figure 3.5 *(facing) Histoire(s) du cinéma* and the history of the Holocaust: the opening phrase of the first movement ("Fantasie") from Paul Hindemith's Sonata for Viola and Piano, op. 11, no. 4, amid sonic interference by the Quadrille from *Carmen*, sutures a montage including a fictional film and documentary footage.

Figure 3.6 Stevens superimposed: Taylor cradling a corpse and Clift.

representation: only after filming the camps could the director grasp the cost of showing a happiness that might otherwise remain unseen. Hence his superimposition of Elizabeth Taylor cradling Montgomery Clift in *A Place in the Sun* with a shot of corpses at Ravensbrück (figure 3.6); hence the return of Hindmith's "Fantasie" at this very moment.

Godard was fond of the opening lines of the poem "L'image" by the surrealist Pierre Reverdy, which say that an image "cannot be born of a comparison, but from the *rapprochement* of two more or less distant realities. The more distant and just the ties between the realities, the stronger the image will be."[45] Two meanings of *rapprochement* are resonant here: juxtaposition and approach, or *re*approach. Not unlike Kluge's combinations of *Kultur* and *Krieg*, Godard juxtaposes the "distant realities" of Holocaust and Hollywood to explore how they may be approaching each other. In *A Place in the Sun*, Taylor plays the society girl Angela, who becomes the demise of Clift's character, George. Working his way up in his uncle's factory, George begins dating his coworker Alice, who expects him to marry her after she becomes pregnant. Falling in love with Angela, George kisses her passionately at a dance, and when they go on a date at the paradisiacal lake, she tells him how a couple drowned there the summer before. George later takes Alice to the lake and she drowns when their boat capsizes by accident. Having failed to rescue her, George is sentenced to death for murder. Before the execution, a remorseful Angela visits him in his cell, a Magdalene-like figure who has caused his downfall and now becomes his redemption. The film ends with George walking to the electric chair and their passionate kiss returns as a superimposition, accompanied by the dance music that had soared in Franz Waxman's orchestral underscore (figure 3.7).

Angela's *fatale beauté*—the title of the second part of *Histoire(s)*—may have inspired Godard to make one head from the pile of corpses in Stevens's concentration camp footage dissolve into the head of an anxious Clift in Taylor's arms. The shot of the corpses is preceded by a series of horrifying heads (see figure 3.8): the head of Murnau's Nosferatu alternating with a detail from Picasso's *Le sauvetage* ("The Rescue"), also turned 90 degrees to show a woman stretching her arms upward for an embrace. Then the heads of two resistance fighters hanged by the Nazis

Figure 3.7
Superimposition at the end of *A Place in the Sun*: George, on the way to his execution, recalls kissing Angela.

Figure 3.8
(*facing, top*)
A series of horrifying heads, underscored with "Bella Ciao."

Figure 3.9
(*facing, bottom*)
Double projection as superimposition through quick alternation of images and verbal recollection (rendered in subtitles): a bomb drops into the arms of a woman from Picasso's *Le sauvetage* ("The Rescue") while Godard remembers *Guernica*, and later the woman "embraces" Murnau's Nosferatu.

in Minsk in 1941, though Godard's voiceover mentions the execution of the French philosopher Valentin Feldman. Then the shackled head from a group of three prisoners Goya prepared for *Los desastres de la guerra*. Then the nightmarish heads and faces from Goya's *Caprices* (no. 64, entitled "Buen Viagge" and identified on-screen as "Bon Voyage"). Finally, the bloody head from the pile of corpses spilling out from a freight train dissolves into George cradled by Angela before turning into Taylor's own head. "Bon Voyage"?

The series of horrifying heads that lead to a bizarre conflation of the Pietà and Mary-with-infant iconography seems to validate Wyler's assertion that Stevens had not been the same since he saw the corpses at Dachau. Godard never relinquishes his belief that cinema must and can address the horrors of war and genocide. He surely knew that *A Place in the Sun* itself ends with that superimposition of George walking to the electric chair remembering Angela kissing him in an ardent embrace amid beautiful music. This, perhaps, inspired not only the cut from Clift's anxious face to the colored "Ecce Homo" still of a dead Holocaust victim—possibly an allusion to Léon Bonnat's famous 1880 portrait of Job—but also the subsequent superimposition of Angela and Mary Magdalene, whose arms reach for the body of the risen Christ (see figure 3.10). Is she the "angel of resurrection," as Jacques Rancière claimed, or an angel of death, as Céline Scemama contends?[46] Or is she not both: an angel of resurrection as an angel of death?

Let us ponder these questions by asking how music's involvement in the "sweet miracle of our blind eyes" might make the juxtapositions and superimpositions of distant realities *just* in Reverdy's sense. We may

read Godard's dizzying montages as a rapprochement between distant realities. Or we may *sense* an affective affinity between them. Reading and sensing must combine to grasp fully what James S. Williams aptly describes as the "dense rhetorically motivated formations" of Godard's montage, which are "off-set by nondiscursive moments of association, confluence, contiguity, conjunction, and coincidence, moments that trace the interrelations of human form at the level of silhouette, shape, and figure. These far more basic and spontaneous associations . . . are material, proximate, local, and specific, and as such they offer a purer, more inclusive moment of seeing and feeling than the more mental act of cognition and interpretation."[47]

Reading and sensing belong as much to the domain of music as they do to the image. As music makes the rapprochement between the distant realities of an image legible, it can catalyze their emotional rapport, as suggested in later lines of Reverdy's "L'image": "What is great is not the image but the emotion which it provokes. The emotion thus provoked is true, poetically, because it is born outside all imitation, all evocation, and all resemblance."[48] The two pieces of music in Godard's montage pertain

Figure 3.10 Superimposition of distant realities mediated by music: After a change from D major to G♭ major, the viola reaches up just as Liz Taylor adds a third arm to reach down for the hand of the risen Christ in Giotto's *Noli me tangere*.

to this discursive and affective dimension: a segment of the antifascist song "Bella Ciao" and, again, the opening of Hindemith's "Fantasie." The song fades in with the shot of Nosferatu that starts the sequence of horrific heads. Lifting "Bella Ciao" from an iconic recording made by the Gruppo padano di Piadena (founded in 1962) with Giovanna Marini as the soloist, Godard may have been attracted by the striking superimposition of the folk and partisan versions of the song. While the former gives voice to a laborer saying goodbye to a beautiful woman when leaving for work in the rice fields, the latter belongs to the voice of a partisan fighter expecting to die in the mountains and to be buried "under the shadow of a beautiful flower." Godard clipped a twenty-second segment from the recording where the group fades out, repeating the last two lines—"È questo il fiore del partigiano / Morto per la libertà" (This is the flower of the partisan, who died for freedom)—while the solo voice reprises the first two lines of the folk version: "Alla mattina appena alzata / O bella ciao bella ciao bella ciao, ciao, ciao" (In the morning, barely woken up / O (my) beautiful, goodbye, (my beautiful, goodbye, (my) beautiful, goodbye, goodbye).

As a song of farewell, "Bella Ciao" is also a song of remembrance: the beautiful flower is a memento for the life lost in the fight against fascism. Hence the two versions form a palimpsest where the words of partisan resistance are grafted onto the folk song—a practice familiar from the creation of contrafacta, which substitute or alter the text of a song with another while keeping the melody, often taking advantage of the original meaning instead of erasing it. Performing this palimpsest, the quickening pace of the partisan version overlaps with the slower beginning of the folk tune. Godard may have noticed the critical interference of this sonic superimposition, combining a call for future action with a return to the past, thereby giving voice to a powerful solidarity between partisan and peasant. The sonic layering echoes the series of shots preceding the sequence of horrific heads: here, two rapidly alternating paintings of Mediterranean towns—briefly lingering on one overlaid with the title *Histoire(s) du cinema*—are followed by war footage of a destroyed building, buried in billowing black smoke, and of a plane dropping bombs. Remarkably, the plane alternates so quickly with the detail from *Le sauvetage* that the latter remains almost invisible to the naked eye (figure 3.9).

Amid these sonic and visual superimpositions, Godard's voiceover adds another layer of critical interference: "We've forgotten that small town and its white walls shaded by olive trees. But we remember Picasso, that is, *Guernica*." While Picasso's *Le sauvetage* remains invisible on-screen in its momentary superimposition with the shot of the bomb-dropping plane, Godard's mention of *Guernica* projects Picasso's most famous painting on the viewer's mental screen, colliding with *The Rescue* in the viewer's unconscious. But when Godard starts the segment from "Bella Ciao" with the shot of Nosferatu, he inserts the detail from *Le sauvetage* no fewer than seventeen times to emerge from unseen to seen. The miracle of the blind eye is the mechanism of the optical unconscious: the rapprochement between the plane and Picasso's painting reveals a figure reaching up to rescue another. Adding the acoustic dimension, voiceover and music enter into this rapprochement through double projection: we hear "Valentin Feldman" and see the fighters at Minsk. We are reminded of Goya's chained prisoner, and the image appears as if called up from memory by the words. And throughout, we hear "Bella Ciao" projecting the peasant and partisan onto the prisoner.

Although *Historie(s)* constantly overwhelms viewers with the complexity of audiovisual montages, they remain readable to the patient interpreter devoted to deciphering their meaning. Yet the pleasures of painstaking philology can only do partial justice to sensing their aesthetic effect. Richard Neer suggests that Godard's montages work in the way Ludwig Wittgenstein understood "'connecting links' between artifacts and events in historiography": a "hypothetical connecting link should . . . direct attention to the similarity, the relatedness, of the *facts*. As one might illustrate an internal relation of a circle to an ellipse by gradually converting an ellipse into a circle; *but not in order to assert that a certain ellipse actually, historically, had originated from a circle . . .* but only in order to sharpen our eye for a formal connection."[49] In Godard's montages, historical reality takes the form of superimposition, juxtaposition, and alternation of images and sounds. As Neer puts it, "It is not that certainty is merely fantastic, but that the fantastic has all the efficacy of what we call certainty."[50] For Christopher Pavsek, cinematic utopia involves the deep link between the film on-screen and the inner film, "by dint of its privileged address to the faculty of *Phantasie*."[51]

This kind of imagination is essential for counterhistorians like Godard and Kluge, whose insights emerge from observing noncausal coincidences.[52] While Kluge hopes that the *Zusammenhang* between "particles of reality" emerges spontaneously, Godard fashions formal synchronicity in the montage of visual and auditory elements. Aligning "Bella Ciao" with the sequence of horrific heads leads to the assertion that Stevens could not have shown Taylor's precarious beauty in *A Place in the Sun* without having filmed the atrocities of the concentration camps—a stark claim made just as the head of a Holocaust victim is "held" in Taylor's arms. Godard underscores this claim by letting Hindemith's "Fantasie" begin right after a dissolve from the victim's head to a close-up of Angela's head talking to George. The effect is uncanny, as in silent films when musical accompaniment seems oblivious to conversations on-screen. While music and image exist on different planes, there are correspondences of gesture: the viola winds down to that sonorous D3 just as Angela bends down to kiss George, shown in the slow motion of intermittent frames. From measure 3 to 4, the shift from D major to G♭ major (changing F♯ into G♭) occurs with the superimposition of Giotto's Mary Magdalene; and the viola quickly rises on an arpeggiated F♯-major chord to reach D♯5 while Angela adds a third hand to those of Mary Magdalene reaching down to the risen Christ (figure 3.10). If the viola's chromatic descent over the piano's variant of the opening melody—now in A♭—is barely audible, it is because Godard turns down the volume, his voice channeling Bernanos: "O, how marvelous to be able to watch what one can't see. O sweet miracle of our blind eyes!"—a variation of "O sweet miracle of our empty hands" from Bernanos's 1936 novel *Diary of a Country Priest*, which inspired Robert Bresson's 1951 film. What are we to see that cannot be seen?

Godard's paraphrase of Bernanos is so perplexing because we heard the opening of Hindemith's sonata just a few minutes earlier while watching one of the most disturbing moments of *Histoire(s)*: the guard wrestling down the emaciated inmate of a death camp. Now the music reprojects these images internally over the images by Stevens and Giotto superimposed on-screen. The "Fantasie" thus catalyzes the faculty of fantasy, mustering its mnemonic power. But the music does not just reproject; it also creates new projections—those "'horizontal' moments of confluence, contiguity, conjunction, and coincidence" that occur "*within* the 'vertical' pull of Godard's rhetorical and imaginary maneuvers."[53] Inasmuch as the "Fantasie" enables us to *read* the correspondences between the superimposed images on-screen, it makes us *sense* the image that intrudes from our memory—no less than a critical interference within a formal synchronicity.

Musical Buoyancy

Hindemith's "Fantasie" belongs to a group of pieces that move sideways within late Godard's oeuvre: integral to the fabric of a single film or connecting different films like a thread woven into a larger tapestry. Even if such music comes with previous associations or is first tied to a specific scene, the mnemonic bond can become unstable, turning these pieces into sonic particles that retain or regain some free agency. Snippets of the second movement from Beethoven's Seventh Symphony recur, for example, in Godard's *Adieu au langage* (2014). The movement had featured prominently in *Allemagne 90 neuf zéro* (1991), his film essay on German unification and the end of the Cold War, where the Allegretto's opening quasi-sforzato chord functions like a stinger or its solemn conduct evokes a funeral march.[54] Although Beethoven's Seventh seems to belong to the natural, cultural, and political landscape of Germany, it begins to drift away from such attachments and turns into mere mood, expressive gesture, pure sound. Here music becomes buoyant, and this buoyancy is akin to what Deleuze and Guattari describe as the deterritorialization of the refrain.

For Deleuze and Guattari, the Wagnerian leitmotif exemplifies the opposing forces of territorialization and deterritorialization inherent in the refrain. While Claude Debussy dismissed the leitmotif as a mere "calling card," they defend Wagner by noting that these motifs eventually "conquer *their own plane*, become autonomous from dramatic action, impulses, and situations, and independent of characters and landscapes; they themselves become melodic landscapes and rhythmic characters continually enriching their internal relations."[55] Deterritorialized, a motif's function as an *aide-mémoire* is attenuated, no longer recalling something else, but only itself. Deleuze and Guattari observed the same phenomenon in *Swann's Way*, the first volume of Proust's *In Search of Lost Time*, where "a little phrase" from Vinteuil's sonata "connects with Odette's face" and catalyzes Swann's passion for her. At first the little phrase acts for Swann as a leitmotif, "as if it reassured Swann the Bois de Boulogne was indeed his territory, and Odette his possession."[56] But then the motif develops in a Wagnerian manner: no longer "tied to a character" but itself a character, appearing, in Proust's own words, as "the plenitude of a music that is indeed filled with so many strains, each of which is a being."[57] As Deleuze and Guattari put it, the little phrase of Vinteuil's sonata "turns back onto itself, opens onto itself, revealing until-then unheard-of potentialities, entering into other connections, setting love adrift in the direction of other assemblages. Here, Time is not an a priori form; rather, the refrain is the a priori form of time, which in each case fabricates different times."[58]

Miriam Heywood has made the tantalizing suggestion that Godard's repeated use of the opening from Hindemith's "Fantasie" may be an allusion to the *petite phrase* that "emblematizes Swann's love for Odette," whose "relationship to the 'phrase' is reflected in Marcel and Albertine's infatuation with the sonata."[59] In *La prisonnière*, the fifth volume of *À la recherche du temps perdu*, Marcel plays Vinteuil's sonata while awaiting the arrival of Albertine, suddenly recognizing the resemblance of the little phrase to Wagner's *Tristan*. Yet when the phrase later returns in Vinteuil's septet, Marcel notes how its amorous association has been absorbed into "something more than a work in which the little phrase reappears."[60] According to Heywood, "the expanding associations forged by the 'phrase,' the sonata and then the septet might indeed seem to reflect that gradual synthesis that characterizes Marcel's story of enlightenment"—a process foundational to Proust's mode of writing and Godard's cinematic technique, where the arrangement of visual, verbal, and sonic particles in *Histoire(s)* strives toward to a "retrospective unity."[61] At first the opening of Hindemith's sonata becomes "part of a signifying series of fragments that immediately disassociates the music from its essential musicality," but later this musicality is recuperated, like Vinteuil's *petite phrase*, through its formal placement within "the video's own aesthetic regime."[62] The little phrase from the "Fantasie" thus partakes in the interaction of territorialization and deterritorialization that underwrites Godard's understanding of the relation between music and image, as he described it to Jean-Luc Douin:

> Music expresses the spiritual, and it provides inspiration. When I'm blind music is my little Antigone; it helps to see the unbelievable [*l'incroyable*]. And what has always interested me is the fact that musicians have no need for the image although people involved with images need music. I've always wanted to be able to pan or track during a war scene or love scene, in order to see the orchestra at the same time. And for music to take over at the moment when there is no more need to see the image. For music to express something else. What interests me is to see music—to try to see what one is hearing and to hear what one is seeing.[63]

The passage is remarkable not just because it testifies to Godard's quasi-romantic faith in music, but also because it illustrates how Hindemith's "Fantasie" can make us "see the unbelievable" once it takes over "at the moment when there is no more need to see the image." Music lies at the heart of the "sweet miracle of our blind eyes" and the "marvelous" paradox of being able "to watch what one can't see." Even though a piece of music can in the context of film accrue a palimpsest of past projections, its images may fade from memory and fail to reproject. Music, expressing "something else," becomes buoyant.

The little phrase from Hindemith's sonata performs this paradox in episode 2B of *Histoire(s)* (entitled "Fatale beauté"), when Godard returns to his claim that photography is "neither an art nor a technology, but a mystery." In *Histoire(s)*, paintings, drawings, etchings, and still photography acquire new agency when projected as fragments. For example, while the words "un mystère" show on-screen, Godard calls out, "Albertine," and a detail appears from Georges Seurat's *Une baignade, Asnières* (1884): the head of a boy with a red hat from the right side of the painting, cupping his hands and shouting into the space off-painting. Ventriloquizing the boy, Godard repeats, softly, "Albertine . . . disparue," and the boy dissolves into the head of a girl from Pierre-August Renoir's *Baigneuse blonde* (1881). It is as if he had called out to her, across time and space, across a bit of history. Over this dissolve—during the very pause between "Albertine" and "disparue"—the little phrase of the "Fantasie" begins for a third time (figure 3.11). "Albertine . . . gone. For a long time I used to go to bed early." "Longtemps, je me suis couché de bonne heure" is the iconic sentence that opens *À la recherche*, whose narrator, Marcel (Proust's persona of sorts), begins a complicated relationship with Albertine from her youth until her accidental death (*Albertine disparue* is the title of the sixth volume). If the recurring shot of Godard hammering away at his typewriter invokes a comparison between the novelist and "the man of the cinema," the pairing of the two paintings, the quotation from Proust, and Hindemith's music suggests that a director is able to tell us something in this sequence "without saying anything." Note how the dissolve from Seurat's boy to Renoir's girl coincides with the phrase "Albertine . . . disparue," the opening chord of the "Fantasie" entering precisely during the ellipsis. If Albertine's disappearance is undone with the appearance of Renoir's girl, she is summoned by Hindemith's *petite phrase* like Elizabeth Taylor's Angela superimposed over Giotto's Mary Magdalene, and like Liza, the guard from *Pasazerka* watching over genocide. Now the little phrase reprojects these cinematic angels of death against the image of Renoir's Albertine—fatal beauty indeed.

And yet, amid this proliferation of musical projections, the fourth and final iteration of the "Fantasie" makes those images vanish (figure 3.12). Here, the music "takes over" by expanding Hindemith's *petite phrase* through measure 14, such that it is heard two more times: the

"Albertine... ... disparue"

Figure 3.11 Godard, ventriloquizing Proust's Marcel through Seurat's boy, calls out to "Albertine," and when he says "disparue," the phrase from Hindemith's "Fantasie" (seen here as a score to show the timing) coaxes her to appear as Renoir's "Baigneuse blonde."

second time played by the piano, starting in measure 5, and the third time played by the viola again, starting in measure 10, with a lush and vivacious accompaniment (now in B major—a tritone above the tonic key). Godard introduces this sequence by saying the word *mystère* once again, but goes silent over a dark screen. The "Fantasie" starts when the words "tout seul" appear on screen, as if to seize the silence, similar to the pause between "Albertine" and "disparue." What follows aligns with the phrase in a purely gestural manner. First, a red-tinted shot from Rossellini's *Viaggio in Italia* (1953)—a film about a troubled marriage—showing the Phlegraean Fields where Ingrid Bergman's character blows cigarette smoke into a fumarole as if to make smoke emit from the surrounding earth. Then, over a very gradual dissolve (exquisitely matched to the viola's drawn-out C5 in triple pianissimo in measure 5) to a shot of a supine woman from Rodin's *Gates to Hell* (likely an allusion to a later scene in *Viaggio*, showing the excavation of a couple killed during the eruption of Mount Vesuvius), the piano sounds the second statement of the phrase.

As the viola extends the phrase, we see the photograph by Man Ray of Proust on his deathbed with the word "Marcel" projected on-screen. Then, an iris opens onto the faceless head of a woman from Max Ernst's *Les visiteurs du dimanche*. Once the head is fully visible and "Marcel" has given way to the word "Albertine," the viola plays the third statement of the phrase in B major while Julie Delpy reads from Bresson's *Notes sur le cinématographe* (1975), a passage Godard had quoted earlier: "Soit sûr

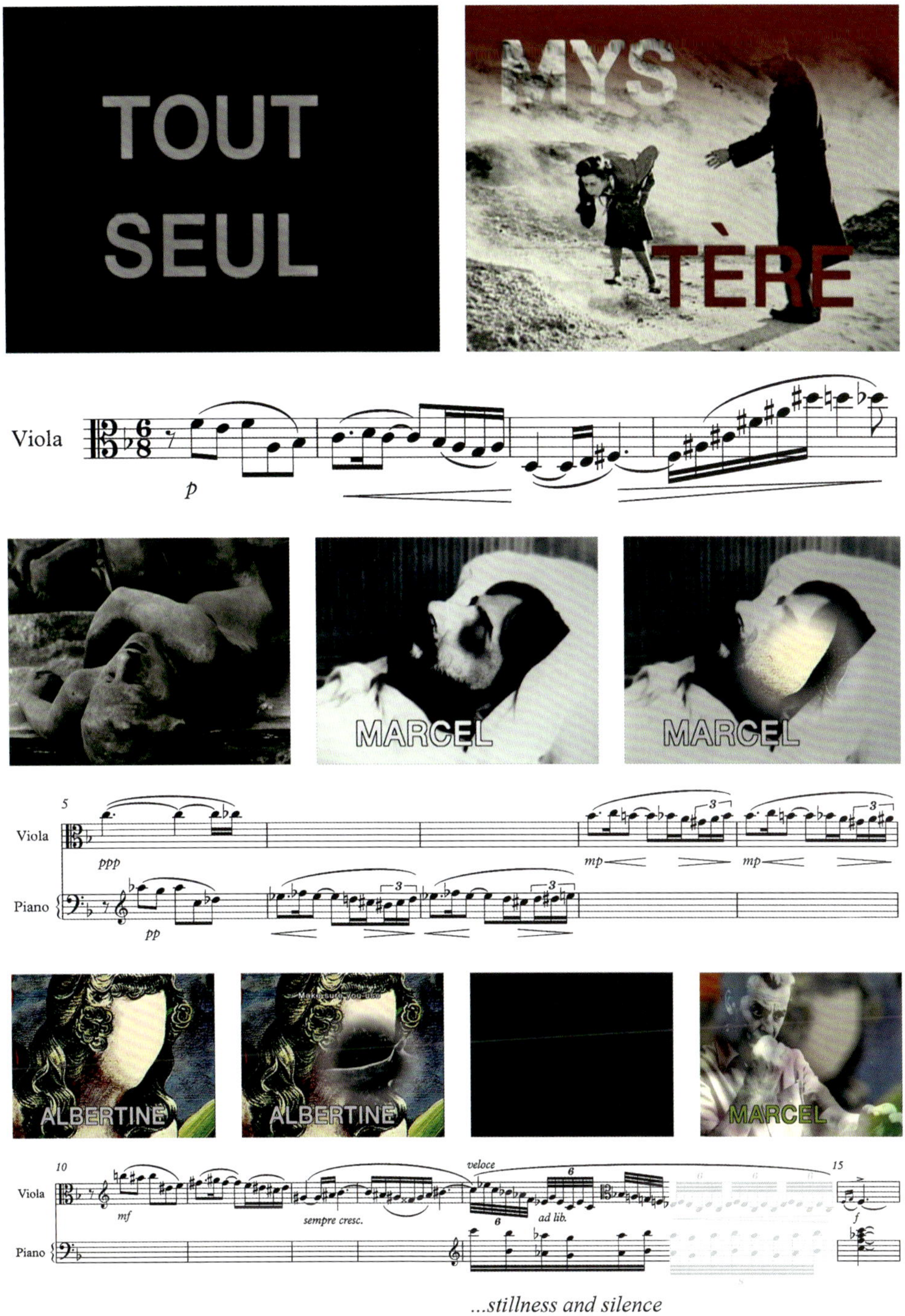

Figure 3.12 Music "takes over": all three statements of the "little phrase" from the opening of Hindemith's "Fantasie" enter into an extended montage that assert music's power to sear and obliterate the image.

d'avoir épuisé tout ce qui se communique par l'immobilité et le silence" (Be sure of having exhausted all that is communicated by the stillness and the silence). The first clause, "Be sure of having exhausted," is repeated while another iris obliterates the woman's faceless head from *Les visiteurs du dimanche* and opens onto a black screen, just as the "Fantasie" approaches its first climax, in measure 14. But as Delpy continues with, "all that is communicated by the stillness and the silence," the music cuts out after the word "silence," right on the last two eighth notes of measure 14, while the image track cuts to a photograph of the novelist and filmmaker Marcel Pagnol, superimposed over a washed-out background of the faceless woman. The sudden stillness and silence is jarring, even though it lasts for no more than two eighth notes, as Godard cuts back to the chord on the downbeat of measure 15—and stops.

Just as it is cut short, Hindemith's "Fantasie" has become buoyant. Not that the music suddenly "sheds all associations," but it does "take over at the moment when there is no more need to see the image." The increasingly expressive iterations of the little phrase seem to "sear" the image when the opening iris simulates a burning film stock—as if music's emotional power ignites, in Benjamin's words, "the tiny spark of contingency, of the here and now."[64] The *petite phrase* expands to expresses something new and something more, similar to the soirée performance in *La prisonnière* (the fifth, so-called Albertine novel of *Recherche*), where the septet takes on "a new red color, so absent from the tender, rustic, and candid sonata."[65] If Godard had first introduced the little phrase of Hindemith's "Fantasie" with a deeply shocking combination of lyricism and atrocity, now the mnemonic lock between beautiful music and horrific image loosens, and the little phrase explodes before returning to stillness and silence. The viola no longer lends a voice to the moving lips of Angela's muted mouth, but rather sings its own melody issued from Albertine's disappearing face—a song without words, an instrumental vocalise, a piece of pure music.

Deleuze and Guattari hold that *faciality* stands at the intersection of signification and subjectification. This is manifest in "a little phrase" of music that first "connects with Odette's face," then leads to the passion Swann develops for her. On the one hand, the face is a white wall, a surface onto which signs are projected and from which they reflect back; on the other hand, the face is the black hole that becomes a target of affective investment. The migration of preexistent music into the movie theater came with the risks and rewards of reprojecting internally images that could interfere with the external projections on-screen. But becoming buoyant again, music loosens its ties to the visual in ways vexing or viable. The creative and critical spark in Kluge's and Godard's cinema stems from their romantic faith in a musical imaginary and its modernist undoing. They make us see something otherwise unseen, or let it disappear.

CHAPTER FOUR

Auratic Replays

Halfway through his seminal study of transtextuality—*Palimpsests: Literature in the Second Degree*—Gérard Genette takes an unexpected turn from discussing parody and travesty in Cervantes and Marivaux to classical Hollywood:

> The title of Woody Allen's *Play It Again, Sam* (1972) acts for film connoisseurs as a contract of cinematographic hypertextuality (hyperfilmicity). They recognize it as the most famous, albeit misquoted, line from the Michael Curtiz film *Casablanca*, in which Humphrey Bogart asks the pianist at the bar to play for him, once more, "his" song. The tune is an emblem of Bogart's sacrificed passion for Ingrid Bergman; it is the Vinteuil sonata of *tough* cinema. Allen's title itself can be seen as emblematic of all hypertextual activity, for isn't it always a question of "replaying," in one way or another, the same undying old song?[1]

In this chapter, I consider cinematic representations of replay as examples of hyperfilmicity where it falls to sound and music to make a movie persist in cultural memory. Because the soundtrack often conjures memorable scenes, it helps viewers to reenact them in real life. Although Genette focused on literature, his sprawling array of categories for hypo-hypertextual relations—ranging from parody and pastiche to travesty and transposition—has been used to explain forms and practices of intertextuality in popular music as well as the remaking of movies.[2] In cinema, hypotextual sounds and images may enter into the hypertext as independent elements: a film may quote a scene from one film and combine it with the music from yet another. The audiovisual mnemonic often works like a palimpsest where music appears as the parchment onto which various visual memories are penned. Think of the images evoked by the uses of Samuel Barber's *Adagio for Strings*: David Lynch's *The Elephant Man* (1980), Oliver Stone's *Platoon* (1986), George Miller's *Lorenzo's Oil* (1992).[3] Film music may entice viewers to relive emotionally contagious scenes. Music can also facilitate the interplay between screen and audience, especially when dramatized as a "dance" between a spectator entering the world of the movie or a character stepping into the outside world. Finally, recalling a film's underscore in everyday situations may give viewers the sense of being directed in a cinematic plot.

My examples—Woody Allen's *Play It Again, Sam* and *The Purple Rose of Cairo* (1985) as well as Nora Ephron's *Sleepless in Seattle* (1993)—are not only films about films, but also movies about watching movies and reenacting them.[4] Since such reenactments can be found throughout the history of film, up to recent cosplay, representations of replay are part of the evolving self-awareness of cinema about its potent effects: viewers living their lives through movies by reciting dialogue, acting out scenes, and remembering music—symptoms of an obsessive immersion in on-screen dream-worlds. Characters replaying their favorite movies not only mirror the special conditions of audiovisual memory in the age of technologically produced mass media. They also show that hyperfilmicity, as manifest in reenactment, is less a relation between texts than between events. The poetics of replay in *Play It Again, Sam*—whose antihero of sorts is Allan Felix (played by Allen), a cineaste aspiring to become like Humphrey Bogart—prompts us to reconsider Benjamin's diagnosis that technological reproducibility makes the aura of artworks "wither" by attenuating their presence effects. Movies, I will argue, acquire their own aura with specific modes of spectatorship that contribute to what Miriam Hansen has called "cinematic experience."[5] For the main protagonist of *The Purple Rose of Cairo*, this aura materializes as a precarious balance between contemplative distance and haptic nearness; as a spectator's gaze returned by a character; and as an interpenetration of image space and body space. Above all, auratic replay involves "mimetic innervation," which enables films to access the optical unconscious by tapping into associative and bodily memory, and thereby relies on what I will call "mnemonic innervation."[6]

Sleepless in Seattle lacks the fantastic elements of Allen's eccentric allegories of cinema, yet its leading character, Annie, still believes that classic Hollywood romance provides plot lines for life, along with the promise of true love and a magic sense of destiny. Like Allen, Ephron made self-conscious use of music, with contemporary covers of popular standards commenting on the plot, or cueing Annie's actions with the underscore from her favorite film, *An Affair to Remember* (1957). Although *Sleepless* is openly nostalgic along those lines, the pull of classical Hollywood has receded, allowing Ephron to reimagine *An Affair* in a distinctly late twentieth-century context, that is, with a post-1989, pre-9/11 focus on personal matters over larger political problems. Amid concerns of critical theory about the propensity of mainstream cinema to foster false consciousness, I will suggest that mimetic practices of intertextuality have followed a utopian impulse even in middlebrow films. The phenomenon of music-driven replay lends support to Benjamin's claim that cinema reconfigured the experience of reality by creating a "space for play" through the activation of viewers' mimetic and mnemonic capabilities. With the rapidly growing consumption of movies, film music came to fulfill an important role in linking cultural and individual memory by blurring the boundary between the soundtracks of films and the soundtracks of life.

Figure 4.1 *Play It Again, Sam*, opening credits: "Here's looking at you, kid": Bogart/Rick is "looking" at Allan Felix/Woody Allen.

Enacting Hyperfilmicity

Play It Again, Sam opens by cutting back and forth between the ending of *Casablanca* and shots of Allan Felix's engrossed face paired with the title credits (see figure 4.1). The lenses of his glasses cast back the light from the silver screen: they are spectacles in more than one sense. Their reflection is a double projection of sorts, for the underlying soundtrack from *Casablanca* prompts us to see Allan, and to see what he is seeing. When Rick says to Ilsa, "Here's looking at you, kid," it seems as if Allan were not just looking, but looked at. Throughout his oeuvre, Woody Allen's affinity with auteurist cinema has led to a self-reflexive style where the boundary between film and reality is porous and permeable. When Allen adapted his own Broadway version of *Play It Again, Sam* for the screen, he decided to probe this slippage in ways that are both banal and profound. At the end of the film, Allan Felix has been transformed from spectator into actor. If we saw him first *watching* the denouement of *Casablanca*, he will eventually *act out* that very denouement by replaying the role Bogart has played in his imagination—the tough man who renounces his love for a higher purpose.

Allen devised a clever plot with a love triangle to make this possible. Recovering from an acrimonious divorce, Allan is encouraged by his best friend, Dick, and Dick's wife, Linda (Tony Roberts and Diane Keaton), to go on blind dates, which only show that Allan suffers from a crisis of masculinity. Lost in the aftermath of the sexual revolution, his repressed psyche holds on to the model of manhood mythologized by classic Hollywood cinema. A movie buff whose apartment is plastered with film posters, Allan takes advice from the ghost of Humphrey Bogart in his *Casablanca* coat (impersonated by Jerry Lacy, who perfectly replicated Bogart's lisping way of speaking)—a spectral presence that is visible and audible only to him. The plot thickens when Allan falls in love with Linda, who shares his neurotic disposition. After Dick returns from a trip to Cleveland, he confides to his friend his suspicion that Linda is having an affair. Dick decides to go back to Cleveland, Linda runs after him to the airport, and Allan runs after her. He catches up with Linda near the runway, and the scene is set for a remake of *Casablanca*'s ending. Figure

Figure 4.2 Replaying the airport scene of *Casablanca*.

4.2 pairs shots Allan saw in the movie theater (left) with corresponding ones from *Play It Again, Sam* (right): the lovers meeting on the foggy airfield, the starting aircraft engine (accompanied by the characteristic stinger from Max Steiner's score), the trio's reaction to the noise of the engine. Reciting some of Rick's iconic lines, Allan replays *Casablanca* in a way that is partly remembered and partly reimagined:

Casablanca	*Play It Again, Sam*
ILSA: You're saying this only to make me go.	LINDA: You're not just saying that to make things easy?
RICK: I'm saying it because it's true. Inside of us we both know that you belong with Victor. You're part of his work. The thing that keeps him going. If that plane leaves the ground and you're not with him you'll regret it.	ALLAN: I'm saying it because it's true. Inside of us we both know you belong to Dick. You're part of his work. The thing that keeps him going. If that plane leaves the ground and you're not on it with him you'll regret it. . . .
ILSA: No.	

RICK: Maybe not today or tomorrow, but soon and for the rest of your life.

Maybe not today or tomorrow, but soon and for the rest of your life.

LINDA: That's beautiful.

ALLAN: It's from *Casablanca*. I waited my whole life to say it.

Allan knows these lines by heart because watching movies habitually is a form of audiovisual entrainment. Pointing to Jean Paul Belmondo's imitation of Bogart in Godard's *A bout de souffle*, Richard Dyer notes how a star's image "can become part of the coinage of everyday speech."[7] Mimicking his idol, Allan conflates the character with the actor, whom he addresses always as Bogart, not Rick. When kissing Linda earlier, Allan seemed to *in-habit* Bogart's body (figure 4.3). Intercut shots from *Casablanca* converge in gestural detail (the women's arms around the men's necks) but diverge in awkwardness (Allan ecstatically rolling his

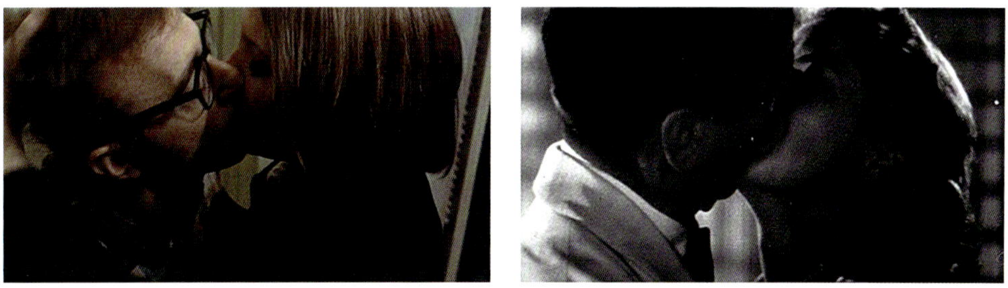

Figure 4.3 Amid the rhapsodic strains of "As Times Go By," Allan and Linda (*left*) are kissing passionately like Rick and Ilsa (*right*).

eyes). These shots could be extradiegetic flashbacks meant to reveal the hypotext; but they also work diegetically, suggesting that Allan has internalized the classic to the extent that his memory directs his moves. Viewers familiar with the original may experience a strange mode of double projection, seeing the original flash before their inner eye as the new version unfolds on the external screen. This is why allusions to an earlier film sometimes amount to what John Biguenet has called the "double take" of the remake.[8]

Umberto Eco describes how "magic frames" can turn a film into a "cult movie" and may reappear in other narrative situations to provoke "a sort of intense emotion accompanied by the vague feeling of a *déjà vu* that everybody yearns to see again."[9] But cult movies have more than magic frames; they also have magic lines or magic music. Indeed, Allen's remake of Rick and Ilsa's kiss is scored with a rhapsodic piano version of "As Time Goes By," first heard in the iconic scene when Ilsa shows up in in Rick's American Cafe, asking his pianist, Sam, to "play it." Rick does the same later that night over a bottle of gin ("You played it for her, you can play it for me"). This is "their" song because it takes them back to their romance in Paris, when Ilsa believed that her husband had been killed trying to escape from a concentration camp. As I have shown elsewhere, recollection is rendered differently for each lover. When Ilsa listens to Sam, we only see her face and can only imagine what she might be remembering; when Rick listens, we actually see what happened in a flashback. I explain the difference between Ilsa's internal and Rick's external projections by distinguishing music's *transport* into an emotional state from music's *transportation* to and of the past.[10] But there is more to this.

As Genette observes, the title *Play it Again, Sam* acts as a contract of hyperfilmicity because cineastes recognize it as a *misquoted* line from *Casablanca*: Ilsa and Rick urge Sam to "play it," but they do not actually say "play it *again*." Yet this "again" is inherent in the hyperfilmic structure of the plot where the two lovers must come to terms with their own backstory. Paris is the hypotext, Casablanca the hypertext—and music the missing link. "As Time Goes By" allows Rick to relive his romance, and then renounce it for a greater cause. At the end of *Play it Again, Sam*, Allan Felix replays this heroic sacrifice. "Play it again, Sam" has become "Play it again, Allan." For Genette, the "unchanged text" recited by Allan is "being travestied solely through a change in the speakers," but results in a "skillfully managed twist . . . that goes beyond being funny."[11] The serious nature of Allan's hyperfilmic enactment stems from the difference between field memory and observer memory: the latter is a visual memory where we observe ourselves from an outside perspective; the former, a memory recalled from our own point of view within the field of action. Both types of memory appear already in the opening credits sequence. Some shots show Allan as a spectator sitting in the movie theater watching *Casablanca*, his head barely visible in front of the right side of the screen (figure 4.4, left); other shots take his point of view by

Figure 4.4 Allan's observer memory of watching *Casablanca* (*left*), his field memory of the screen seen from within the field (*top right*), and his reimagined observer memory replaying the plot in the field (*bottom right*).

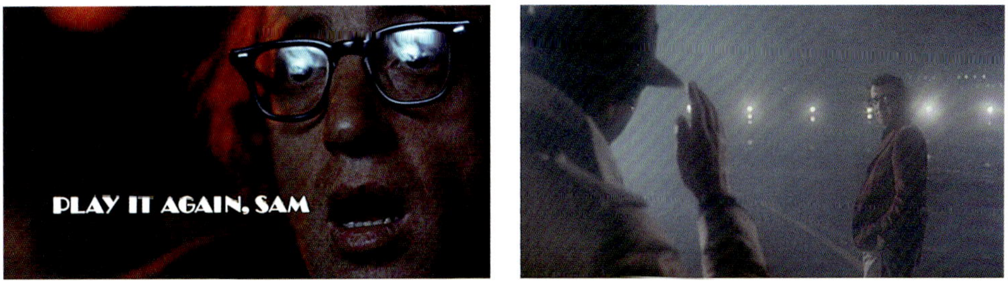

Figure 4.5
"Here's looking at you, kid" (beginning and ending).

showing the film full frame (figure 4.4, top right). But when Allan replays the ending of *Casablanca*, he places himself into the field of his reimagined memory of the film (figure 4.4, bottom right).

Note how the shot at lower left shows Allan sitting in the movie theater with the silver screen positioned slightly to the left and on the right side of the frame the bigger back of another viewer watching the viewing. The large shadow is a placeholder for the generic spectator who partakes in the hyperfilmic replay. As such it prefigures the slippage between Rick, Allan, and us looking at Victor and Ilsa, or Dick and Linda, walking to the plane. Walking back into the field memory, Bogart/Rick then emerges from the fog to tell Allan that he did "great," that he really developed himself "a style," and that he won't be needing him anymore: "There's nothing I can tell you now that you don't already know." Allan's answer could be Allen's: "I guess the secret is not being you but being me," to which Bogart/Rick responds, touching the brim of his hat, "Here's looking at you, kid" (figure 4.5).

Play It Again, Sam has come full circle. If Rick initially "looked" at Allan from off-screen, he is now looking at him from within that magic frame, speaking that magic line. And when Allan walks off into the fog, the closing credits begin with Sam's magic song as performed by Dooley Wilson in *Casablanca*. The contract of hyperfilmicity drawn up during the opening credits has been fulfilled, but only the closing credits can put a seal on this contract by playing that "undying song." Only now does Sam play it *again*. Its return may be Woody Allen's response to Ilsa's famous question "What about us?," asked before boarding the plane, prompting Rick's equally famous answer, "We'll always have Paris." *Play It Again, Sam* has no Paris. Yet as Sam's song trails off, it assures us that *we* will always have *Casablanca*—because we will always have "As Time Goes By."[12]

Mnemonic Innervations

Woody Allen's perhaps most compelling metafilm tells the story of Tom Baxter (Jeff Daniels), a character from a fictitious RKO production called *The Purple Rose of Cairo* who breaks the fourth wall and steps outside his diegetic world because he is attracted to Cecilia (Mia Farrow), a waitress

Figure 4.6
The Purple Rose of Cairo: Cecilia plays the ukulele when singing with Gil (*left*), and replays a scene from one of Gil's films while moving her hand on the ukulele as if she were playing along (*right*).

who has been watching him in this movie numerous times, escaping the desolate reality of the Great Depression. Maladroit at her job and stuck in an abusive marriage, Cecilia is one of those "little shopgirls" Siegfried Kracauer recognized as a growing portion of film audiences in the 1920s and 1930s.[13] Cecilia's plight exemplifies what Hansen described as a "discrepancy between these women's new economic relevance, primarily as consumers and cheap labor, and their lack of real equality in social and legal status and the workplace increased their need for compensatory fantasies."[14] Cecilia must decide between the chivalrous character Tom, who is innocent but genuine, and his cunning actor, Gil Shepard (also played by Daniels), who saves the movie industry and himself by winning over Cecilia and sending his alter ego back into the film from which he emerged.

The scene when Gil and Cecilia visit a music store is pivotal. After he buys her a ukulele, an instrument she played as a child, they sing a couple of tunes, which leads to the following exchange (figure 4.6):

CECILIA: That was wonderful. Oh, you [. . .] after the Lindbergh movie, you should do [. . .] a musical, really [. . .]

GIL: (*Overlapping Cecilia, gesturing*) [. . .] you know I did a, one bit in one once. It's uh . . .

CECILIA: (*Overlapping Gil, gesturing*) [. . .] I know [. . .] I saw *Dancing Doughboys*, sure.

GIL: (*Overlapping, laughing*) *Dancing Doughboys*!

CECILIA: (*Overlapping*) Yeah!

GIL: You remembered!

CECILIA: (*Overlapping*) Yeah, that was great. I remember you-you-you turned to Ina Beasley and you said: "I won't be going south with you this winter."

GIL: (*Gesturing, moving closer to Cecilia*) That's exact—Right, right!

Cecilia laughs; she hugs the ukulele. The Camera moves in closer to the couple.

GIL: (*Reciting his lines from* Doughboys*, his eyes on his hips, intensely*) "I won't, I won't, I won't be going south with you this winter. We have a little score to settle on the other side of the Atlantic."

CECILIA: (*Reciting the heroine's lines from the movie, her eyes on Gil, her hand moving up and down the ukulele's neck*) "Does this mean I won't be seeing you ever again?"

GIL: (*Reciting his lines, his eyes on Cecilia*) "Well, 'ever' is a long time."

CECILIA: (*With emotion, reciting the heroine's lines*) "When you leave, don't look back."

GIL: (*Laughing after a beat*) You remember that, you remember it perfectly. (*Gestures*)

CECILIA: (*Overlapping Gil, her eyes not leaving his face*) Oh sure.

GIL (*Taking Cecilia into his arms*) And then, and then I took her in my arms and, and I kissed her, knowing it was for the last time. (*Pauses, sighing*) God, you're beautiful, Cecilia.

CECILIA: (*Shaking her head, the ukulele still to her chest*) Was it fun? Kissing Ina Beasley?

GIL: (*Shrugging*) Oh, it was jus—, you know, it's a movie kiss. You know, we professionals, we can put that, that stuff on just like that.

CECILIA: (*Overlapping, sighing*) It looked like you loved her.

Gil gives Cecilia a lingering kiss. Romantic music begins to play.[15]

Making music together prepares Cecilia and Gil for replaying the farewell scene from *Dancing Doughboys*. A minute detail suggests the equivalence between singing and acting: during the conversation, Cecilia holds the ukulele and moves her hand up and down its neck *as if she were playing*. Singing puts them in sync. Cecilia's excessive consumption of movies has made her prone to conflate reality and fiction. Another whimsical detail suggests this to us, as self-conscious spectators: the strings enter the underscore just as Gil bends down to kiss her, revealing a violin pinned to the wall. Even in real life, the star has the edge. While Tom only knows the one film in which he is a character, Gil has appeared to Cecilia in so many different roles that she can recite any scene by heart.

According to Hansen, Benjamin's notion of mimetic faculty was not "a category of representation . . . but a relational practice . . . involving sensuous, somatic, and tactile, that is, embodied, forms of perception and cognition." The effects of this practice can either create a "noncoercive engagement with the other" or facilitate a "compulsive assimilation to the products of the culture industry."[16] Whereas Adorno and Horkheimer worried about the latter, Benjamin saw in film the potential for a mimetic "innervation"—a concept appropriated from Freud to describe how cinema had fashioned a new "mode of regulating the interplay between humans and (second) technology."[17] Films created a special space—a room for play (*Spiel-Raum*), for a new physis developed by technology. While bourgeois art had been beholden to the idea of beautiful semblance, Benjamin noted that "in film, the element of semblance has been entirely displaced by the element of play."[18] Cecilia's bizarre affair with a character who steps out of a movie literalizes the experience of cinema as an extension of surrealist experiments: the "interpenetration of reality with the apparatus" brings about "new configurations of body and image-space at the levels of both representation and reception."[19] Hansen recovered the idea of innervation from the original (later excised) layer of Benjamin's artwork essay, where the utopian body of Disney's Mickey Mouse becomes emblematic for the "new realm of consciousness" that he saw as emerging with film. In the first handwritten draft, the section on the optical unconscious was actually entitled "*Micky-Maus*."[20] In his earlier essay "Experience and Poverty," Benjamin even suggested that Mickey Mouse would offer a "dream to make up for the sadness and discouragement of the day" by leading a life of "miracles that not only surpass the wonders of technology, but make fun of them."[21]

The Purple Rose of Cairo revolves around such miracles. The evolution from semblance to play maps onto Cecilia's experience of cinema. At first, the silver screen is a reflective surface for the projections of her escapist fantasies; it then becomes a portal that enables these projections to pass through and materialize. The first mode is representational: here movies are an illusory semblance to be watched from afar. In the second mode, however, cinematic experience becomes relational, as the spectator begins to play with screen characters. Benjamin discussed such participatory reception in section 18 of the artwork essay, noting the difference between concentration and distraction: "A person who concentrates before a work of art is absorbed by it," while "the distracted masses absorb the work of art into themselves."[22] What matters is that the former is optical and the latter tactile, as illustrated in that we can look at architecture or use it. Tactile reception comes about by habit in the state of distraction, which, for Benjamin, "finds in film its true training ground."[23] Thus Cecilia initially consumes movies in the state of concentration, where she becomes absorbed in their semblance; but as a habitual spectator, she experiences them in the state of distraction, where she absorbs them into herself. Optical reception gives way to the tactile reception that can be seen in the shots that show Tom and Cecilia stepping in and out of the screen, and in the parallel shots that show them dancing on either side (figure 4.7).

Cecilia's progression from concentration to distraction, from optical to tactile reception, from representational semblance to relational play maps onto Benjamin's account of the decay of aura, suggesting that movies may possess their own aura and thereby share its predicament. Benjamin pinpointed the loss of aura by invoking Luigi Pirandello's view of the cinematic actor as "exiled not only from the stage but also from his own person."[24] At stake is the actor's physical presence. In the theater, the aura of Macbeth is tied to the actor playing him, but once the camera takes the place of the audience, "the aura surrounding the actor is dispelled—and, with it, the aura of the figure he portrays."[25] Cecilia

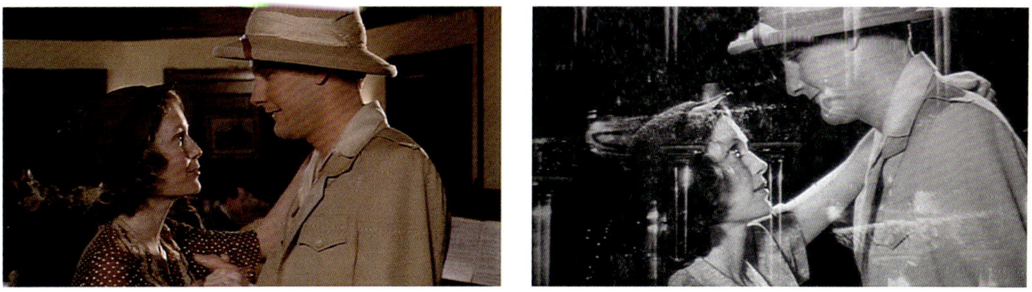

Figure 4.7
Interpenetration of image space and body space: Tom and Cecilia dance on both sides of the screen—after Tom exits the image space and after Cecilia enters.

witnesses this split between actor and character in the contest between Gil and Tom. She assumes that Tom must be real because he is genuine, and that Gil must be genuine because he is real, but the aura of both is dispelled during their face-to-face encounter, as shown in the corresponding frames where Tom confronts Gil from a place on and outside the screen (see figure 4.8). These encounters dramatize what Benjamin describes as the "film actor's estrangement in the face of the apparatus," where "the mirror image has become detachable from the person mirrored" and, transported to "a site in front of the masses," becomes subject to their control. Although Benjamin saw the revolutionary potential of such control, he was aware that the film industry already used it for counterrevolutionary purposes by making "the cult of the movie star" work hand in hand with its counterpart, "the cult of the audience."[26] While political issues are not the explicit focus and concern of Allen's film, Tom Baxter's escapade does suspend the projection of *The Purple Rose of Cairo* and thereby brings the entire industrial production of movies to a halt. Inasmuch as narrative cinema relies on the identity between star actor and character, exposing that identity as a fabrication poses an existential threat to the dream factory and its manufactured aura.

Cecilia's encounters with Tom and Gil reveal that their resemblance is false and as such becomes a central problem of a cinematic aura. This is evident from Benjamin's two main definitions of the phenomenon. The first understands aura as "a strange weave of space and time: the unique appearance of a distance, however near it may be" (or, "however close the thing that calls it forth"); the second explains aura as a quasi-human response to "inanimate or natural objects" so that "to experience the aura of an object we look at means to invest it with the ability to look back at us."[27] Initially, *The Purple Rose of Cairo* literalizes the possibility of a cinematic aura as a reciprocal glance between film character and spectator: Cecilia's concentrated gaze prompts Tom to look back at her when that gaze becomes habitual. The resulting change from optical reception to tactile reception dispels his aura as he becomes absorbed into her world: Tom steps out of his film and takes Cecilia's hand to run away with her (figure 4.8, bottom right). She seems set to revert to the optical mode of reception after Tom returns to his diegetic world because he is too unreal

Figure 4.8 Face-to-face confrontations between character and actor (*top*), and cinematic aura as returned gaze (*bottom*).

and Gil escapes to Hollywood because he is too real. But when Cecilia returns to the movie theater in the final scene, her renewed attraction to cinema restores its aura while integrating elements from the tactile mode of reception. As a film about film's aura, Cecilia's story is an allegory of its loss and recovery, reconfigured through mimetic innervation as a new equilibrium of nearness and distance whose "complementary poles" facilitate the interpenetration of image space and body space.[28]

How this plays out in the film's poignant conclusion rewards a close reading. When Cecilia arrives at the movie theater where she was to meet up with Gil and elope to Hollywood, the manager tells her that Gil left alone to shoot his next movie as soon as Tom had returned to his world behind the screen. As the camera focuses on Cecilia realizing her double loss, we hear the manager say, "Don't forget Cecilia, Fred Astaire and Ginger Rodgers start today." Here a pensive piano piece (written and performed by Dick Hyman) enters on a close-up of Cecilia's dazed face and continues over a slow dissolve to a remorseful Gil sitting on an airplane. This is the very music we heard during those magical moments that Cecilia and Tom spent earlier in an empty amusement park at night. Entitled "Carousel Memories," the wistful tone of the cue has already marked it as music of loss and nostalgia—expressed by the solo piano at the end of other films by Allen from the 1980s, notably *Stardust Memories* (1980) and *Hannah and Her Sisters* (1986).

But *The Purple Rose of Cairo* does not end on this note. The piano gives way to Irving Berlin's "Cheek to Cheek," from *Top Hat* (1935) with Fred Astaire and Ginger Rodgers—the song from the opening credits, which now returns with its original footage to suggest a more upbeat conclusion to the film. When the music starts, the camera pushes in on Gil. Allen then cuts directly to *Top Hat* before cutting to Cecilia, who enters the movie theater and settles into her seat just as the most famous number from Astaire and Rodgers's most successful collaboration appears on-screen:

Heaven, I'm in heaven [A]
And my heart beats so that I can hardly speak
And I seem to find the happiness I seek
When we're out together dancing cheek to cheek

Heaven, I'm in heaven [A]
And the cares that hung around me through the week
Seem to vanish like a gambler's lucky streak
When we're out together dancing cheek to cheek.

Oh I love to climb a mountain [B]
And to reach the highest peak
But it doesn't thrill me half as much
As dancing cheek to cheek.

Oh I love to go out fishing [B]
In a river or a creek,
But I don't enjoy it half as much
As dancing cheek to cheek

Dance with me [C]
I want my arm about you
The charm about you
Will carry me through

Heaven, I'm in heaven [A]
And my heart beats so that I can hardly speak
And I seem to find the happiness I seek
When we're out together dancing cheek to cheek.

If Berlin's lyrics are programmatic for Cecilia's story, the song also provides a blueprint for her experience of cinema.[29] The heavenly bliss of dancing cheek to cheek described in the first two stanzas (A) eclipses the solitary activities in the bridge (B) and leads to the eight-bar interlude (C), starting with the line "Dance with me" (figure 4.9). The invitation to dance comes with a stirring harmonic change to the parallel minor and a melodic leap up to E♭, followed by three falling sixths with each subsequent line, before moving, via V/V and V7, back to the A section.

The opening credits suggest that "Dance with me" is a call to go to the movies. At this moment of the song, the black credit screen gives way

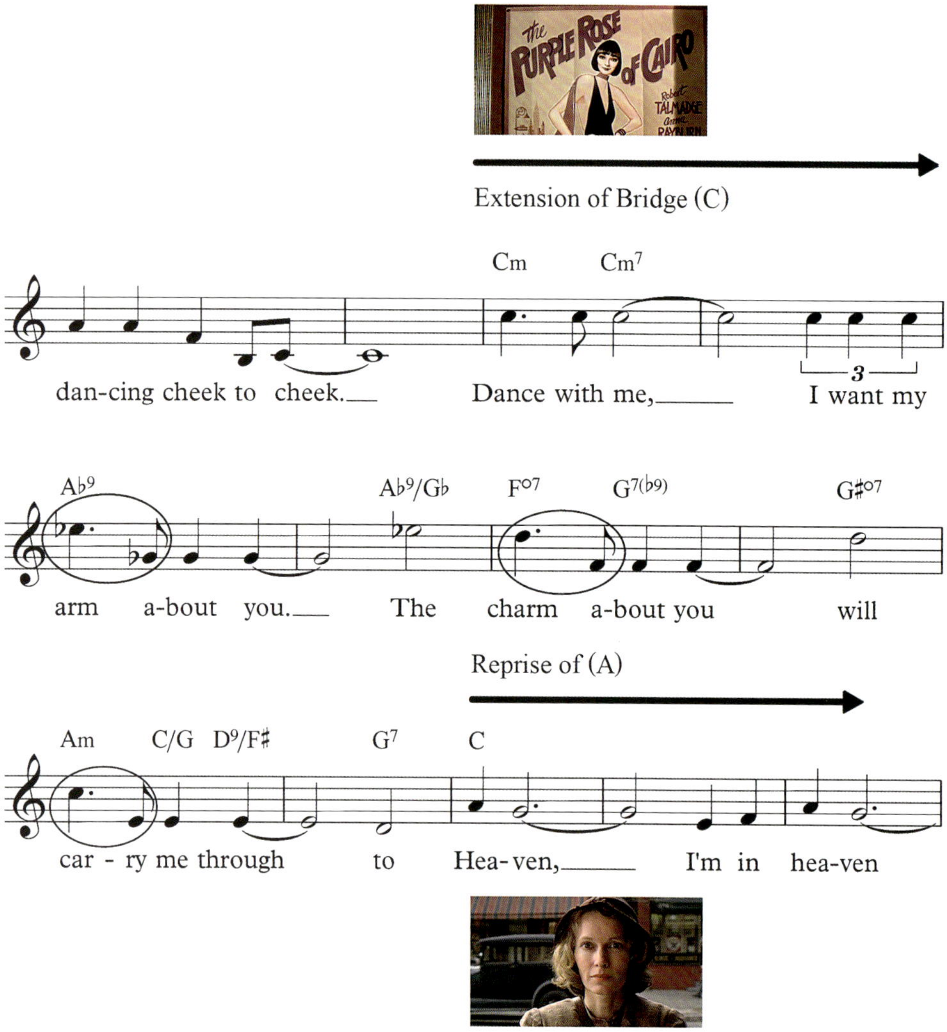

Figure 4.9 The "Dance with me" interlude in "Cheek to Cheek" invites Cecilia to go to the movies to watch *The Purple Rose of Cairo.*

to the poster of *The Purple Rose of Cairo*. Then a cut to Cecilia looking at the poster coincides with the reprise of A (figure 4.10, top). The two female leads, Cecilia and Kitty (Tom's love interest from the film and the film within the film), thus face each other in shot and reverse-shot. This sets up the very opposition between image and body space that Cecilia will breach when she enters Tom's diegetic world and meets Kitty, who faints when she touches Cecilia, realizing that she is "real." If shot and reverse-shot first render the relation between the diegetic viewer and the diegetically viewed as a divide, they now share a two-shot that bridges this divide. The physical encounter between viewer and viewed must be seen next to the two-shot of Cecilia and Tom dancing, which in turn parallels what Cecilia sees in the movie theater later on: Fred and Ginger dancing.

The opening gambit of Cecilia looking at the movie poster returns at the end of the film when she watches "Cheek to Cheek" in the movie theater. Her eyes downcast at first, she looks up at the end of section B, just before the interlude after the bridge. Why does she glance up at that moment? The answer requires a detailed look at the way "Cheek to Cheek" becomes an occasion for dance in the musical. As he so often did, Astaire builds his routine with the song first sung in the context of social dance and then transitions to pure dance while the melody is replayed as instrumental music. After Astaire has finished singing, the music modulates, via C7 and B7, to land on a striking E-minor chord to begin the "Dance with me" interlude. Instead of cadencing in E major at the end of the section, as one would expect, the cellos pick up the melody and launch the instrumental reprise of the entire song in D major. As the tonal trajectory of the number moves upward from C (for the song) via D (for the dance) to E♭ (the coda)—the E-minor in the transition delivers a burst of tonal energy that triggers the pure dance section (see figure 4.11).

With an ingenious stroke, Astaire used the transition to move from the confined social space of the dance floor *over an actual bridge* to an adjacent stage that gives free rein to his choreographic imagination. Now the A sections give rise to sweeping movements across the stage, while the first four measures of the contrasting B section are used for a lighter step dance. The number's climax coincides with another repetition of the A section, introduced one last time by the interlude. This time, however, the music does not modulate smoothly, but rather shifts upward more abruptly by a half-step to the "Dance with me" chord in E♭ minor, with the three falling sixths leading to the final return of section A in E♭. This harmonic highpoint is shored up by a powerful orchestral tutti, which prompts the dancers' most dynamic turns yet. As if in a final rush, Astaire lifts Rodgers so forcefully into the air that her dress literally traces her energetic moves with a spectacular trail of white tulle. At the end of *The Purple Rose of Cairo*, Allen condenses the number into a sequence of its most important moments, masking the cuts with reaction shots of Cecilia's face. This telescoped version heightens the effect of the rising harmonic trajectory, and with it, the mounting energy of the choreography.[30] Importantly, this shorter version preserves the invitation to dance, as acted out by Astaire and Rodgers when moving over the bridge to the stage to show the virtuosic style that was the main attraction of their films.

This spectacle appears to have a palpable effect on Cecilia, who begins to smile ever so slightly. However minute, her smile registers the change from song to dance. As such, it becomes the *physical* reflex of cinematic innervation. We cannot see what she sees, but we can glean it from her face, brightened by the light from the screen. The corners of her mouth move up to the final flourish of the dance, where Ginger and Fred spiral gracefully, cheeks touching, to the melody of the last line: "When

Figure 4.10a From invitation to innervation. As "Dance with me" is sung during the opening credits, Kitty "looks" at Cecilia (shot and reverse-shot, *top*), but then "touches" her after Cecilia has entered the screen world (two-shot, *middle*)—a world where Tom and Cecilia dance like Fred and Ginger (*bottom*).

Figure 4.10b Watching *Top Hat*, Cecilia, ukulele in hand, looks up (*top*) to see how Fred and Ginger, during the phrase "dance with me," move across the bridge from social dance into the spectacle of pure dance (*middle*); she begins to smile when Fred and Ginger end their dance, cheek to cheek (*bottom*).

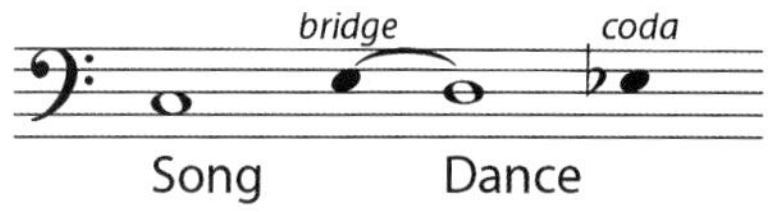

Figure 4.11 The rising tonal trajectory of "Cheek to Cheek" as a song-to-dance number in *Top Hat*.

we're out together dancing cheek to cheek." As the film returns to the opening shot of Cecilia looking, it offers the movie's final moral about watching movies habitually. Although the fourth wall has been resealed, movies can still be a source of mimetic innervation—they always were and always will be. Even after losing Tom and Gil, Cecilia can become so engrossed in the cinematic experience that it makes her smile again. The lyrics have it no other way: the "cares" that "hung around" her "seem to vanish like a gambler's lucky streak." One mustn't merely dance, but dance cheek to cheek—with the screen.

Is this ending hopeful or heartbreaking? Its ambivalence is symptomatic of Benjamin's argument with Adorno over the effects of mimetic innervation in mass culture. For Adorno, the laughter with which audiences responded to Disney's cartoons or Chaplin's slapstick comedy was all too easily seized by the capitalist forces that put film at the service of fascism. The flip side of collective therapy was collective terror. In a now notorious letter, Adorno criticized Benjamin for being too optimistic about the political potential of a "dreaming collective" or "collective unconscious." A laughing audience, he noted, "is anything but salutary and revolutionary; it is full of the worst bourgeois sadism instead."[31] This stance relied on the widespread belief that Mickey Mouse and jazz made audiences prone to the pleasures of submissive identification.[32] Benjamin's more optimistic view of Mickey Mouse was based on the optical unconscious, enhanced by sound. Just as dance is visualized music, the optical-acoustic unconscious arises with the technology of sound film. The tight synchronization of music and action that Disney perfected—called "Mickey Mousing" in industry jargon ever since—was not only common in cartoons and slapstick comedy but characteristic of the film musical, whose numbers were routinely lip-synched and choreographed to prerecorded sound. Perhaps Benjamin removed Mickey Mouse in later versions of the artwork essay because he came to realize that the political potential of collective innervation had been usurped by fascist propaganda after all. And yet, as Hansen suggests, we may conceive of "the movie-going collective" as being "made up of individual viewers" who would engage in "the kinds of mimetic engagement Benjamin found in the surrealists, the child, the beholder of old photographs, or, for that matter, Proust."[33]

About a dozen years after *Play It Again, Sam*, *The Purple Rose of Cairo* offered a strikingly Benjaminian take on cinematic experience as the interplay between film and spectator. Its bittersweet ending resonates with Benjamin's ambivalence about the redemptive powers of cinematic experience rather than Adorno's concerns about its commodification. The ending seems to change regressive reproduction into profane illumination, rendered literally auratic when the light from the silver screen is reflected on Cecilia's smiling face. In the cinema, aura receives a new lease on life through music, which animates the dialectics of semblance and play. With *Top Hat* projected on screen, the ukulele that Cecilia holds close to her chest remains a token of her tactile encounter with film. Breaking into song, Cecilia and Gil became children again to recover their mimetic faculty; watching Fred and Ginger dance, Cecilia relives how she danced with Tom. Musical numbers may be escapist but may also create the space for auratic replay through mnemonic innervation. Hence her smile.

Mimetic Magic

In a well-known scene from Nora Ephron's *Sleepless in Seattle* (1992), Suzy (Rita Wilson) and Greg (Victor Garber) are catching up with their friend Sam (Tom Hanks), who has moved from Chicago to Seattle to start a new life after the death of his wife. Sam has just told them that on Christmas Eve his son Jonah called into the radio show of psychologist Marcia Fieldstone, telling her that his dad needs a new wife and eventually getting Sam on the line. Sam's moving account of his wife and his struggle to adjust has since prompted a flood of letters from all over the country, including one from Annie (Meg Ryan), who proposes meeting Sam on top of the Empire State Building on Valentine's Day. Suzy immediately makes the connection:

SUZY: Oh, it's like that movie.

SAM: What movie?

SUZY: *An Affair to Remember*, did you ever see it? Oh, god, Cary Grant and Deborah Kerr. Is it Karr or Kerr?

SAM: Karr.

GREG: Kerr.

SUZY: Okay, she's gonna meet him at the top of the Empire State Building, only she got hit by a taxi. And he waited and waited. And it was raining, I think. And then she's too proud to tell him that she's, uh, (*wells up*) . . . crippled. And he's too proud to find out why she doesn't come. But he comes to see her anyway, I forget why, but oh, oh, it's so amazing when he comes to see her, because he doesn't even notice that she doesn't get up to say hello. And he's very bitter. And you think that he's just gonna walk out the door and never know why she's just lying there, you know, like, on the couch, with the blanket over her shriveled little legs and . . . (*stops, sobbing*)

JONAH: Are you all right?

GREG: She's fine.

SUZY: (*crying*) And suddenly he goes . . . "and they sold the painting" . . . and he, like, goes to the bedroom, and he looks, and he comes out, and he looks at her, and he kinda, just, they know, and then they hug again, it's so . . . God!

SAM: That's a chick's movie.

GREG: I would say so.[34]

Improvised on the set, Wilson's emotional summary of Leo McCarey's *An Affair to Remember* (1957) immediately became famous, not only for its over-the-top delivery but also for Sam and Greg's response, faking their own weepy account of the war thriller *The Dirty Dozen* (another hilarious impromptu performance by Hanks and Garber). Such male mockery follows a well-established blueprint for light entertainment, trading in gender stereotypes for comic effect: women are emotional; men have difficulty expressing their feelings. *Sleepless* remained true to this template but raised the stakes by adding a bit of melodrama to the mix. Women take charge of its plot not merely because tears come easily to them but because their tears are presented as genuine and transformative.

Jeff Arch, who wrote the original screenplay and collaborated with Ephron on the final script, has noted in an interview that *Sleepless* was based on an unusual premise, not only that the people falling in love do not meet properly until the very end of the movie, but that Annie is the one moving the plot forward (with Jonah as an accomplice) because Sam is still paralyzed by grief and thus lacks the "desire" needed to drive the action.[35] Since a satisfying conclusion of the film required rebalancing the affective economy between the sexes, Arch endowed an emotional Annie with a surplus of desire, while Sam gradually becomes ready for a new relationship. The success of the script lies in weaving together Annie's professional instinct to go after a good story (she is a reporter for the *Baltimore Sun*) and her personal quest for the right man. What makes this quest credible are plausible alternatives: Sam makes an effort at going on dates, and Annie is already engaged to the sweetly perfect, but boring, Walter (Bill Pullman), whom she met while switching up sandwich orders—a coincidence, she readily admits. Indeed, what nurtures her doubts about Walter is a nagging belief in true love as a result of destiny, not chance. Hence, she is prone to reading events as "signs," which allows her to lapse into a deeper longing, fueled by cinematic fantasies—above all, the romance between Cary Grant and Deborah Kerr's characters in *An Affair to Remember*.

Annie is, of course, a habitual spectator—a late twentieth-century kin of Kracauer's "little shopgirls" and Allen's Cecilia, more grown-up but still hooked on classic Hollywood romances with their premise and promise that true love may be possible. In a pivotal scene, Annie, preoccupied with the idea that she must write a letter to "Sleepless in Seattle" (Sam's tagline on Dr. Fieldstone's program), is watching *An Affair* at home with her friend and colleague Becky (Rosie O'Donnell, perfectly cast as the comic sidekick). To fill in a few essential plot details, *An Affair* is about playboy Nickie Ferrante (Grant) who meets nightclub singer Terry McKay (Kerr) on a cruise ship. Though both are already engaged to be married, they fall in love on the journey. When the ship docks at Madeira, Nickie introduces Terry to his grandmother, who tells her that the young Nickie had shown considerable talent as an artist, and that she hopes he will return to painting upon settling down with the right woman. The implication is that Terry is the one, made obvious when Nickie's grandmother sits down at the piano and plays the song "Ce bel amour, qui ne peut mourir," composed for the film by Harry Warren, sung by Vic Damone during the opening credits and serving as a recurring theme in Hugo Friedhofer's score. Terry joins in, but the ship horn calls the travelers back on board, cutting short the last two verses, translated in the English version as "That we may live and we may share / A love affair to remember." The song marks the moment when Nickie falls in love with Terry, and he proposes to her the night before their arrival in New York. Passing the skyline the next morning, they agree to wait six months to see whether he can support himself as a painter, and then meet at the top of the Empire State Building ("the nearest thing to heaven in New York," as Terry puts it).

Annie is shown drafting her letter to Sam just when Nickie asks Terry the fateful question about her fiancé—"Are you in love with him?"—and Terry answers, "I am not now." This becomes Annie's cue: "Now those were the days when people *knew* how to be in love. . . . They *knew* it. . . . It was right. It was real, it was . . ."—here Becky cuts in—". . . a movie. That's your problem. You don't want to be in love. You want to be in love in a movie." But Becky shares Annie's deepest desires, which is why her "favorite part" includes, as the script has it, one of the most memorable lines from *An Affair to Remember*:

> Deborah Kerr says: "It's now or never." And Cary Grant says: "We'd be fools to let happiness pass us by." Deborah Kerr: "Winter must be cold for those with no warm memories."[36]

The fear of a future "with no warm memories" also haunts the main protagonists of *Sleepless*. Both Becky and Annie are *lip-synching* this sentence—a detail not in the original screenplay (figure 4.12). They know the film by heart, they inhabit it, and they simulate replaying it while Friedhofer's main theme underscores their conversation and the dialogue from *An Affair*. This is why Becky lifts from their favorite film its famous plot device, telling Annie to suggest that Sam meet her at the top of the Empire State Building on Valentine's Day, and then mailing the crumpled-up letter to him after Annie has thrown it away. And this is what Suzy's emotional summary of *An Affair* gets at: will Annie meet Sam on the Empire State building, or will she, like Terry, be hit by a taxi and miss him, only to reunite, shriveled legs and all, in a final scene?

But *Sleepless* is not a remake. The meeting on Valentine's Day sets up the question of how people know whether they are meant for each other. Annie's obsession with this question makes her open to believing in the miracles of serendipity, even though she is prone to misreading them as providence. Amid the messages imparted by old movies, the omnipres-

Figure 4.12 Watching *An Affair to Remember*, Becky and Annie lip-synch the famous line "Winter must be cold for those with no warm memories" which is underscored by the film's main theme.

ence of modern media plays a pivotal role, because they transmit such messages in unexpected ways. Early on, Annie, having announced her engagement to Walter to her family on Christmas Eve, is driving to her future in-laws to do the same. She turns on the radio, switching channels to avoid the fabrications of seasonal jollity, but stays with Dr. Fieldstone's show when hearing Jonah talk about his dad, and Sam about trying to get on with his life.

DR. MARCIA FIELDSTONE (*V.O.*): Sam, tell me what was so special about your wife?

SAM (*at home in Seattle*): How long is your program? Ah, well, it was a million tiny little things, that, when you added them all up, it just meant we were supposed to be together. And I knew it. I knew it the first time I touched her. It was like coming home, only to no home I'd ever known. I was just taking her hand to help her out of a car. And I knew it. It was like . . .

ANNIE (*in the car in Baltimore*): . . . magic.

SAM: . . . magic.

DR. MARCIA FIELDSTONE (*V.O.*): Well, folks, it's time to wrap it up. I'm Dr. Marcia Fieldstone in Chicago and to all my listeners, a magical and merry Christmas. (*Music on the radio fades in.*) And to you, Sleepless in Seattle, we hope you'll call again soon and let us know how it's going.

SAM: Oh, you count on it.

On the soundtrack Ray Charles singing "Over the Rainbow" swells to full volume:

> . . . That's where you'll find me.
> I know somewhere over the rainbow
> The Bluebirds glide
> Birds fly over the rainbow
> Why, then, oh why, can't I?[37]

The scene stages the magic of meeting the right partner at the right moment—not just Sam taking the hand of his wife, but also Annie "meeting" him for the first time on the air. The latter meeting qualifies as a variant of what James George Frazer famously described in the late nineteenth century as "sympathetic magic," which assumes "that things act on each other at a distance through a secret sympathy, the impulse being transmitted from one to the other by means of what we may conceive as a kind of invisible ether, not unlike that which is postulated by modern science for a precisely similar purpose, namely, to explain how things can physically affect each other through a space which appears to be empty."[38] It is striking how premodern conceptions of magic remain influential in popular culture at a deep level of belief. Indeed, Frazer's distinction between two types of sympathetic magic—homoeopathic, or imitative, magic and contagious magic—are at work in *Sleepless* as inexplicable yet palpable powers. While imitative magic is based on the law of similarity—"like produces like" or "an effect resembles its cause"—the law of contact or contagion establishes "that things which have once been in contact with each other continue to act on each other at a distance after the physical contact has been severed."[39]

Magic is literally in the air, through the technology of wireless transmission: two people in Seattle and Baltimore are sutured by invisible sounds from Chicago to create an intimate encounter over the ether where the physical absence of the other person is overcome by poignant gestures of completion (figure 4.13). Tears running down her cheeks, Annie does Sam's work of mourning. Rendered in crosscutting, their emotional sympathy suggests that the contingent may be the transcendent: that Annie is destined to become Sam's new wife. As the plot unfolds, imitative magic and contagious magic work together: the similarity between Annie and Sam's wife becomes increasingly obvious, as if her

Figure 4.13 Sympathetic Magic mediated by radio: talking in Seattle, listening in Baltimore.

actions were caused by a profound affinity between them. Annie comes to sense this, when Sam recounts how he touched his wife's hand: anticipating his final word, "magic," she speaks his heart and her own in near synchrony—a touching of voices. From then on, the plot is driven by what Michel Chion calls the "epiphany of the acousmêtre," the desire to discover the source of a sound: Annie must *see* Sam so that they can touch hands.[40] After he hangs up the phone, music, presumably resounding from the end of the show, brings this point home: Ray Charles's soulful cover of "Over the Rainbow" enters with the last line of the bridge—"That's where you'll find me"—to wrap up the program and the scene with the most longing lines of a song ranked by the American Film Institute as the greatest of all time.

Ephron had an uncanny knack for quoting magic lines and magic songs from cult movies. "Over the Rainbow" is surely a favorite, deployed too in her other Hanks-Ryan vehicle, *You've Got Mail* (1998). After subtle hints in the underscore it emerges when the two protagonists meet in the last scene, in what is—similar to *Sleepless*—another plot driven by an epiphany of the acousmêtre: email pals can *see* that they are not business rivals, but rather meant for each other.[41] For Ephron, covers of classic tunes not only serve as commentary but showcase how popular music has become an ineluctable strand of personal and collective remembrance. In the soundtrack of life, music endows events with meanings that linger as memories. Jimmy Durante's growly version of "As Time Goes By" accompanies the title credits, which follow the opening shots of Sam at his wife's funeral in Chicago—a city he must leave because it reminds him of her at every corner. But even in Seattle, he is haunted by her memory. After Sam has tucked Jonah in on New Year's Eve and returns to an empty living room, Nat King Cole's legendary version of "Stardust" drifts in from the underscore: "Sometimes I wonder why I spend the lonely night dreaming of a song. The melody haunts my reverie, and I am once again with you."[42] Ephron uses the song to summon a spectral visit of Sam's wife offering a New Year's toast, quoting another magic line: Rick's cheer to Ilsa from *Casablanca*—"Here's looking at you"—to which Sam responds, "Here's to us."

In *Sleepless*, it is an entire movie, *An Affair to Remember*, whose magic romance leads the plot to a new ending. McCarey's 1957 version was itself a remake of his 1939 film *Love Affair* (starring Irene Dunne and Charles Boyer), and Glenn Gordon Caron added a third remake in 1994 (starring Warren Beatty and Annette Bening). All three versions had the same basic plot line, adapted to their decades' ambience and lifestyle. *Sleepless in Seattle*, by contrast, is not an update, but an attempt to capture the "true" romance of the earlier classic. Yet *Sleepless* does not slip unabashedly into nostalgia. Instead, it engages in a hyperfilmic conversation about the presence of the cinematic past, clipping just enough from the 1957 version—a cult film by the 1990s thanks to cable television showings and VHS rentals—to renew the quest for romantic love. These clips contain not just the magic frames or magic lines whose effect Eco describes as "a sort of intense emotion accompanied by the vague feeling of a *déjà vu* that everybody yearns to see again."[43] They also come with magic music that sustains those emotions and intimates those vague feelings.

Music played an important role in *Love Affair* and its two remakes, not least in the visit to Nickie's grandmother—an elderly aunt, in the 1994 version—who sits down at the piano, with Terry humming and singing along (figure 4.14). In all three versions, a broken-hearted Nickie—"Michel" in 1939, "Mike" in 1994—returns to her house after his missed rendezvous with Terry, now finding himself alone at the piano, his grandmother having passed away in the meantime. As he touches the instrument, his memory of the two women performing the song fades in on the soundtrack before the housekeeper hands him a package with the shawl his grandmother wore during his last visit, and which she wanted Terry to have. The song's lyrics speak directly to his "affair" as a wondrous *thing* to remember, like "a page . . . torn out of time and place." McCarey had, in 1939, chosen the well-known eighteenth-century air "Plaisir d'amour,"

Figure 4.14 "Ce bel amour, qui ne peut mourir"—the source melody for the main theme in *An Affair to Remember*: first, Terry sings the song accompanied by Nickie's grandmother (*top*); then, after his grandmother's death, Nickie remembers Terry singing (*bottom*).

whose refrain notes that the short pleasures of love are painfully remembered for the rest of one's life.[44] His 1957 lyrics emphasized less the loss than the love, with Warren writing a song whose contemporary elegance Terry could showcase in her last nightclub performance before moving to New York.[45]

As Friedhofer weaves Warren's melody into his Oscar-nominated underscore, it foreshadows a sense of growing attachment when Nickie and Terry visit the chapel on his grandmother's estate, and later colors the pivotal conversation on the ship in which Nickie proposes to her. It is only logical that the pertinent portion from that cue—entitled "The Proposal"—returns in the final scene, when Nickie, in a surprise visit on Christmas Day, presents his grandmother's shawl to Terry, suddenly realizing that she was the woman in the wheelchair who had asked for his unsold painting of *both* women wearing that shawl. As he discovers the painting in her bedroom, the song's melody enters in the strings, swelling with a reaction shot of Nickie, *wincing* (figure 4.15). As Dan Wang put it beautifully, "The wince is the impact of narrative on the body: of the moment when the events of the story, up until now indecipherable to him, are supplied with the interpretive key that makes them spring into a causal chain, as a magnet will do to a scatter of shavings." The moment makes a consummate case for how music can clinch the bittersweet

Figure 4.15 After Nicki finds out that Terry bought his painting (*top*), he "winces" as the melody of "An Affair to Remember" swells in the orchestral underscore (*bottom*).

ending of romance tinged with remorse. Again, Wang: "The wince is a clue that the climactic resolution of the love story exists not only as the arrival of an emotion that is indexed by the love theme, but also more primally as affect."[46] Hence the return of the melody is more than a felicitous drop into the underscore. For, on some level, the melody seems to be *replaying* in Nickie's head—no longer the faint singing he heard when touching the piano at his grandmother's house, but a poignant orchestral reprise of the moment he and Terry fell in love.

The ending of *Sleepless* is quieter but no less effective, reprising the music from "The Proposal" during its heartwarming denouement on the observation deck of the Empire State Building. Jonah's friend Jessica, after watching *An Affair to Remember* ("the best movie I have ever seen"), had grasped the import of Annie's letter and used her parent's credit card to book him a flight to New York on Valentine's Day. And so Jonah waits all afternoon on the observation deck for Annie, while a frantic Sam is on his way from Seattle. In the meantime, Annie, on a date with Walter, finally opens up to him about her doubts, and he graciously takes back her engagement ring, after which she hurries to the Empire State Building to the jubilant orchestral strains of Warren's song. By now, however, Sam has recovered his son and the observation deck is closed, though the security guard allows her to go up (*An Affair* is also his wife's favorite), and we are left with Annie wandering around and wondering. Time dilates and a wistfully ruminating piano brings back songs from two earlier scenes.

Why those songs? The first is Carly Simon's glossy cover of "In the Wee Small Hours of the Morning," heard when Annie, lying sleepless next to Walter one night, gets up and walks into her kitchen. She switches on the radio and—miraculously—the music continues as if it had been playing all along, its smooth saxophone interlude now underscoring a rerun of "The best of Dr. Marcia Fieldstone" that includes Sam's account of what was so special about his wife: "How long is your program? Ah, well, it was a million tiny little things. When you added them up, it just meant we were supposed to be together. And I knew it, I knew it the first time I touched her. . . . I was just taking her hand to help her out of a car. And I knew it. It was like magic." As Sam speaks, Annie puts down the apple she had started to peel in long strips (an important detail) and begins to well up, as she had when listening in her car on Christmas. But now the camera slowly pushes in on her face to reveal the gradual onset of tears in what is one of Ryan's finest performances. The second song is "Bye Bye Blackbird," entering on piano when Annie discovers Jonah's backpack on the observation deck. It recalls a scene in which Sam comforted his son at night, wondering whether he should sing that song to him as his wife used to do when Jonah had a bad dream. After Jonah says that he is "starting to forget her," Joe Cocker's impassioned cover of "Bye Bye Blackbird" enters the underscore and Sam recalls with a smile that "she could peel an apple in one long curly strip." Clearly, the ruminating piano links these two scenes, pointing to one of those "million tiny little things" that count as sign and not coincidence. The connection through sympathetic magic that Annie has felt twice over the radio is now confirmed by what Frazer defined as the law of similarity: Sam's wife and Annie are alike. Holding the backpack with Jonah's teddy bear in her hands, we know she is ready to become his new mother.

Yet Sam has only *seen* Annie, not *touched* her—and this is what the denouement must deliver. He accidentally saw Annie at the airport when she was arriving in Seattle to research a story about him, and they faced each other during a botched encounter at the beach when she was almost run over by a truck.[47] That scene had also combined fragments of music heard before: instrumental snippets from the upbeat "A Wink and a Smile," composed by Harry Connick Jr., for Annie's investigation; a jumpy, sitcom-ish version of the opening phrase from Warren's "An Affair"; and, when Annie faces Sam across a busy street, the echo of a mysterious-sounding waltz, first heard when Annie tried on her grandmother's wedding dress, with her mother recounting her first date with Annie's father: "At one point I looked down, at our hands, and I couldn't tell which fingers were mine and which were his. And I knew . . . magic. It was magic." If these three jumbled segments did not form a continu-

Figure 4.16 Annie "hears" the cue "The Proposal" cueing action: it first radiates from her face (*top*), and then Sam touches her hand (*bottom*).

ous cue, the ruminating piano that accompanies Annie on the Empire State Building does create a coherent sequence of songs that transitions seamlessly into the very moment when the strings pick up the opening of Warren's song in Friedhofer's "The Proposal."

This is the most memorable melody from Annie's favorite film, which she has watched countless times. She has heard it in the opening credits; heard it sung by Terry three times, the third time as recalled by Nickie when revisiting his grandmother's empty house; and heard it underscoring his proposal on the ship, as well as its redemption in the final scene. Now this melody, retrieved from the movie-imbued memory track of her life becomes a soundtrack of sorts: it is music she seems to hear, in some way, in her head just as Sam shows up on the top of the Empire State Building with Jonah to retrieve his backpack (figure 4.16).

Called up from her optical-acoustic unconscious, the love theme from

An Affair appears not just to supply the fitting score for Annie's first real meeting with Sam, but to have had the power to make such a meeting happen. This is the magic of the replay: it enters into their story, to use Eco's formulation, as that "intense emotion accompanied by the vague feeling of a *déjà vu* that everybody yearns to see again." After Sam's earlier encounters with Annie at the airport and on the street—a "very French *déjà vu*," he tells Greg and Suzy—the emotion elicited by the music from *An Affair* now makes Annie's replay auratic, bridging nearness and distance, image space and body space, semblance and play. Ever since her mother mentioned touching her father's hand for the first time and *knowing* that he was the right one, Annie has been searching for "signs" that would direct her to the right man, so that she, too, may hold his hand. When she finally meets Sam, she hears that music as a "sign," now radiating from her face and legible to him, as if the halo of soft strings—the very timbre of tender affection—is aura as returned gaze. As if answering Jonah and Sam's question ("You are Annie?"), the music underscores her "Yes," prompting him to extend his hand: "We better go. Shall we?" The last reprise of Friedhofer's "Proposal" *cues* Sam's proposal. Now that sympathetic magic has done the work of imitation it also completes the work of contact. Only now, touching hands, they both know.

The happy ending of *Sleepless in Seattle* thus reclaims those "magical correspondences" that Benjamin saw as being lost with the decline of the mimetic faculty, raising the pressing question of modernity: "whether we are concerned with the decay of this faculty or with its transformation."[48] At stake is the human need to recover the sensuous mimetic script underwriting the nonsensuous semiotic of language. Annie ultimately overcomes her difficulty reading signs by acting out the script of *An Affair to Remember*, as cued by the music. She realizes what Hansen describes as "the possibility of a resurgence of mimetic powers *within* the disenchanted modern world."[49] When touching Sam's hand like his wife, Annie's radiant smile (more so than Cecilia's) shows that her auratic replay has reclaimed the mimetic faculty and renewed its mnemonic magic.

CHAPTER FIVE

Panoramic Flashbacks

Panoramic memory, a term used by the neurologist Samuel Alexander Kinnier Wilson in 1928 to describe certain symptoms of uncinate epilepsy, has long been associated with the experience of total recall in near-death situations.[1] Thomas De Quincey reported the experience as early as 1845, relating the account of a woman who had been rescued from drowning as a child: "In the twinkling of an eye, every act, every design of her past life lived again, arraying themselves not as a succession, but as parts of a co-existence."[2] The episode seemed intensely illuminating in quite a literal sense: "light fell upon the whole path of her life backwards into the shades of infancy" and effectively "poured celestial vision upon the brain, so that her consciousness became omnipresent at one moment to every feature in the infinite review." Introducing the woman's account, De Quincey distinguished between the "vellum palimpsest" and "our own heaven-created palimpsest, the deep memorial palimpsest of the brain." In the former, life events have "by pure accident . . . consecutively occupied the roll," while in the latter "fleeting accidents of a man's life" that seemed "irrelate and incongruous" appear in the "retrospect" of "dying moments" to follow "organizing principles which fuse into harmony, and gather about fixed predetermined centres, whatever heterogeneous elements life may have accumulated from without." De Quincey compared this revelatory experience to a "pall, deep as oblivion" that was drawn up suddenly "at the signal of a blazing rocket sent up from the brain" to expose the "whole depth of the theatre."

Douwe Draaisma, a historian of psychology, has shown that descriptions of near-death experiences are historically specific, noting that "by far the most common metaphor in recent descriptions of panoramic memory is *film* and its associated terms like flashback, replay and slow motion."[3] If cinematographic conventions such as eerie lighting have shaped how people relate near-death situations, in turn, "the metaphor of film for the experience of panoramic memory has *itself* become a cinematographic convention."[4] Early examples of flashback narration include Paul Fejos's 1928 *The Last Moment* (now lost), where the central character drowns himself and recalls significant moments from his past as he is dying, and Mervyn Leroy's 1932 *Two Seconds*, where Edward G. Robinson plays a convicted murderer whose life runs before his inner eye as he is electrocuted.[5] These films are variants of the frame-tale narrative, where the moment of death provides the occasion for a whole-life retrospective. Once the narration starts, however, the review unfolds like a regular film. A related convention is the story told from beyond the grave (often using voiceover) by a narrator who is already dead when the film begins, as, for example, in Billy Wilder's *Sunset Boulevard* (1950) or more recently Sam Mendez's *American Beauty* (1999).

Since flashbacks are ubiquitous across genres, cinematic representations of panoramic memory need not be triggered by actual near-death situations, nor do panoramic flashbacks have to span an entire lifetime. In Frank Capra's *It's a Wonderful Life* (1946), an angel gives the banker George Bailey (about to commit suicide in despair over his imminent bankruptcy) an opportunity to see a version of his life from which he has been excised, as if he had never lived—a stark contrast to the actual life "screened" for the angel by his superior to prime him for George's rescue. Here the simulated flashback enables what James Chandler has called a sentimental mode—wherein sentiment becomes an emotion "mediated by a sympathetic passage through a virtual point of view."[6] There is also a fluid line between flashback narration, which covers a whole film, and the shorter flashback montage, which condenses the past into a synoptic retrospection. While flashbacks may become whole-film montages with linear or nonlinear narration, as in auteurist films such as Chris Marker's *La Jetée* (1962) or Andrei Tarkovsky's *The Mirror* (1975), *American Beauty* uses a nonlinear flashback montage from the moment of death to frame a traditional flashback narration from beyond the grave.

If the flashback triggered by sound or induced by music is a longstanding device in cinematic storytelling, panoramic flashbacks raise the stakes for the music by highlighting its importance for the remembering character as well as for his or her remembered life. The selection of records that cues Julie's recollection in *Penny Serenade* (1941) interweaves personal and period memory, not unlike Woody Allen's *Radio Days* (1989) and Terence Davies's *Distant Voices, Still Lives* (1989), where the experience of music belongs to the "soundtrack of life" embedded in mass media, such as radio and film. Through music, with music, or *like* music, panoramic memory becomes a time-out moment, an altered state, a special condition with heightened emotion and enhanced perception that catalyzes the expanded perspective of a larger whole. While the term "flashbulb memory," alluding to a device to enhance exposure during photography, has been used to illustrate how memories of emotionally intense events are retained as vividly as snapshots, music may boost this effect.[7] De Quincey's description of how life events "fuse into harmony" captures the sense of detached euphoria in panoramic memory. Physiologically, the feeling of having "fallen into heaven," reported by people who survive falls from great heights, may stem from a rush of adrenaline in response to danger, the production of endorphins in anticipation of a painful impact, and the stimulation of neural correlates responsible for the recollection of memories.[8]

Cinematic representations of panoramic memory have drawn on music to simulate an altered state of heightened consciousness where its power to harmonize becomes the power to coordinate: music not only can express a sense of elation but can suture a rapid sequence of images onto a coherent flashback montage or assemble a flashback narration into a cogent account. Representations of total recall and quasi-divine omniscience make us aware of film as a medium of memory, highlighting the differences and similarities between technological and organic memory. Most pertinent is Benjamin's observation that situations of mortal danger lead to the recollection of "profound moments," unconsciously captured in life like photographs—an idea that I extend to music's ability to record visual memories and replay them later. Music also participates in the experience of panoramic flashbacks in ways that highlight its role in the soundtrack of life: as a sign of habit, as a souvenir of events, and as the sound of euphoria—even transcendence. These roles are relevant to the one case study in this chapter, Max Ophüls's *Letter from an Unknown Woman* (1948). At first, the film takes the cinematic convention of panoramic memory back to traditional issues of film music, such as the slippage between source music and underscore, the difference between preexistent and newly composed music, and music's narrative function. The unusual story, however, told from beyond the grave by a woman in a letter to a pianist who failed to remember her, offers a new perspective on the phenomenon, as the woman assumes, through her hypertrophic memory, quasi-directorial powers to cure his amnesia by recalling the past through music.

This chapter's concern with the momentousness of end-of-life situations is particularly conducive to what may be described as a shift from meaning to the meaningful. In the face of death, the search for the meaning of life can give way to a need to find meaning *in* life, a unique opportunity to assess how life has been, or might have been, meaningful. Here the synoptic review of panoramic memory may not only impart new insights and prompt a reevaluation, but also offer an occasion for reconcilement and redemption. In this regard, the panoramic flashback can create a sense of closure, an easing of the process of dying.

Hypertrophic Memory

Letter from an Unknown Woman revolves on unequal memory. Based on a novella by Stefan Zweig, the film unfolds through flashback narration in the form of a letter addressed to Stefan Brand (Louis Jourdan), a philandering pianist in turn-of-the-century Vienna. In the opening scene, Brand returns to his apartment late at night, instructing his servant John to prepare for a quick departure so that he can escape the duel awaiting him in the morning. John (who is mute) hands him a letter that arrived that evening and Stefan begins to read, intrigued by its portentous opening: "By the time you read this letter, I may be dead. . . . If this reaches you,

you will know how I became yours when you didn't know who I was or even that I existed." We hear the voiceover of the letter writer Lisa Berndle (Joan Fontaine) and the screen dissolves to show her story. Or rather *their* story. Since Stefan has no recollection of the woman, the letter is to make his memory equal to hers. The flashback narration unfolds as an intricate mixture between the letter's limited point of view and a broader narrative perspective gained by its writer after her death.

The flashback begins when Stefan moves into the apartment building where the fifteen-year-old Lisa lives with her widowed mother. Lisa develops a crush on him, cut short when her mother relocates to Linz to remarry. Now a young woman, Lisa becomes engaged to a military officer, but breaks off the engagement to move back to Vienna. She follows Stefan and his career from a distance, keeping a nightly watch outside his apartment, where he eventually notices her without remembering who she is. Their meeting turns into a one-day affair, and after spending the night together, Stefan promises to contact Lisa when he returns from a two-week concert tour. He never does, and Lisa never reaches out to him, even after the birth of their son, also named Stefan. Years later, having entered into a marriage of convenience with a wealthy general, she encounters Stefan (whose career has been floundering) at a performance of *The Magic Flute*. Once again, he has only a vague sense of having seen her "somewhere." Hoping to rekindle their relationship, Lisa separates from her husband and puts her son on the train for a two-week stay in the countryside. But when she visits Stefan at his old apartment, he still cannot place her. Distressed, Lisa leaves. Before long their son dies of typhus (which he caught on the train) and Lisa falls gravely ill herself, writing to Stefan with her own death looming. After reading her letter, he has a flashback of key moments with Lisa, finally remembering the girl and woman, whose name John writes down for him on a piece of paper. The clock strikes five, too late for Stefan to escape, but he no longer has a reason to run away from his challenger, who turns out to be Lisa's husband. The film ends with the carriages of the dueling parties pulling away, suggesting that Stefan will meet his fate and be united in death with Lisa—no longer an unknown woman.

Letter is perhaps Ophüls's best-known film, made in the United States after fleeing from Nazi-occupied Europe, where he had built an impressive reputation—first in Germany, then in France—with a string of highly innovative films since the early 1930s. Hollywood presented plenty of challenges for Ophüls, and it was not until after the war (partly due to support from Preston Sturges) that his dormant career resumed. *Letter* became the pilot project of Rampart Productions, launched in 1948 by William Dozier (formerly at Paramount and RKO) and Fontaine, his wife. In collaboration with screenwriter Howard Koch and producer John Houseman, Ophüls tried to create a film that would include his signature long takes and mobile camera against a prevailing aesthetic that relied on the much more cost effective technique of continuity editing. Although initial reception was mixed, *Letter* eventually became a canonical film, spawning plenty of critical and scholarly commentary that sought to explain and validate the director's auteurist aspirations. While Ophuls's unusual use of flashback narration and his fondness for varied doublings offer an object lesson in cinematic style, his focus on female protagonists (prominent in several of his other films) has lent itself to interpretations involving psychoanalytical and feminist perspectives by writers ranging from Stephen Heath, Robin Wood, and Stanley Cavell to Kaja Silverman, Laura Mulvey, and Karl Siereck.[9] The 1987 publication of the continuity script (together with variants of the shooting script, as well as reviews, essays, and interviews) was followed in the mid-1990s by two major monographs on Ophüls, by Susan White and by Lutz Bacher.[10] The latter deals specifically with Ophüls's Hollywood years, offering not only a detailed account of the director's rocky relations with the studio system, but also minute descriptions of the production process, in which he had to grapple with financial and logistical constraints. The most sustained musicological treatment of *Letter* appeared a decade later in a chapter of Heather Laing's *The Gendered Score*, a study of 1940s melodrama and the woman's film, with Lisa exemplifying a "female listener."[11]

Amid such ample coverage, I want to review and rehear *Letter* by considering the role of music's mnemonic power in the panoramic retrospective. This angle emerged from the prominent role Ophüls and Koch accorded to music when adapting Zweig's story (which originally involved a writer, not a musician) for the screen, and it evolved quite dramatically from the Final Shooting Script to the film's final version, including Daniele Amfitheatrof's score, which has never been scrutinized in this regard. Given the larger concerns of this book, I am particularly keen on music's function in the two distinct cinematic manifestations of panoramic memory that pair up in the film: Lisa's flashback narration and Stefan's flashback montage. Both are stylized forms of synoptic retrospection—one extensive, the other intensive—and they align with Lisa's and Stefan's changing ability to remember each other through music. I will argue that Lisa's memory is *hypertrophic* and that her ability to associate Stefan with music in life shapes her posthumous panoramic flashback as an all-seeing and all-hearing narrator. As an example of what Maureen Turim describes as film characters with "obsessive memory," Lisa's omniscience plays out in Amfitheatrof's underscore, suggesting that she has mastery over that aspect of the narration as well.[12] Stefan, by contrast, appears largely oblivious to the mnemonic powers of music. It is only in his concluding flashback montage—a brief recollection of his meetings with Lisa—that music helps conjure up these encounters and brings about a change of heart.

Ophüls had already deployed music's mnemonic capacity as a plot device in his award-winning *La Signora di Tutti* (1934), for which Amfitheatrof had also written a score that similarly serves a dual role in character memory and character narration. Much of *La Signora* is constructed, not unlike the later *Lola Montès* (1955), as a panoramic flashback of the main protagonist, a famous singer and movie star, who reviews her life during a narcotic sleep on the operating table after a suicide attempt (both film and flashback end with her death). Taking up the trope of the moment-before-death flashback, *Letter* is unusually self-conscious about music's role in cinematic representations of remembrance, exploring how parallels between mechanical and human memory reflect back on film as an audiovisual medium capable of recording and reprojecting the past. The unequal memories of Lisa and Stefan drive the plot and structure the narration, and music is integral to this difference, making transparent how *Letter* benefited from the influence of cinema on the culture of memory. Inasmuch as Lisa's panoramic flashback came to dominate Koch's adaptation of Zweig's novella, Ophüls had to acquiesce to Dozier's demand for a conventional and morally acceptable dramatic ending, leading to the insertion of the flashback montage that confirms Stephan's *visual* recognition. Created from existing footage during postproduction, the flashback was to motivate his willingness to die in the duel.[13] But this need to fully remember Lisa visually, I will suggest, made it necessary that Stefan eventually share her aural and musical mode of knowing him.

Commentators have routinely remarked that Lisa's flashback narration represents events from a perspective that she could not have assumed during her life.[14] Often-cited examples include two similarly framed shots that were already prominent in the original Final Shooting Script and that were (not surprisingly) created on the same day: the first shows Stefan coming home at night with a woman, as observed by the adolescent Lisa from higher on the staircase (and shot over her shoulder); the second shows Stefan returning home several years later during his one-day dalliance with the adult Lisa, with no upstairs observer (figure 5.1). The pairing implies that Lisa has become yet another of Stefan's conquests (showing the womanizer's propensity for loveless repetition), but the second shot also draws attention to a vantage point external to her letter. This has raised questions about Lisa's status as a narrator.

Although the flashback starts out as a visualization of the letter, Robin Wood notes that the "tendency of the film to draw us into her vision is balanced and counterpointed throughout by a conflicting tendency to detach us from the 'dream' and comment on it ironically, hinting at a prosaic reality that Lisa excludes."[15] However, the discrepancy between partial and total vision can be explained quite differently in light of Lisa's death. By the time Stefan reads the letter, she has passed away, as confirmed in a postscript: "This letter was written by a patient here. We believe it was meant for you as she spoke your name just before she died."[16] Lisa's death thus accounts for her surplus of knowledge, allowing her to relate her story from the point of view of a supernatural entity, perhaps

Figure 5.1
The twin shots: Lisa observes Stefan coming home with a woman (*top*); and later, as omniscient narrator telling the story from beyond the grave, she observes herself comes home with Stefan (*bottom*).

a divine being, whose omniscience is akin to that of a director who has complete creative control over the story and its telling. Indeed, Ophüls and Koch created a deliberate slippage between the limited outlook of Lisa's letter, written on her deathbed, and her position of speaking from beyond the grave. To invoke narrative theory, the former results from the "internal focalization" of Lisa as a character, while the latter has the "zero focalization" typical for an omniscient narrator. This narrator pairs the first stairwell shot with a second shot, creating a sense-making narrative that sees (and conveys) meaningful parallels from the posthumous point of view.[17] With this perspective, Lisa assumes quasi-directorial powers that transform the letter into a flashback narration, changing mimesis into diegesis. Put differently, as Lisa-writer evolves toward Lisa-director, her flashback is no longer a reproduction of events from her letter but their representation, cinematically *rendered* as a panoramic memory from the double perspective of a homodiegetic narrator that elides the difference between protagonist and observer, character and storyteller, or subject and object of the subject gaze. In short, Lisa's panoramic memory enables her, in De Quincey's words, to view "the whole depth of the theatre" after drawing up the "pall."

For Stefan, however, this pall is drawn up only gradually. We do not know how specific his recollections are. Initially, he can only *imagine* what the living Lisa wrote, while the dead Lisa can *show* it through her augmented powers of directorial omniscience. Occasional cuts back to Stefan reading at his desk remind us of the difference between letter and film as media of remembrance. Cognizant of Stefan's poor memory, Lisa has included photographs of their son in the letter, one of which shows her and little Stefan in the basket of a mock hot-air balloon (figure 5.2).[18] We see Stefan looking at them through a magnifying glass—a prosthetic aid that emphasizes his perceptual shortcomings, his lack of imagination, his weak recollection. But why do these photographs still fail to remind him of the woman he recently saw at the opera and who came to his house afterward?

This question points to the aforementioned disagreement between Ophüls and Dozier, who strongly believed that a dramatically satisfying denouement required that Stefan remember Lisa *visually*. If Lisa's letter affords Stefan a second look at his life, he can only fully understand and see their story *after* he has finished reading. Dozier's insistence led to the inclusion of Stefan's flashback montage, which follows the convention of representing diegetic memory: the camera pushes in on Stefan's face and a dissolve discloses what he sees through his teary eyes. This condensed array of images, akin to near-death panoramic memories, is triggered by the melodramatic too-late trope ending Lisa's letter: "My life can be measured by the moments I've had with you and our child. If only you could have shared those moments, if only you could have recognized what was always yours, could have found what was never lost. If only . . ."[19]

Since all of the images in Stefan's flashback montage stem from Lisa's flashback narration, some crucial questions arise: How is it that Stefan can recall those very same images now? How can his montage draw from her narration? How can he see what we saw? To answer these questions we need to go back to the ending of Zweig's novella. If the rationale for the diegetic flashback is that Stefan's visual recollection of Lisa will motivate him to "man up" for the duel, Ophüls's reluctance to be overly explicit originates with the novella's final paragraph, where the writer's memory remains shrouded in a mist:

Figure 5.2
Stefan looks at a photo of Lisa and their son, Stefan.

The letter fell from his nerveless hand. He thought long and deeply. Yes, he had vague memories of a neighbour's child, of a girl, of a woman in a dancing hall—all was dim and confused, like the flickering and shapeless view of a stone in the bed of a swiftly running stream. Shadows chased one another across his mind, but would not fuse into a picture. There were strings of memory in the realm of feeling, and still he could not remember. It seemed to him that he must have dreamed of all these figures, must have dreamed often and vividly—and yet they had only been the phantoms of a dream. His eyes wandered to the blue vase on the writing-table. It was empty. For years it had not been empty on his birthday. He shuddered, feeling as if an invisible door had been suddenly opened, a door through which a chill breeze from another world was blowing into his sheltered room. An intimation of death came to him, and an intimation of deathless love. Something welled up within him; and the thought of the dead woman stirred in his mind, bodiless and passionate, like the sound of distant music.[20]

There is much to cherish in Zweig's description of these "vague memories": as shadows not fusing into a picture, as a string of feelings, as oneiric phantoms. Bacher has shown that Ophüls was deeply invested in the novelist's vision of vagueness but sought to reconcile it with the dramatic imperative that Stefan gain a more definite sense of Lisa in the end. The original Final Shooting Script developed the motif of flowers sent annually by the unknown woman to the writer—a material link that became less prominent once the film put greater emphasis on Stefan recalling her visually—and musically. One cannot help being struck that the very last clause of the novella likened the "thought of the dead woman" stirring in the writer's mind to "the sound of distant music." By turning the writer into a musician, the screenplay offered an opportunity not only to make this music heard, but also to have musical memories call forth a visual recollection of the unknown woman. Because music could help to "fuse into harmony" the "fleeting accidents of a man's life," it eventually became integral to Lisa's panoramic flashback narration as well as Stefan's flashback montage.

Given the critical change in the screenplay, Lisa and Stefan are initially set apart by their ability (or lack thereof) to remember through music. As Lisa writes at the outset of the letter, the second beginning of her life (her "second birthday") was the beginning of her *consciousness*: "Nothing is vivid or real in my memory before that day in spring, when I came home from school and found a moving van in front of our building." We hear the sound of a harp before we see it being unloaded from the van. This is a small detail, but the order of appearance—sound before image—anticipates Lisa's infatuation with the pianist, whom she hears playing for days before meeting him face to face. As Laing has noted, music contains for Lisa "the key to an intimate understanding of Stefan."[21] When Stefan is practicing Liszt's concert etude in D♭ major, "Un sospiro," the screenplay specifies how the music literally enters Lisa's body. Sitting on the swing below his window and looking at her hands, "she rhythmically removes them and then replaces them on the ropes of the swing."[22] This is a primal scene of sorts, sublimating the sexual sense invoked by Lisa's prurient girlfriend, who relates flippantly how a certain boy outside of their school "doesn't keep his hands to himself." Since Lisa can feel Stefan's playing hands, she already knows him without having laid eyes on him. Her flashback narration relates this knowledge through an added point of view: the young Lisa who feels Stefan's hands cannot see him play, but the film cuts to him playing the piano because the narrating Lisa has access to those images. Knowing Stefan through music is not only the source of her emerging obsession with him, but also the basis of her excessive memory of him. As Lisa's fixation on Stefan grows, she is shown listening to him through transom windows, perusing scores in the library, and looking at programs of his concerts—all amounting to a kind of finishing school that will make him say on the day of their affair, "You know far too much about me already, and I know almost nothing about you."[23]

Double Takes

Stefan is introduced as a performer prone to memory lapses. After botching the cadenza in measure 37 of "Un sospiro," he interrupts his practice with a sense of frustration—a key moment, which becomes Lisa's cue to rush to the doorway through which he will leave the building. It is here that they see each other for the first time, with Lisa standing behind the glass door she holds open for him. This is another primal scene, but one without music. On his way out, Stefan notices Lisa. He stops. A medium shot shows them looking at each other through the glass door, followed by a medium close-up of Stefan's face from Lisa's point of view (figure 5.3). "Thank you," he says charmingly. Before stepping out onto the street, Stefan stops and looks once more, seeing Lisa still standing behind the door.

Their first visual encounter is pivotal. This is not only because it occurs at a doorway, a threshold, a liminal space, but also because it will replay at the end of the film. Stefan will leave through the same door for the duel; he will turn around once more and see Lisa's ghostly image—a spectral reprojection of his first encounter—but no longer unknown. Like the twin staircase shots, this doubling shows how self-conscious Ophüls's cinematic style was about relying on acts of remembrance. Already during preproduction, he had argued against the return of Lisa's shadow as "a little corny" and planned for another version without Stefan turning back.[24] He had similar qualms about the flashback montage, yet with the latter in place, Lisa's spectral return at the door reinforced the dramatic rationale for Stefan's redemptive death. More importantly, the doubling of the door scene raises the question of whether the narrative frame—Stefan returning home, reading the letter, and leaving for the duel—might be envisioned by Lisa, suggesting that the entire film, not just the letter, springs from her posthumous perspective.

Letter invokes parallels between human and mechanical memory, suggesting that photography and sound recording may be understood in terms of an optical-acoustic unconscious. Stefan's first meeting of Lisa at the door is no less than an occasion for taking a mental picture (figure 5.3). The Final Shooting Script describes how his glance has a "special quality" evocative of a camera bringing an object into focus: the

Figure 5.3 The first encounter: after playing Liszt's "Un sospiro" Stefan sees the young Lisa for the first time in a first take (*top pair*) and second take (*bottom pair*).

"concentration" of his glance "is so intense that nothing or no one else seems to exist other than its immediate object."[25] But since this first look at her through the glass screen appears to be insufficient, he turns back for a second look, or rather, a retake—a shot that was missing even in the Final Shooting Script.[26] Stefan's "double take" is symptomatic of his mnemonic weakness, a combination of poor perception and diminished storage that affects both vision and hearing.

Lisa's first look at Stefan has the opposite outcome: "From that moment on, you have never left my thoughts. . . . Perhaps it was the way you looked at me that first time."[27] She senses something in Stefan's glance that he will come to understand only years later: his music. Her mental picture of him only adds to what she already knows about him through music: his image simply attaches itself to Liszt's etude. Music becomes Lisa's vehicle for visual memory, bolstered by listening to him practice

“Un sospiro” from the hallway at night. On the day her family moves to Linz, she runs back to her apartment to hear the piece resound through the empty apartment. The sonic design of the scene is telling. The Lisa who wanders through the empty apartment recalls “Un sospiro” echoing with added reverb in her mind as a diegetic memory. Yet the Lisa who narrates the incident remembers her reminiscing self through an aura of added strings. Moving from source to underscore, the music connects her moment of remembrance with how she recalls that moment later on. Hypertrophic memory in life powers narrative omniscience after life. Lisa’s superior recollection of music turns it into a means of remembrance: first resounding within the limits of field memory, Liszt’s etude permeates the unbounded memory of the postmortem observer.

This musical glue in Lisa’s flashback narration—akin to De Quincey’s sense of “harmony” as an “organizing principle” in panoramic memory—becomes a recurring plot device of *Letter*. The corresponding key moment is Lisa’s second face-to-face encounter with Stefan, which takes place near his apartment one night after her return to Vienna. A band of street musicians plays the aria “Nur für Natur” from the second act of the 1881 operetta *Der lustige Krieg* by Johann Strauss Jr.—an immensely popular tune recycled in his so-called *Kuss Walzer* (“Kiss Waltz”), op. 400, whose ear-wormish melody includes a memorable turn to the flat seventh (figure 5.4). As Lisa—who has been stalking Stefan for weeks—settles into her usual spot at a street corner, he passes her to give the musicians some money. When they play the melody again—this time without vocals, to make room for the dialogue—he notices her.

STEFAN (*removing his hat*): I’ve seen you before . . . (*She looks down.*) . . . a few nights ago . . . right here. Oh, you live near here?

LISA: No.

STEFAN: Do you like to listen to street singers?

LISA (*looking down*): Yes.

STEFAN: Neither do I.[28]

“Nur für Natur” is the second piece by which Lisa will remember Stefan all her life. Though he effectively pays for an encore, he fails to make that association and will not recall the music until after reading the letter.

The common practice of working source music into the underscore takes on special significance in *Letter*. As Lisa’s musical memory permeates her beyond-the-grave narration, it becomes apparent what a keen listener she has been in life, even when hearing seemingly inconspicuous music. Three examples may suffice. The first stems from the Linz episode when Lisa and the lieutenant seeking her hand attend an open-air concert of a music corps on the town square, including Wolfram von Eschenbach’s heartfelt “O thou my fair evening star” from Wagner’s *Tannhäuser*. The “arranged” marriage between a tender melody and a

Figure 5.4 The second encounter: after a band plays the aria "Nur für Natur" by Johann Strauss Jr. (*right*), Stefan approaches Lisa who has been listening and watching from the distance (*left*).

military band puts an ironic twist on the ill-starred proposal of a secondary suitor.[29] Years later, when Stefan follows Lisa into the foyer at the opera, Papageno's aria "Ein Mädchen oder Weibchen" (sung in Italian) can be heard from the stage, the carefree bird-catcher inadvertently glossing Stefan's careless pursuits.[30] However coincidental, all this music does not merely offer an extradiegetic commentary by an implied author, or, to use a term by Jerrold Levinson, an implied filmmaker. We can also hear these pieces as being *heard* by Lisa, who surely grasps their meaning for her current situation: while the arrangement of Wolfram's aria prompts her to cancel the fraught engagement, Papageno's frivolity seems to approve of Stefan's allure.[31]

A third, more subtle, example of coincidentally efficacious music is the scene in which Stefan takes Lisa out to dine in the *chambre séparée* of an elegant restaurant on their evening together. Selections of two waltzes by Johann Strauss Jr. seem to resound from the adjacent main room, as if played by a salon orchestra.[32] The popular melody from the first section of *Wiener Blut* ("Vienna Life"), op. 354, is followed by the second section, creating a rounded ternary when the opening returns.

Such makeshift arrangements were of course common in film music, providing here the appropriate Viennese ambience to accompany Stefan's urbane talk about food and wine. But there is more to the choice of the second waltz. When the server interrupts the couple with a request from another guest—a countess who compliments Stefan on his afternoon concert ("Mozart himself could not have done better") and asks for him to sign the program—Lisa recalls that four years prior the *Morning Review* had also compared him to "the young Mozart." Yet Stefan plays down the comparison ("I *was* very young") and continues to expound on the virtues of the Valpolicella ("The Italians say it's such a good wine because the grapes have their roots in the valley and their eyes on the mountain"). Here the music switches to the second number from Strauss's *Künstlerleben* ("Artist's Life"), op. 316, whose ending lends a touch of yearning to a lilting melodic descent. And Lisa insists that he "talk about himself":

STEFAN: The truth is I've had rather an easy time of it. People accepted my music very quickly, perhaps too quickly. Sometimes, it's easier to please others than oneself. What were you going to say? You know you don't talk very much.

LISA: Well, I can't say it very well, but . . .

STEFAN: Yes.

LISA: . . . sometimes I felt when you were playing that . . .

STEFAN (*listening intently*): Go on.

LISA: . . . that you hadn't quite found—I don't know what it is—what you're looking for.

STEFAN (*leaning back in his seat*): How long have you been hiding in my piano? Never mind explaining. I'll just assume that you are sorceress and that you can make yourself very tiny. (*Lisa laughs nervously and looks down and away from Stefan as he continues with mock seriousness.*) It might be a good thing to have a sorceress for a friend. Who knows, you may be able to help me someday.[33]

The Final Shooting Script is quite specific about the effects of this phrase: "the words 'you may be able to help me' take on an unexpectedly serious and sincere meaning. Their eyes hold."[34] Of course, that "someday" will be the day of Stefan's duel, the day of reading Lisa's letter, the day of his death. On that day Lisa will indeed help him, with her magical grasp of music, to make sense of his life as an artist. We catch a glimpse of that grasp in the way she recalls the conversation with its seemingly accidental change of waltzes. Surely Amfitheatrof was playing a game of recognition for insiders who could hear how the music tracks the shift in the conversation from Stefan's hedonism to his failed artistic aspirations. Yet given the acuity of Lisa's ear, when she narrates that evening, the change to the *Artist's Life* waltz seems to "fuse into harmony" the relevant parts of their conversation, as if to cue her request that Stefan talk about himself.

Figure 5.5
Cue no. 52, "The Letter Ends," recalls "Un sospiro" and "Nur für Natur" (*Kuss Walzer*). Conductor's score of *Letter from an Unknown Woman* (voiceover added). Courtesy Margaret Herrick Library, Academy of Motion Picture Arts and Sciences.

As Lisa the listener tunes into her musical environment, coincidental music can become consequential: it enters into her flashback narration because she remembers it as being meaningful. One might say that her memory of music—surely a trademark of the film composer—allows her to "score" her own flashback, both supplementing and supplanting her voiceover. Heard this way, the source music that seeps into the underscore issues from an expanding narrative voice that extends her limited perspective as a character. Lisa's memory of music organizes her recollections, so that, in De Quincey's formulation, certain pieces function as "fixed predetermined centres" that "gather . . . whatever heterogeneous elements life may have accumulated from without." "Un sospiro" and the *Kiss Waltz* are most prominent in Lisa's extended narrative voice, since portions of their melodies often recur reworked in the same cue or in adjacent cues. (The studio's cue sheet lists both Liszt and Strauss

Jr. together with Amfitheatrof as arranger.) For example, after Lisa has put her son on the train, she searches for Stefan in the coffeehouse near his apartment. Here the melody of the *Kiss Waltz* is worked into a subdued adagio for strings, giving way to the hopeful strains of "Un sospiro" when she approaches Stefan's apartment and runs up the stairs after buying a bouquet of white roses from the same vendor from whom Stefan had bought her a single white rose years earlier (these cues are entitled "Kiss Waltz" and "White Roses"). Similarly, the cue "Heartbreak," which sounds when Lisa leaves Stefan's apartment in despair after realizing that he does not remember her, begins with the melody of Liszt's etude as she passes John on the stairs, and ends with the melody of the *Kiss Waltz* as she wanders alone across a deserted square.

This cue runs into the next, entitled "The Letter Ends," as the shot dissolves into Lisa at the hospital, writing to Stefan that his son has died. Just after her voiceover says, "If this letter reaches you, this, remember this," the piano version of "Un sospiro" enters with added strings before she continues: "I love you now as I always loved you. My life is measured by the moments I've had with you and our child" (figure 5.5). Yet something quite striking happens when Lisa ends the letter, whose final lines bear repeating: "If only you could have shared those moments, if only you could have recognized what was always yours, could have found what was never lost. If only . . ." Here the solo violin *joins* Liszt's etude by alluding to the characteristic turn to the flat seventh in measure 9 of "Nur für Natur"—an evocative counterpoint that unites the two key moments when Lisa had met Stefan face to face.

Aural Recognition

Lisa's hypertrophic memory, then, turns her into a homodiegetic narrator who weaves the music she heard in life meaningfully into her flashback. *Letter* dramatizes Lisa's and Stefan's differing ability to store memories by invoking, more or less explicitly, technologies of reproduction. Given Stefan's mnemonic deficiency, the visual retake may be his last resort, but to little avail. To illustrate this failure, Ophüls created one of his most media-conscious scenes for the couple's off-season visit to the Prater, Vienna's famed amusement park. Here they go for a "ride" in a myriorama—a train carriage that simulates travel as scenery is pulled past the compartment window (figure 5.6, top). Lisa, all chatty, tells Stefan of her childhood "journeys" around the world, staged by her father using brochures from a local travel bureau. With travel thus set up as playtime and media event, the myriorama ride and its embedded reminiscence perfectly illustrate the protagonists' mnemonic strengths and weaknesses. If Lisa seems to know everything about Stefan—every concert he has given, every piece he has played, every review written about

Figure 5.6
At the Prater, Lisa and Stefan "travel" by train to Venice in a myriorama (*top*). The "conductor" moves the panorama roll with his feet and operates an orchestrion with his left hand to provide musical "underscoring" (*bottom*).

him—he must admit that he knows nothing about her except that she has "traveled a great deal." He is so taken with their journeys that he pays to see all the rides a second time: "we revisit the scenes of our youth." But for him the repeated rides remain as inconsequential as the encore of the *Kiss Waltz* he paid for when meeting Lisa on the street earlier that day.

The parallel between the myriorama and music is critical. James Chandler has noted that the "proto-cinematic" myriorama exemplifies a moment of "sentimental reflection, a form of medium-self-consciousness" that suggests "the kind of reflective self-knowing that cinema itself can (and cannot) offer." Ophüls's invention of the scene turns cinema into "the medium of analysis" that "challenges Freud in his own 1900 moment and his own Viennese backyard."[35] That medium of analysis includes music: since none of the music seems to stick to Stefan's mind, nothing seems to stick to the music, even though the Prater's soundscape teems with well-known tunes, ranging from a simple barrel organ playing Juventino Rosas's famous waltz "Sobre las olas" ("Over the Waves") and the popular tune "The Carnival of Venice" (in German-speaking lands known as "Mein Hut der hat drei Ecken") to the *Sorgenbrecher* ("Care-Breaker Waltz"), op. 230 by Johann Strauss Sr., periodically wafting over from the dance hall next to the myriorama. The title of the waltz is telling with a twist: this is memorable music meant to make us forget all troubles, but not the good time of getting away from them.

This is why these ambient pieces, complete with the conductor's whistle, alternate with the soundtrack for the train journey provided by that "conductor," who moves the scenery with a contraption akin to a stationary bicycle, while his left hand turns a wheel that powers an orchestrion (figure 5.6, bottom). For the latter, Amfitheatrof used the cue "Greenwich Village," written by Hans Salter for a street fair–like scene in Fritz Lang's *Scarlet Street* (1945).[36] Born and trained in Vienna, Salter had been Ophüls's first choice for scoring *Letter*, and the air of Old World fairground music surely befits a scene that the director remembered from his own visits to the Prater, where the so-called Central Station (*Zentralbahnhof*), offering "journeys" to Constantinople, Nice, or Paris, had been added as an attraction in 1919—an upgrade of comparable rides installed the late nineteenth century. A 1934 newspaper article reported how visitors traveled in shaking train cars with the scenery "rushing by" as "beautiful bright panoramas unfurled" with "images so vivid [*plastisch*] that one is tempted to jump out of the window right into the blooming landscape."[37] If the myriorama was a precursor to travelogue films—Stefan takes Lisa on a ride as he might have taken her to the movies only a few decades later—this most memorable attraction in the Prater only sets up the most heartrending result of Stefan's amnesia when Lisa visits him years later in his apartment after their meeting at the opera. "Do you travel a great deal?" he asks after mentioning his recent trip to America. Originally absent from the shooting script, the question was added almost like a punch line that drives a stake through her heart.[38] Lisa records and remembers. Stefan repeats, but forgets. And the outcome is fatal.

Cavell notes that in *Letter from an Unknown Woman* "repetition signals death."[39] "I'll see you in two weeks, two weeks," he quotes Stefan shouting to Lisa the morning after their trip to the Prater, as he boards the train to Milan for a concert tour he had "forgotten about." Their exchange deserves a second hearing:

STEFAN: Say "Stefan" the way you said it last night.

LISA: Stefan.

STEFAN (*shaking his head*): It's as though you said it all your life.

CONDUCTOR (*walking behind them in the background*): Better hurry, sir!

STEFAN (*to the conductor*): Yes! (*To Lisa, kissing her hand*) Goodbye.

WOMAN (*calling, off-screen*): Stefan!

STEFAN (*to the woman*): Yes. (*Starting away, to Lisa*) Goodbye. (*off-screen, calling back to Lisa*) It won't be long. I'll be back in two weeks! (*hanging from the train*) Goodbye! Two weeks!

VOICEOVER: Two weeks. Stefan, how little you knew yourself. That train was taking you out of my life.[40]

"Goodbye . . . goodbye!" "Two weeks . . . two weeks!" In the Final Shooting Script, Lisa's voiceover actually begins by repeating the repetition: "Two weeks . . . two weeks," expressing more pointedly what the Lisa on the platform already sensed: Stefan's reiterations are empty. They are not recorded and therefore do not record. Quoting from memory, Cavell forgot to mention that Stefan wedged another "goodbye" between the two iterations of "two weeks." Empty repetition is a form of forgetting that signals his nonreturn. (When the young Stefan later reminds his mother twice of his own short trip to the countryside—"two weeks . . . two weeks"—we know that he, who had been conceived the night before his father's farewell, is bound to die.) Again, the Final Shooting Script is explicit: "A sudden look of terror crosses her face. Those words 'two weeks,' the departing train, the waving Stefan on the platform—the sudden reminiscent blend of circumstance are subjectively charged with finality."[41]

But what about "Stefan . . . Stefan"? By asking Lisa to repeat his name, Stefan requests no less than an *aural* retake—a crucial change from vision to hearing. Instead of speaking and remembering *her* name, he wants to hear her say *his* name once more, as if turning Lisa's voice, which we have heard all along "at the interior of the narrative," into an acoustic mirror.[42] Inasmuch as Stefan is caught up in narcissistic reflection, he somehow senses that the elusive magic of memory has an auditory dimension. But he is not yet ready to attach memories to music. Nowhere is this more palpable than the night before, when he danced with Lisa to Carl Michael Ziehrer's popular waltz *Weaner Mad'ln* ("Viennese Girls"), op. 388, played by an all-female orchestra in the Prater (figure 5.7, top):

STEFAN (clapping): You are a sorceress. Now I'm sure. How else could we dance this way unless we've danced together before? (*Lisa looks down, and Stefan places his finger under her chin to lift her face up to him.*) And yet if we had, I should have remembered.[43]

Let us recall Benjamin's description of Proust's *mémoire involuntaire*: how it consists of images "we have never seen before we remember," how these images were "developed in the darkroom of the lived moment," how "our most profound moments have been equipped—like those

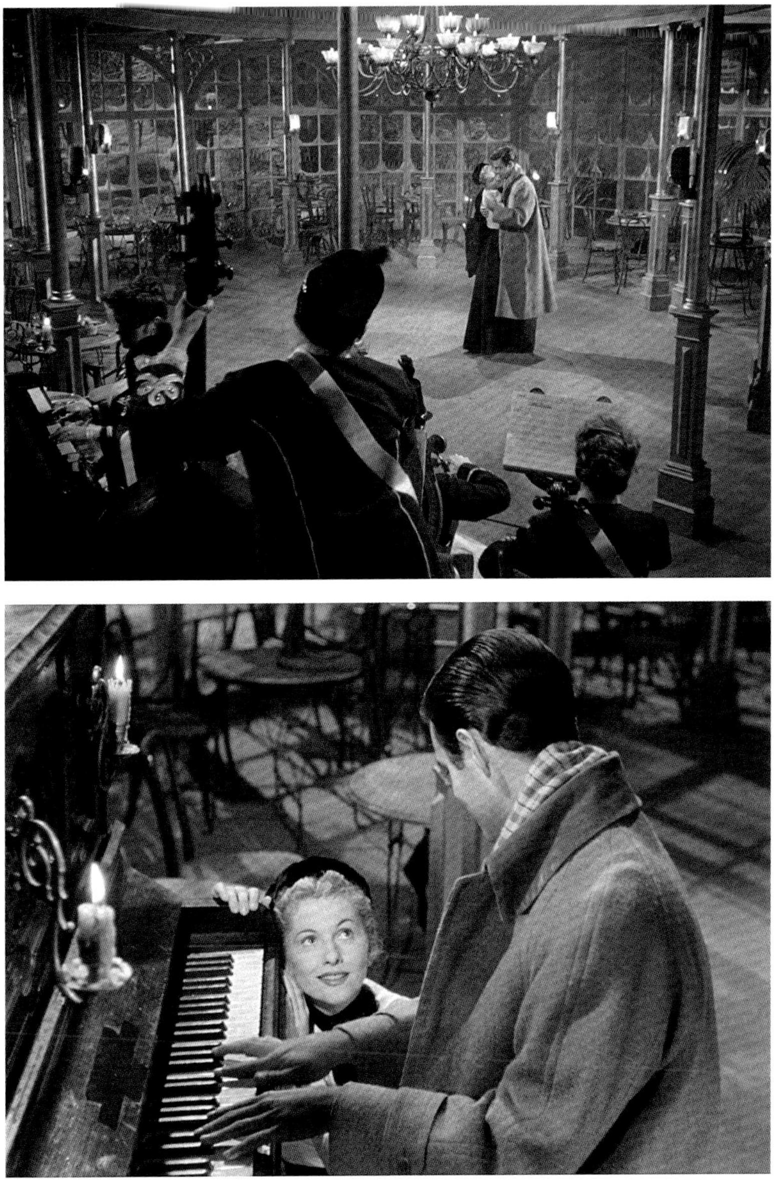

Figure 5.7
Lisa and Stefan dance to Carl Ziehrer's waltz "Viennese Girls" (*top*) and Stefan replays it for Lisa after the orchestra has left (*bottom*).

cigarette packs—with a little image, a photograph of ourselves." Benjamin explicitly refers to panoramic memory, noting how "that 'whole life' which, as they say, passes through the minds of people who are dying or confronting life-threatening danger, is composed of such little images," and how these images "flash by in as rapid a sequence as the booklets of our childhood, precursors of the cinematograph."[44] Amid such affinity between organic and mechanical reproduction, Benjamin assumes that involuntary memory and photography share the magic of an automatized unconscious encoding, which can be recalled under extraordinary conditions similar to the experience of panoramic memory

ily invested in psychoanalytical and psychiatric treatment as indicative of gender difference, *Letter* is not easily parsed that way. Although its protagonists come across as case studies of female hysteria and male amnesia—played out as Lisa's hypertrophic memory and Stefan's insouciant forgetfulness—the film's construction and representation of gender is unstable, not least because it combines both pathologies into a complex reversal. Tania Modleski, above all, has noted how Lisa's "impending death releases her from her vow of silence" and with it from being an object like Stefan's other women, while he, in turn, appears as a "feminized man" who becomes an object of her desire, in a rejection of patriarchal men.[47] One might detect a similar rejection in Ophüls himself, hiding his agency behind the quasi-directorial perspective of Lisa's posthumous narration, which continues her role as Stefan's analyst, helping him to recover his memories and thereby discover what was lacking from his music. As a cure, Lisa's letter is not only doing the talking, but also teaching him to listen. The letter recovers her voice—which we hear as voiceover before Stefan recalls it—and thereby recovers his vision.

"What motivates these images?" and "Why does their knowledge constitute an assault?" Cavell asks about Stefan's flashback. At their most basic, they show that the letter has succeeded in making Stefan suffer from reminiscences he now shares with Lisa. Flashback narration and flashback montage converge in regret over his failure to recognize her. Knowing these images leads to the painful realization that his encounters with her were missed opportunities or, as Cavell would put it later in a postscript to *Contesting Tears*, "missed appointments, say disappointment."[48] In the book he had summed up Stefan's gesture, covering his eyes (figure 5.8 bottom), as

> both warding off his seeing something and warding off at the same time his being seen by something, which is to say, his own existence being known, being seen by the woman of the letter, by the mute director and his (her?) camera—say, seen by the power of art—and seen by us, which accordingly identifies us, the audience of film, as assigning ourselves the position, in its passiveness and its activeness, of the source of the letter and of the film; which is to say, the position of the feminine.[49]

What Cavell could have pointed out is that Lisa, too, is shown covering her eyes after finishing her letter perhaps because she has seen herself as that source of the letter *and* of the film (see figure 5.8, top). In both cases, their face-covering is scored with a stinger chord, a standard gesture of film music that often signals life-threatening danger or the impact of a character suddenly realizing something of major import. The stingers express the very horror that Cavell (in the postscript) saw in Stefan's reaction to the "death-dealing" set of images from his flashback mon-

Figure 5.8 After the flashback montage, Stefan covers his face (*bottom*), as Lisa did after finishing the letter (*top*).

tage.[50] These images are a subset of the death-dealing images in Lisa's flashback narration. It is the sound of Lisa dropping her pen—exhausted by the illness that has already killed her son—that prompts the lethal force of the stingers, which deal death to remembered music here and later: first cutting off the counterpoint between "Un sospiro" and the allusion to the *Kiss Waltz*, then cutting short Stefan's encore of *Viennese Girls* at the end of his montage. The stingers are no less than twinned sounds for the twinned shots of faces covered with hands, showing that Lisa's posthumous perspective encompasses both the narration of her letter and its narrative frame. When joining her in death, Stefan himself will attain this perspective—"his own existence . . . seen by the power of art"—to fulfill a deep longing that has haunted him all his life.

Cavell suggests that the "death-dealing" images, which delay Stefan's escape from the duel, are followed by "death-enhancing" images, above all, Lisa's spectral appearance at the door: "Both modes of returning images raise the question of how desires, and their images, are of death; of the relation of film as such, always coming after, immortalizing events, to death."[51] This Barthesian question about the experience of a future anterior through photography returns us to Cavell's claim that *Letter* is, in some sense, a film about film. I take this to mean that cinematic images are *remembered* images pointing toward some form of immortality in the face of death. However banal, these images are a reminder of a life lived when seen from a vantage point closer to death or beyond death. *Letter* evinces cinematic recall not only through the form of the flashback, but also through different modes of repetition—either meaningful or empty—to distinguish Lisa's mindful remembrance from Stefan's mindless forgetting. If Stefan lives by being present only one moment at a time, Lisa's hypertrophic memory has made her in death present to all moments of her life. One might say that he belongs to the single frame, while the entire film belongs to her. His "now" and her "ever" share the condition of being out of time, albeit it on different terms that must be reconciled. "For us," Stefan says during Lisa's last visit, "all the clocks in the world have stopped." And yet, as Lisa writes later, "I had come to tell you about us, to offer you my whole life, but you didn't even remember me." [52]

Her letter makes good on that offer: imparting her whole life stops the clock of his. Such stoppage is marked by death-dealing stingers. When Stefan comes home at the beginning of the film, a stinger signals not only how the letter grabs his attention but also how reading it entails a suspension of time. He must forget the present to remember the past, but the past eventually catches up with the present. Of the two stingers that mark the end of Lisa's and Stefan's flashbacks, the second is more forceful, for it coincides with the first of five clock strikes that announce the hour of the duel, giving notice that his lifetime is up. Although Stefan's fate is sealed by the time it takes him to read the letter, the final scene requires a transition toward a union in death with Lisa, who already exists out of time. The version that evolved from the Final Shooting Script (which still lacked the flashback) not only increased the role of the visual, but also created an increasingly close sonic connection with Lisa, which enables Stefan to recognize more fully what he had not recognized before.

This recognition takes shape in three stages, of which the first two were already in the Final Shooting Script: acknowledging Lisa's name, taking one of the white roses from her last visit, and seeing her phantom image at the door. In the Final Shooting Script, the ending of the letter dissolves directly to Stefan asking John, "*You* remembered her?" in a "deeply remorseful" tone: "What was her name?" And when his servant writes it down, Stefan repeats it aloud "almost caressing the name."[53] In the final version of the film, Amfitheatrof scored question and answer by quoting the melody of "Un sospiro," first in the cello and then in the oboe. Giving voice to the obsequious love for and profound understanding of Stefan that John (otherwise excluded from the sonic register) shared with Lisa, the music also expresses this vocal caress. The quotation from the etude begs to be heard by Stefan—after all, this is the piece that he had played just before meeting Lisa for the first time. But unlike the diegetic *Kiss Waltz* and *Viennese Girls* remembered in his flashback, it remains unheard. When John writes "Lisa Berndle" next to a piece of score paper with notated music, the silent letters release only the sound of her name, now spoken by Stefan for the first time (figure 5.9, top).

Figure 5.9
John writes Lisa's name, which Stefan speaks aloud (*top*). Stefan picks a rose from the bouquet, hearing Lisa's voice (*bottom*).

The next two stages of recognition inch closer to Stefan's sonic communion with Lisa. As he gets ready to leave his apartment to the dirgelike opening of the final cue ("Duel in the Shade"), he pauses before the bouquet of white roses that Lisa brought at her last visit, picks one, and looks at it while the final words from her letter resound: "if only you could have recognized what was always yours, could have found what was never lost" (figure 5.9, bottom).[54] In the Final Shooting Script, the scenario was significantly different: "Stefan's glance returns to the letter. He reads the last lines aloud as though addressing them to himself." Then, when the time for the duel arrives, he selects a "still unfaded" rosebud, "takes it out tenderly," and "fastens it to the lapel over his heart."[55] Why the change from speaking to hearing in the actual film? While we have never heard Stefan *hear* Lisa say these words, he hears them now—finally forging a bond between her writing and her voice, which appears to speak through the flowers as a material trace of her existence. Once again, the incipit of "Un sospiro" returns in the viola, now punctuated by harp arpeggios, pointing to Lisa's supernatural presence in the narrative frame. If Stefan remembers Lisa's voice, he *almost* hears this melody, whose subsequent reprise in the cello and oboe beckons even more insistently from the beyond before he shakes John's hand in a final farewell.

To actually *hear* such music, however, Stefan must take one more step toward death. Leaving through the very doorway where he saw Lisa for

the first time, he turns around for a last retake (figure 5.10, first still). What he sees, however, is not a memory image (as in his flashback montage) but an apparition conjured together with an eerie echo of the *Kiss Waltz*. The moment is uncanny and represented as such visually and sonically: just as the transparent body of the young Lisa hovers behind the door, another ethereal harp arpeggio ushers in a muffled whole-tone version of Strauss's melody, played by the C and G flutes in their lowest register and dangling in midair from a spooky violin tremolo (figure 5.10, second still embedded in score excerpt). It is only now that Stefan seems to see *and* hear as well as hear *and* see. For the image of meeting Lisa the girl materializes with the music from meeting Lisa the woman—the two encounters that he should have remembered and that he does now remember, *together*. Even as the vision of Lisa at the door vanishes, the melody of the *Kiss Waltz* lingers for a reaction shot of Stefan looking back long enough to suggest that he has also seen a mental image of Lisa on the street. After the faint melody of the waltz fades out in the flute pair, he lowers his eyes and his head in a gesture of acceptance (figure 5.10, third still). Only then does he walk up to the carriage that will take him to the duel and to his death.

Figure 5.10 Leaving for the duel Stefan turns and, after seeing Lisa's specter by the door and "hearing" the eerie whole-tone echo of the *Kiss Waltz* (measures 36–39, marked by arrows; *facing page*), lowers his eyes (page 152). Excerpt from cue no. 55, "Duel in the Shade," reproduced from the copy of the conductor's score; courtesy Margaret Herrick Library, Academy of Motion Picture Arts and Sciences.

Dozier may have insisted so adamantly on Lisa's spectral return—nicknamed the "President's Shot" by the production team—because it gave audiences a tried-and-true formula for transforming the tragic into the bittersweet and thereby offered an emotionally and dramatically more satisfying, even cathartic, conclusion.[56] At the end of *Maytime* (discussed in chapter 1), the lovers separated in life are united in the afterlife when the ghostly spirit of the young Marcia leaves her aged body to join the ghostly spirit of the young Paul in a reprise of "their" song, "Will

- 4 -
33
34
35
SLOWER
36
FLUTE
(VIBRATO)

37
38
39
FASTER
40
3 HNS (CLOSED WITH FIST)
PIANO
HARP
TIMP

You Remember." Although Ophüls initially preferred to be less concrete and less corny, the increasing closeness between Stefan and Lisa in the final version of the film created a denouement that opened the door to their imminent reunion. While Stefan's flashback montage counts as an observer memory, his encounter with the ghostly girl is akin to a field memory. For Cavell, the death-dealing images of the grown Lisa are different from the death-enhancing image of the young Lisa "in being located in the same space with Stefan, as if he is taking some present part in this quasi-hallucinatory image."[57] Here again, music must be taken into account, for it not only belongs to that space but also opens a pathway to a supernatural existence. In fact, what Cavell describes as the combined erotic and religious life of *Letter*—"the transcendental presencing of . . . death-dealing and death-enhancing images, as from outside the world, 'beyond' it"[58]—is mediated by music, as suggested at the end of Zweig's novella: "the thought of the dead woman stirred in his mind, bodiless and passionate, like the sound of distant music." If the image of Lisa's apparition turns this thought into the appropriate ethereal sight, the eerie echo of the *Kiss Waltz* certainly qualifies as "distant music." The addition of the close-up reaction shot of Stefan is explained in production records as "registering that he has found the final link in his remembrance of Lisa."[59] Although Ophüls had planned to prepare a version without this shot, the final link in Stefan's remembrance occurs between the outer reprojection of the young Lisa and the inner reprojection of the older Lisa, summoned by the otherworldly trace of the *Kiss Waltz* by two flutes—a double projection of sorts.[60] Stefan's recognition of this connection is reflected in his face: eyes lowered, no longer covered by his hands.

To invoke Martin Jay's momentous 1993 book *Downcast Eyes*, one might understand Stefan's lowered eyes as a shift in the acquisition of knowledge from a predominantly visual to a musical imaginary. Although it would be anachronistic to pin the entire critical paradigm of denigrated vision onto *Letter*, its visual prowess is clearly mediated by the potency of sound and voice as well as the mnemonic power of music. The void in Stefan's artistic imagination has been his inability to see and remember through music. Lisa's spectral return suggests that Stefan has, as Cavell noted, "internalized" her image, "a fixated image of his past."[61] Yet it is sound that directs his vision inward: speaking her name, hearing her voice, and remembering the music they heard together. If images of Lisa took possession of Stefan in the flashback, he finally takes possession of Lisa's image by approaching a transcendental position "beyond time." Stefan's resolve to die becomes a resignation from looking. Lisa's vision is vanishing because "what was yours" has become truly his, with the help of music she had come to associate him with all along. Already the Final Shooting Script had stipulated how this might be illustrated in the final moments of the film: when Stefan "disappears into the dark hall" after meeting John's eyes "in mutual understanding," the music that was to come up in the underscore was "fragments of the piece Lisa heard Stefan play years ago."[62] Then the camera was to focus on the bouquet of white roses: "With the morning light full on them, they seem to recapture their freshness and beauty. Only underneath them on the piano top a few fragile, while petals have fallen."[63] The actual ending of *Letter* is much less governed by the visual—merely a shot of carriages pulling away. Instead, the last musical cue culminates in a rousing climax that indeed features the most recognizable melodic fragment of "Un sospiro." While breaking off Liszt's etude presaged the end of Stefan's career before he met Lisa for the first time, now the unearthly reprojection of that meeting leads to an apotheosis of the etude's characteristically rising melodic head in the full orchestra, as if to say that Stefan will soon be ascending, transfigured, into Lisa's embrace.

Laura Mulvey ends the latter of two essays on Ophüls's adaptations and on repetition and difference in three of his doomed romance films with a "somewhat subjective, even whimsical note," suggesting that "the womaniser might be a figure for Ophüls's own desiring, cinephilic, engagement with the mobile camera and the extended shot in contradistinction to the rigidity of the studio style." Despite this stance, the director "flourished" in Hollywood because he took advantage of the "*mechanisms* of the cinema," including crews, cranes, sets, moving walls, staircases—in short, the whole machinery of production.[64] Mulvey concludes:

> His films (first emerging at the last gasp of modernity in the early 1930s, often looking back to its early appearance at the turn of the century) celebrate the

excitement of the machine itself and its metaphoric relationship to desire. For me, this fusion is represented above all, first, in *Liebelei* when Fritz and Christine dance to a little mechanical juke-box, surrounded by mirrors and caught by the movement of the camera, and, second, in Stefan and Lisa's journey on the fairground train in *Letter from an Unknown Woman*. Both involve linking a mechanism of modern popular culture to the paradoxical constraints and liberties of love, of history, and of cinema.[65]

The director's affinity with the womanizer as a quasi-machine returns us to Stefan's pursuit of Lisa at the opera, where he wonders whether he might have seen her before at one of his concerts, admitting, however, that he hasn't given any concerts lately:

LISA: You don't play any more?

STEFAN: Oh, it's not quite as final as that. I always tell myself I'll begin again next week and then when next week comes, it's this week, so I wait for next week again.

LISA (*shaking her head*): What are you waiting for?

STEFAN: That's a very disturbing question!

LISA (*interrupting him*): My carriage.

STEFAN: You can't ask such a question and just walk away.

I have the feeling—please, don't think I'm mad. I know it sounds strange, and I can't explain it, but I feel that you understand what I can't even say, that you can help me.

Have you . . . have you ever shuffled faces, like cards, hoping to find the one that lies somewhere just over the edge of your memory, the one you have been waiting for?

Well, tonight when I first saw you and later when I watched you in the darkness, it was as though I had found that one face among others. Who are you?[66]

One of the striking reversals of *Letter* is how Lisa redirects Stefan's desire to her as an object, but does so by turning him into an object of her desire, masking the director's cinephilia. It is Lisa who is shuffling Stefan's deck of cards by presenting herself again and again as the face that emerges from the edge of his memory, making him wonder: I have seen you; I have heard your voice; we have danced together before.

Stefan's plea for help is a plea for a release from his machinelike mode of seduction, described in the Final Shooting Script (during Lisa's last visit) as the "automatic reflexes of an unexpected conquest" that have become a "shop-worn, almost-ritualistic technique of the professional seducer."[67] Both as a performer and as a person, Stefan's routines are repetitive and his charm is shallow. They break down like the portion of "Un sospiro" where the etude's soul—the melody—gives way to the flashy surface of virtuoso flourishes. Yet his nonchalant, if increasingly nagging, sense that something is amiss does give him the feeling that

Lisa's superhuman insights may be able to save him. Not surprisingly, her sorcery resorts to the magic of human memory, tapping into Stefan's unconscious: "You are a sorceress. Now I'm sure," he responds after they waltz to Ziehrer's *Viennese Girls*. "How else could we dance this way unless we've danced together before? . . . And yet if we had, I should have remembered." In the ellipsis, Lisa looks down, as a sign not of inhibition but of introspection: she has already *seen* their dance, recorded by her hypertrophic memory and reprojected before her inner eye. The sorcery that Stefan senses is a cipher for cinema as a machine of remembrance. *Letter from an Unknown Woman* showcases and involves its viewers in the workings of the *cinematic unconscious*—an image, a sequence, a scene that has never been consciously experienced before will suddenly be remembered. The cinematic unconscious as optical-acoustic unconscious is the mode of panoramic memory, and this is what happens in Stefan's flashback where the music of the waltz becomes the soundtrack for a recollection of scenes from the Prater. As with the repeated train rides, there is something magically mechanical in the revue-like assemblage of sights recalled by the jukebox-like sounds of the women's orchestra as well as Stefan's reprise of it at the piano. If human memory works like film, film works like human memory, especially when cued by music. This is how they dance together.

Ophüls may have resisted the flashback montage, yet its images sprang from the fulfillment of his own cinephilic desire all the same. The elaborate setup of the scene in which Stefan and Lisa stroll through the Prater caught the attention of the studio's publicity department, which marveled in an unpublished press release at the "near impossible" accomplishment of "Cameraman Frank Planer . . . making a 320-degree shot of Joan Fontaine and Louis Jourdan."[68] The recollection in Stefan's flashback testifies to Mulvey's "mechanisms of cinema," broadly understood, because it carries the market-driven requirement of the studio system that he remember not only dancing with Lisa, but meeting her at the door and, through music, on the street. Similarly, the conventional conclusion of the lover's union in the afterlife, as projected by the apotheosis of "Un sospiro," fulfills the generic requirements of tragic romance, both satisfying censorship demands and catering to audience expectations. What Mulvey describes as the "mechanism of modern popular culture" may have found its most striking expression at the very end of the film: not so much in the overwrought climax of Liszt's etude in the underscore as in the music encored with the closing credits: *Weaner Mad'ln*. The return of Ziehrer's waltz is a gesture of ironic whim from the beyond, after the pall over the film's panoramic flashbacks has finally fallen. Stefan and Lisa, it seems, are now dancing in Hollywood heaven. If we leave the theater with this image swirling in our minds, that would indeed be the last act of Lisa's sorcery.

3

Affect

CHAPTER SIX

Freudian Fixations

Two meanings of "fixation" concern me here. The first is germane to media technology and media aesthetics: the fixation of something evanescent to a physical object for preservation, transmission, or dissemination, notably through processes of mechanical reproduction—a song to a record, an image to a photograph, or a moving image to film. A special case is the fixation of sound to an image or image to sound. Throughout this book, I have been exploring this mechanical fixation, as it has an important corollary: once sound and image are perceived together as an unchanging or "fixed" entity, they become associated in memory in new ways, whereby sound turns into a cue for the image, more often and more effectively than the image serves as a cue for sound. Cinema has thus fostered the belief that technological and organic forms of memory formation, storage, and recall not only operate in similar ways, but work hand in hand, creating a porous line between medium and mind as well as between body and machine.

Freud's theory of psychosexual development offers a second meaning of fixation, defined as a phenomenon whereby an "instinctual component" is "left behind at a more infantile stage," so that this component (also glossed as "libidinal current") then "behaves in regard to later psychological structures as though it belonged to the system of the unconscious, as though it were repressed."[1] Fixation, that is, describes the state of remaining partially stuck in an earlier phase of psychosexual development. For example, a person who has been unable to resolve an issue at the oral stage may continue to seek oral pleasures and thereby develop an eating or drinking disorder, or have problems with smoking or biting fingernails. Freud compared the temporal incongruity in psychosexual development to a malfunctioning relation between the unconscious and consciousness: the instinctual and libidinal element is an unwanted behavior that is prevented from entering into consciousness, as if it were repressed. Importantly, he connected the idea of fixation to traumatic neuroses, where patients are "*fixated* upon some very definite part of their past" from which they are "unable to free themselves," such that they are "completely estranged both from the present and the future."[2] This "fixation upon the moment of the traumatic disaster" makes it possible that patients can relive the traumatic situation in their dreams or under hypnosis: since "every neurosis contains such a fixation," neurotic symptoms, whose meaning is hidden in the unconscious, must be recovered and made known as part of psychiatric and psychoanalytic treatment.[3] The key to curing a traumatic fixation is becoming conscious of it.

Fixation has had little to no media-theoretical currency compared with other Freudian concepts such as repression, fetish, and transference, even though it is linked to them. According to Janet Bergstrom, the "parallel histories" of cinema and psychoanalysis have had two main points of contact: films about psychoanalytical or psychiatric treatment; and psychoanalytic theories of film. If films about psychoanalysis were particularly prominent in the 1940s and 1950s, theories of film that heavily drew on psychoanalysis became prevalent in the 1970s and 1980s, often integrating traditional concerns of film theory, such as spectatorship, with issues of viewer identity and gender. Mary Anne Doane's pioneering study of the woman's film of the 1940s, *The Desire to Desire*, sought "to trace a coincidence of cinematic scenarios and psychoanalytic scenarios of female subjectivity," treating these psychoanalytical scenarios as "models . . . insofar as they are symptomatic of a more generalizable cultural repression of the feminine."[4] My case studies—*The Seventh Veil* (1945) and *Little Voice* (1998)—bear out Doane's suggestion that the woman's film of the 1940s continued to shape conceptions of female subjectivity: they "still have a certain currency."[5] Both films represent the two above meanings of fixation, notably the female body as a medium for the storage and transmission of childhood trauma whose cure requires a cathartic abreaction. Specific to both films is the role of music in the formation of individual and collective memory. This plays out in the context of a British culture at different historical moments—after World War II and after the Thatcher years—where the influence of popular entertainment through mass media is symptomatic of a larger malaise.

As I return to music as a device for recording images, I take up Thomas Elsaesser's view of Freud as a media theorist despite himself. In a series of articles, Elsaesser has pointed to Freud's conception of "the body/mind as a storage and recording medium as well as an input/output device" that, on the one hand, records raw sensory data and, on the other hand, renders processed representations—or memories.[6] In one of his best-known essays, Freud proposed that a new toy—the *Wunderblock* (literally, *magic* writing pad)—could model the "hypothetical structure of our perceptual apparatus" by showing how the seemingly unlimited storage capacity of human memory would be mitigated by partial forgetting.[7] To recall: the magic pad consists of a wax slab covered with a double-layered sheet—the top layer of transparent celluloid, the bottom, translucent wax paper. Writing on the pad with a stylus yields a visible inscription, which disappears when the sheet is lifted from the wax slab. Freud compared the celluloid to a "protective shield against stimuli," serving to "diminish the strength of excitations coming in" while allowing them to pass to the wax slab, where they are recorded as lasting impressions.[8] To show how they could remain legible even after the sheet is lifted, Freud invoked photography: "It is easy to discover that the permanent trace of what was written is retained upon the wax slab itself and is legible in suitable exposure [*Belichtung*]"; thus it would not be far-fetched to compare the "appearance and disappearance of the writing with the flashing-up [*Aufleuchten*] and passing-away of consciousness in the process of perception."[9]

What if the permanent trace were cathected by music? To appreciate the stories told in *The Seventh Veil* and *Little Voice*, we need to extend Elsaesser's notion of a "media unconscious" as an optical-acoustic unconscious.[10] Since patients of psychoanalysts were predominantly female hysterics, Elsaesser suggests that Freud may be seen "as having not so much *medicalized* female subjectivity as '*medialized*' women."[11] Once psychoanalysis had gone culturally mainstream by the 1940s, movies about mentally ill female musicians interwove medical history with media history to dramatize trauma and its treatment. The two films illustrate how two different models of trauma were, and have remained, central to its treatment in the popular imagination, where the musical cure either requires reliving the traumatic event or observing the event from a distancing perspective.

"Stripping Bare a Woman's Mind"

Directed by Compton Bennett, *The Seventh Veil* (1945) is about a suicidal pianist, Francesca Cunningham (Ann Todd) and her turbulent relationship with her guardian and mentor Nicholas (James Mason). Topping the British box office that year, the film competed at the 1946 Cannes Film Festival and won the 1947 Academy Award for Best Original Screenplay by Muriel and Sydney Box (Sydney Box was also the producer). *The Seventh Veil* belongs to group of films from the 1940s that draw on classical music—often a vernacularized variant of the piano concerto genre—to showcase conflicted characters in complex relationships: *Hangover Square*, *Love Story*, *Dangerous Moonlight*, *While I Live*, to name the most prominent. Musicians troubled by madness, haunted by fear, or affected by amnesia were regarded as symptoms of broader social problems, often directly linked to war trauma.

The film opens with a riveting scene—much enhanced by Benjamin Frankel's intense underscore—in which Francesca sneaks away from the hospital at night and throws herself into a river. She is rescued and returned to the clinic, where she remains in a catatonic state. The psychiatrist in charge of her case, Dr. Larsen (Herbert Lom), uses drugs to induce a hypnotic state, facilitating Francesca's regression into the past (figure 6.1). He explains the procedure to his colleagues with a comparison to Salome's dance of the seven veils, noting that it takes extraordinary mea-

Figure 6.1 Under hypnotic regression facilitated by narcotics, Lisa narrates her story in flashback episodes.

sures to remove the last—seventh—veil. (As the promotional tagline for the film had it, "It dares to strip bare a woman's mind.") This sets up the scene of analysis not only as a scene in a film but as a scene about film as a medium of analysis. As Raymond Bellour has noted, "Fictionalized representations of hypnosis are the manifestations, the pre-theoretization, of a fundamental relationship between the cinematographic apparatus and the hypnotic apparatus."[12]

Francesca's flashback narrative—told under hypnotic regression ("narcosis voice" in the script)—revolves around her relationships with three men, but begins with a traumatic incident from her childhood.[13] Having played with a classmate, she was late to school and was punished by her teacher, who caned her hands on the very day she was auditioning for a music scholarship. She failed and never tried again. After her father's death, Francesca is adopted by her cousin Nicholas, who resides alone in a stately but antiquated house. Initially annoyed by the prospect of caring for a teenage girl, he recognizes Francesca's talent and enrolls her at the Royal College of Music. There Francesca meets the North American saxophonist Peter, who moonlights with his band in a cafe. They fall in love dancing to a slow waltz (composed by Frankel). Peter proposes to Francesca, but Nicholas intervenes and takes her, still his underage ward, to train at European conservatories for a career as a concert pianist. This seven-year education abroad, and her rise to fame, makes up the second episode of Francesca's story, culminating with her debut at the Royal Albert Hall, playing Rachmaninoff's Second Piano Concerto. Later that night, she looks for Peter all over the city and eventually finds him working at a new venue. Peter arranges for his band to play "their" waltz, and they begin to dance. Distressed, Francesca breaks off her narration, leaving unsaid what went wrong. Prompted by Dr. Larsen, she then recounts her involvement with Max, a prominent highbrow-ish painter from whom Nicholas commissions a portrait of her. Max helps Francesca, who has forsworn love, to come to terms with her emotional life and free herself from Nicholas's influence. He invites Francesca to travel with him to Italy, but when she informs Nicholas of her plans, he becomes so enraged that he tries to beat her hands with his walking stick, while she plays the slow movement from Beethoven's Pathetique Sonata. A frightened Francesca runs off with Max and they end up in a car accident that leaves them both slightly injured. Awakening in the hospital with bandaged hands, Francesca is convinced that she will never be able to play the piano again. Wishing she had died, she attempts suicide.

Francesca's narration catches up with the present three-quarters of the way through the film, and the plot now proceeds with Dr. Larsen's attempted cure. He sums up her case to Max and his colleagues as a series of traumatic events: first, the "caning at school, resulting in the failure at the music examination and the fear that her hands might be injured"; second, "the attempt by her guardian to smash her hands"; and third, "the car crash and the shock of finding herself in the hospital with her hands bandaged." Dr. Larsen concludes:

> Now all these things together have produced a *fixation*, a barrier in the patient's subconscious mind which is now preventing her full recovery. It is this barrier which we now have to break down and I believe I found a way to do it. That's why I have put her under hypnosis. Now, with the help of music—music which we know she loves—I am going to suggest to her a way to conquer this fixation. If I can make her play the piano, I shall wake her up while she is actually playing and she will know that there is nothing really wrong with her hands.

The ensuing scene is extraordinary (figure 6.2). Dr. Larsen leads Francesca, under hypnosis, to the piano, sits her down, and asks whether she wants to hear some music. She nods. Larsen prompts his colleague to put one of Francesca's records on the phonograph. The recording happens to be the second movement of Beethoven's Pathetique, which Dr. Larsen does not realize is the music she was playing when Nicholas attempted to hit her with his cane. As the music resounds, Dr. Larsen encourages Francesca to play along: "Your hands are on the keys now. Your hands want to play. You want to play, don't you?! Try!" Francesca hesitates, but Larsen's hands guide hers to the keyboard. Tentatively, she begins to play along with the recording, at first joining the melody with the right hand, and then adding the left-hand accompaniment. Everyone in the room looks at her, listening.

In his essay on the magic writing pad, Freud envisioned how the con-

tact between the perception and memory systems left a permanent, albeit hidden, trace, illustrating this point in his final paragraph:

> If we imagine one hand writing upon the surface of the Mystic Writing-Pad while another periodically raises its covering-sheet from the wax slab, we shall have a concrete representation of the way in which I tried to picture the functioning of the perceptual apparatus of our mind.[14]

An evocative picture: one hand that writes; another that makes the writing disappear. The pad illustrates the processes that shield the unconscious from perceptual overload, retaining only relevant information. The device also suggests that there is a material basis for the storage of memories resulting from physical contact, comparable to the effect of light in photographic exposure. Freud's image of the two hands in the moment of inscription has an astounding parallel in the two arms at work in Francesca's reenactment—one mechanical, touching the record with the needle, the other human, pressing down piano keys with fingers. But just as her hands begin to synchronize with Beethoven's "Adagio" during the transitional section starting in measure 16 Francesca breaks off. The recording no longer serves as a cue for musical replay but as a trigger for traumatic recall. Hearing Nicholas's angry voice, Francesca becomes agitated, and precisely at the moment when his cane came down on her hands—the melodic turn that reaches up to G5 on the first beat of measure 22—she cries out and collapses.

Figure 6.2 *(facing)* Cathartic abreaction though musical replay: using Francesca's recording of the Adagio Cantabile from Beethoven's Pathetique (*top*), Dr. Larsen guides her hand to the keys to play along (*middle*), but she breaks off with a scream in measure 22, the very moment Nicholas had tried to hit her with his cane while she was playing the movement earlier (*bottom*).

Dr. Larsen's therapy was very much in line with contemporary cures of traumatic neuroses. Right before starting to work on *The Seventh Veil*, Sydney Box had finished the documentary *The Psychiatric Treatment of Battle Casualties*, writing later that its "enthralling and often heartrending subject" offered him his "first insight into the theory and practice of psychiatry," which in turn then "gave *The Seventh Veil* its unique appeal to audiences."[15] A print of the film has yet to resurface, but it likely dealt with approaches to healing the effects of shell shock, which had been a well-known affliction since World War I. At the core of such treatment was the cathartic method, which involved reliving a traumatic event under hypnosis. Doctors believed that patients who experienced the full intensity of the original emotion would undergo an abreaction of the event. But the psychological mechanism of abreaction had been a matter of considerable discussion. At a meeting of the British Psychological Society in February 1920, three psychiatrists—William Brown, Charles S. Myers, and William McDougall—who had treated shell-shocked soldiers during the Great War, engaged in a debate about the "therapeutic value" of "the revival of emotional memories"—the proceedings of which were later published in the *British Journal of Medical Psychology*.[16] Did the affective release result from the reproduction of the original emotion in the present moment? Or was the emotion, experienced as part of a past event, enabling patients to distance themselves from the trauma and thereby to reintegrate the repressed and dissociated memory?

Sydney Box likely learned about trauma therapy through the work of British psychiatrists such as John Stephen Horsley and William Sargant, who began treating soldiers in 1940 by adding the use of barbiturates to the cathartic method practiced during the Great War. Drug treatment had been developed in the 1930s by Sargant, who recommended using short-acting sodium pentothal "to induce the drowsy, semiconscious, hypnotic state of relaxation that seemed to encourage confessional hypermnesia and recall."[17] This so-called "narco-analysis" aimed at maintaining a high level of awareness that would facilitate the self-recognition needed for the reintegration of the dissociated memory. While narco-analysis amounted to what Ruth Leys has described as a form of "participatory" treatment, the use of barbiturates and ether was "surgical," in that it did not require collaboration with the patient.[18] Sargant actually argued that even invented scenes could contribute to the cure of the patient, thereby downplaying the necessity of the analytical component in treatment. But most therapists maintained that cathartic reenactments were true to the original event and vouched for its reality, however distorted the event might appear in later symptoms. It is by way of this claim of accurate reproduction that the analogy to recording technology became a powerful source of explanation. Thus the American psychiatrist Abram Kardiner noted that "fixation on the traumatic event" was reflected, for example, in changes to the "dream life" of traumatic neurotics.[19] Patients could be plagued by repeated dreams, in which dissociated images were diluted and retarded, playing "*like the picture of a normal piece of action slowed down by the motion-picture camera, the film's being cut off before the action is completed*."[20] Following the Hungarian psychoanalyst Sándor Ferenczi, Kardiner also drew attention to a range of physioneurotic mechanisms through which a traumatic experience was registered by the body. Ferenczi had located the somatic nature of trauma symptoms in tics, which he explained as "an over-strong memory fixation on the attitude of the body at the moment of experiencing trauma . . . [so] as to provoke a perpetual or paroxysmatic reproduction of the attitude."[21] This is exactly what happens in *The Seventh Veil*. Dr. Larsen's effort to cure Francesca by luring her into playing the piano fails precisely because Beethoven's Adagio had become part of such an "over-strong memory fixation on the attitude of the body." Unbeknownst to the psychiatrist, Nicholas's attempt to strike Francesca's hands is paroxysmally reproduced when she is playing the piece along with her recording. Although she retracted her hands before being hit, she later conflates the pain of earlier childhood punishment with the intended outcome of Nicholas's aggression.

This is how *The Seventh Veil* interweaves the cultural history of trauma and media. The initial failure of Francesca's cure exemplifies the underlying opposition between what Leys called mimetic and anti-mimetic conceptions of trauma. The mimetic theory assumed that trauma was a state "in which the victim unconsciously imitated, or identified with, the aggressor," much as in the hypnotic state a patient was subject to heightened suggestibility.[22] However, the fact that people were unable to remember what happened to them during hypnosis suggested that a traumatic scene, too, would be "constitutively unavailable for subsequent representation and recall"; thus, attempts to cure patients through a hypnotic catharsis that would allow them to recollect and reintegrate a dissociated memory could never succeed.[23] This anti-mimetic conception of trauma is connected to a different effect of hypnosis, namely the possibility that a patient could experience a traumatic scene from the specular distance of an observer. Inasmuch as Dr. Larsen understands the power of unconscious fixation that reproduces the traumatic event, he builds his treatment on conscious distanciation from it. Having enabled Francesca to narrate her traumatic experiences from a specular distance, he seeks to maintain that distance by waking her up so that she can integrate the dissociated memory. But this anti-mimetic therapy is thwarted by the unforeseen mechanism of mimetic abreaction, which does not lead to a cathartic cure but instead leaves Francesca in the grip of the traumatic event. Becoming conscious of her playing, she ends up reliving her fear. The resulting impasse becomes a new puzzle for the analyst, who realizes that the music itself—that is, a specific piece of music—might be central to Francesca's traumatic fixation and so a key to its cure.

Musical Transference

If Francesca's romance with Peter represents love that would lead to a middle-class marriage and her affair with Max a transgression of bourgeois norms, her relationship with Nicholas is ambivalent and ambiguous. Her dependency as a ward is offset by her promise as a musician, which becomes a driving force in their relationship. As long as Nicholas is nurturing, Francesca remains devoted to him; when he becomes controlling, she turns rebellious. Although their familial bond licenses mutual affection, it taints their underlying attraction as incestuous. Early on, when Francesca spontaneously embraces Nicholas out of gratitude for his support, he rebukes her. As Francesca's youthful impulsiveness clashes with his parental rationality, their age difference is amplified by Nicholas's Byronic limp. He too may be scarred by trauma. His cane not only supports his fragile physique but also serves as an instrument of discipline and punishment in his Svengali-like pursuit to fashion Francesca into a great artist. To recall, Svengali—in George du Maurier's 1895 novel *Trilby*—is a Jewish musician who turns the title character into a celebrated diva, who sings only under hypnosis. Similarly, Nicholas's ambition casts a strong spell over Francesca. As he becomes the source of her devotion and rejection, *The Seventh Veil* revolves around a psychological struggle to reconcile his artistic aspirations with her personal desires.

Their struggle plays out as a drama of transference and countertransference—that is, a conflict arising from the patient redirecting feelings to the therapist and vice versa. This conflict is driven by Francesca's change from foster child to possible spouse and Nicholas's change from substitute parent to potential lover. Caring for a traumatized child is undermined by his own childhood trauma, whereby he is himself caught between the roles of therapist and patient. In their script, Muriel and

Sydney Box insinuated an Oedipal dimension to that trauma: Nicholas's reluctance to raise an orphaned relative stems from having been abandoned by his mother, who left his father for a singer when her son was twelve. Francesca learns this from a servant, who suggests rather impudently that she has "what it takes" to do the same to her warden someday. Indeed, as Nicholas brings up Francesca, the adolescent woman does eventually take the place of the missing mother. As Tony Williams has noted, the latter's portrait hangs above the mantel in his parlor like those "domineering parental images" found in Hitchcock's *Suspicion* (1941) and later in *The Paradine Case* (1947) and *The Birds* (1963).[24] When Nicholas replaces the portrait of his mother with Max's painting of Francesca, he seeks the Pygmalion-like creation of his warden as an ideal woman and a perfect performer, whose raw musical talent and unruly personality must be refined and reined in.

According to Williams, *The Seventh Veil* should be seen an allegory about the postwar adjustment of homecoming soldiers and, as such, combines two symptoms that had long been associated with war neurosis: the split personality and mourning for the lost mother.[25] Destabilized marriages and unstable males were two sides of the same malaise affecting families and society at large. Thus Francesca's hysteria has its pendant in Nicholas's neurosis, which symbolizes the need for returning soldiers—disturbed veterans, as shown in such films as *Random Harvest* (1942), *I'll Be Seeing You* (1944) or symbolized in *Spellbound* (1945)—to overcome their dissociated battle memories and thereby reintegrate at home and into society.[26] The incompatible personalities Francesca explores in her relationships with men correspond not only to Nicholas's difficulty with reconciling his roles as surrogate parent and potential partner, but also to his struggle to undo the damage of his own life. Francesca's artistic education of becomes a form of therapy, whose underlying drama of transference—including musical transference—becomes the very puzzle Dr. Larsen must solve to determine whom Francesca will chose as her husband.

The idea of *musical* transference may describe how Dr. Larsen tries to relieve Francesca from her fixation by trying to bring about a change from mimetic repetition to anti-mimetic recognition. As noted above, Larsen fails to restore to Francesca's hands the bodily movement stored in her own recording of Beethoven, for the music triggers the traumatic memory of Nicholas's attempt to hit her as she played the piece during their argument about her decision to elope with Max. The quarrel articulates the changing nature of Francesca's transference from obedient love to rebellious hate. This amounts to her refusal to perform on his behalf. In turn, Nicholas, who is fearful of losing control over his protégé, resorts to changing the terms of his countertransference: having nurtured Francesca's talent, he now seeks to break her fingers. In an earlier version of the script, Francesca discovers an old upright piano that has been hidden by

Figure 6.3 Francesca takes over playing Mozart's "Sonata facile."

Nicholas in the attic of the house and plays it as if to retrieve his past.[27] In the final version, she refuses his invitation to play the grand piano in the parlor, but Nicholas sits down to play Chopin's short and simple Prelude No. 7, luring Francesca back to the piano. Moving a little to the left, he then launches into the first movement of Mozart's K 545 (published as "Sonata facile" and designated "a little sonata for beginners"). Now eager to play, Francesca jumps in with her right hand for the melody of the second theme and sits down to finish the exposition alone (figure 6.3). The swapping of bodies on the bench effectively transfers his own artistic ambitions to more able hands.

Here musical transference accesses the physical dimension of psychological transference: making music involves motoric memory that can be manipulated. Knowing Mozart's K 545 by heart means that Francesca has the sonata already in her hands; knowing that she has the music in her hands gives Nicholas access to her heart. These Svengali-like actions rehearse romantic—E. T. A. Hoffmannesque—fantasies of programming a performer to play perfectly, like an automaton. When Dr. Larsen later transfers music from gramophone to performer, he recruits a similar mechanism. If the eager girl quickly swapped seats with her warden in Mozart's sonata, it takes the reluctant woman much longer to recoup Beethoven's Adagio from her own motoric memory. "You want to play, don't you?" Dr. Larsen's suggests. Yet her bodily mnemonic not only reminds her hands how to play but recalls the violence Nicholas directed at them.

In *Introductory Lectures on Psychoanalysis*, Freud noted that it is possible to overcome transference "by pointing out to the patient that his feelings do not arise from the present situation and do not apply to the person of the doctor, but that they are repeating something that happened to him earlier. In this way we oblige him to transform his repetition into a memory. By that means the transference, which, whether affectionate or hostile, seemed in every case to constitute the greatest threat to the treatment, becomes its best tool, by whose help the most secret compartments of mental life can be opened."[28] Dr. Larsen uses transference as a tool but accidentally brings out its threat. The filmmakers represent this paradox as an assemblage of contesting sonic layers. While Dr. Larsen's clear voice encourages Francesca to play along with the gramophone, Nicholas's distorted shouting intrudes to disrupt her recovery:

Figure 6.4 Two traumatic experiences to cure with a recording: dancing to "their" waltz, Peter told Francesca that he is married (*left*); Nicholas tried to hit Francesca's hands with his cane to prevent her from leaving him (*right*).

"If you won't play for me you shall not play for anyone else ever again." Inasmuch as Dr. Larsen's invitation jars against Nicholas's injunction, the clash of recorded sound and live performance is more potent. When Francesca begins to synchronize with her own recording, the difference in frequency between piano and phonograph symbolizes that she is not in tune with her former self. What is the source of this interference? Her collapse at the piano sends Dr. Larsen first to Nicholas, playing for him Francesca's recording of the Pathetique to find out "whether perhaps it has any sentimental associations or is connected with anyone she knew." In the theatrical play created after the film, Nicholas "suddenly limps across the room, takes the record off the gramophone and smashes it by banging it against the side of the radiogram case. In doing so, he drops his cane." He questions whether Larsen "can prove anything from a gramophone record," to which the doctor responds that "one can prove a great deal—when one observes the effect of a few bars of music on somebody's feelings."[29] The musical cue is Larsen's key to the puzzle. Knowing now what Francesca means to her warden, he needs to learn what Nicholas means to her by finding out whether Peter is still in the picture. Paying Peter a visit, he learns that, following Francesca's debut at the Royal Albert Hall, Peter told her that he had married, after which she left without a word. Larsen asks Peter to come to Nicholas's house the next day and bring a record of the waltz they used to dance to (figure 6.4). The stage is set for the final cure.

As Andrew Spicer has pointed out, Sydney and Muriel Box prepared three different endings for *The Seventh Veil*, not disclosing to the cast which would be used until the last day of shooting. In the first, Dr. Larsen asks Peter to play the waltz, "places Francesca's hands on the keys of the piano," and then asks her to join in. After Peter stops playing, she finishes the tune, says "Peter!," and kisses him.[30] While the second ending leaves Francesca's choice open, the third ending, endorsed by the audience in a sneak preview and used in the film, begins with Peter arriving at Nicholas's house with the recording and being led upstairs to Francesca. Waiting in the downstairs parlor with Max, Nicholas explains that Peter is "the man Francesca wanted to marry" and that he is "the apostle of a new religion, called swing." When the recording of the waltz is heard, Nicholas notes that the "tune they used to dance to" is being used in a repeat of Dr. Larsen's "little experiment." The music stops and Peter comes down, mystified: "What's the good of turning the clock back anyway? Never did anyone any good." Then Beethoven's Adagio resounds:

All three men stop and listen for a moment. Both they—and we—are waiting for the moment when the previous experiment failed. Whoever is playing reaches this point, negotiates it successfully and goes on with the Sonata. In a moment, LARSEN appears at the top of the stairs. He is listening to the music as he comes down and is obviously rather pleased with himself.

LARSEN: Doesn't she play beautifully?
MAX: Is *she* playing?
NICHOLAS (*smiling*): Yes, that's my Francesca.
MAX: May I go up now?
LARSEN: It would be a pity to interrupt her.
MAX: But surely she wants me with her?
LARSEN: Perhaps.
MAX: What do you mean—perhaps?
LARSEN: Forgive me, gentlemen. I should have explained to you at once, but the music has put it out of my head. I think I can promise you a complete cure, but you will have to prepare yourselves for a new Francesca—a new and very different person.
NICHOLAS: In what way?
LARSEN: You see, the past is over for her now—quite over. Her mind is clear, the clouds have been swept away and she is no longer afraid. Whether you will be entirely satisfied with the change in her, I do not know, but it might be wise not to expect too much.
MAX: Are you trying to tell me, she— (*he glances angrily at PETER*)?
LARSEN: I am trying to tell you she will want to be with the one she loves or the one she has been happiest with; the one she trusts or the one she cannot do without.
MAX: And who is that?
LARSEN: It would be hardly fair of me to say.[31]

Ann Todd recalls in her memoirs how she attended a private screening of *The Seventh Veil* at Marlborough House, where she was seated next to Queen Mary, who had "tears in her eyes" asking, "Child, you didn't go to that horrid man at the end, did you? I couldn't quite see without my glasses."[32] Yet preview audiences saw that the contest between the "new religion of swing" and the old belief in Beethoven was one Nicholas would win. In the competition between past and present, the waltz fails the test of the cathartic cure not only because it is, as Peter puts it, "kinda corny," but also because it stands for the age of technological reproducibility. Since Nicholas has already smashed the vinyl of Francesca's Pathetique, she can play alone again.

The theatrical version, too, reverted to live performance:

FRANCESCA wanders over to the piano and sits down on the stool. . . . She begins to play the Mozart Sonata in C. In a moment, NICHOLAS appears in the doorway. FRANCESCA looks across at him happily. He walks over to the piano and she makes room for him to sit beside her. MAX and PETER meanwhile go quietly. Soon FRANCESCA and NICHOLAS are playing together. THE CURTAIN FALLS.[33]

Here musical transference is no longer a threat but a tool that resets the relation between Nicholas and Francesca. Guardianship makes way for partnership. Redressing the masochistic and misogynistic undertones of the film, the theatrical ending played up Francesca's new-found freedom. Roles reversed, she is in charge of her choice, ready for the full transfer of her affection to her warden-become-lover, now her equal.

Musical Unconscious—Medium Unconscious

The ending of *The Seventh Veil* was to offer a response to the larger social trauma brought about by World War II. If Francesca and Nicholas suffer the symptoms of a damaged life, music restores them to society as a couple committed to artistic autonomy. The contest between classical and popular music plays on a profound anxiety over the survival of European culture, threatened by the influence of America as an emerging global player, its power epitomized by the reach of its entertainment industry. In a more pessimistic reading, however, Francesca's voluntary return to the piano and to Nicholas is a false fantasy that reinstates psychosocial automatisms. The identification with her aggressor—that "horrid man"—signals, in Lacanian terms, a return to the symbolic order of classical music, which regains its cultural dominance. As the master analyst, Dr. Larsen's confidence in Francesca's recovery is not only driven by a desire for narrative closure, but also comes with the restoration of traditional aesthetic norms. "Doesn't she play beautifully?" he asks, promising a complete cure that reinstates traditional cultural values to heal the wounds war has inflicted on the Old World.

Attaching war trauma to music, *The Seventh Veil* combines medicalized female subjectivity with medialized womanhood, making the parallel histories of cinema and psychoanalysis converge in the figure of the female musician. With the past recorded in the performer's body, contemporary psychiatry enters into an intriguing plot, whose representation draws on the analogy between traumatic fixation and cinematic flashback. Here Muriel and Sydney Box continue the tradition of what Anton Kaes has called "shell-shock cinema."[34] After World War I, its direct or covert portrayals of war trauma had become prominent through two generic variants: comparatively realistic depictions of traumatic neurosis, such as Georg Jacobi's *Toward the Light* (1918), and starkly expressionist allegories, such as Robert Wiene's *The Cabinet of Dr. Caligari* (1920). A quarter century later, *The Seventh Veil* combined the vestiges of the gothic tale with the latest developments in psychiatric medicine. While early shell-shock cinema had seized upon hypnosis as a phenomenon that mirrored the power of film and explained its workings, Francesca's story continued the self-reflective cinematic representation of hypnotic treatment, successfully enlisting music to bridge the gap between mental states and media effects.

Yet the contest between Peter's waltz and Beethoven's Adagio did not simply articulate different aesthetic registers and express cultural preferences; it was also instrumental in staging the converging scenarios of fixation in the mind and fixation in media. Both types are marked by an inability to forget and an inability to remember. Just as Freud regarded traumatic neurosis as a malfunctioning relation between the conscious and unconscious that leaves patients "*fixated* upon some definite part of their past," the problem for mechanically recorded media is the automatic storage of every part of the past. The two forms of fixation coalesce in music, which, as a medium at the intersection of body and mind, records and replays memories. If the different endings of *The Seventh Veil* set up Peter's waltz and Beethoven's Adagio as musically mediated fixations, the piano piece became the more compelling case to dramatize such fixation because it allowed the plot to home in on Francesca's development as a classical performer who fears the loss of her ability to play. The symptoms of fixation—her catatonic state and her inability to use her hands—are two facets of that fear, which frame the film as the ground zero of her traumatic neurosis. Francesca's treatment combines talking cure with playing cure, both of which conjure up this past in ways that allow psychoanalysis and cinema to converge, not only in flashback narration but also in what one might call "flashback performance." Precisely the malfunctioning relation between the conscious and unconscious brings out ways in which the music-making woman is a media-machine who narrates the past from an anti-mimetic distance or replays the past through mimetic reenactment.

Although the term "flashback"—describing the experience of dissociative episodes as a diagnostic criterion of post-traumatic stress disorder—did not officially enter the *Diagnostic and Statistical Manual of Mental Disorders* until its third edition (1987), the phenomenon had long been observed in those terms.[35] In 1918 the psychiatrist Ernst Simmel, who had written his dissertation on dementia praecox, published a short treatise on his treatment of shell-shocked soldiers during World War I, which had a decisive influence on Freud. Simmel noted how the hypermnesia that a patient "commanded" during hypnosis made it possible to repeat an experience, like a film that was made "to roll once again; the patient dreams the whole thing one more time, the sensitized subconscious releases the affect, which in turn discharges in an adequate emotional expression, and the patient is cured."[36] Reporting the case of an aphasic soldier who had lost his speech in 1916 after jumping into a water-filled tunnel during a grenade attack, Simmel describes how he created a cathartic abreaction under hypnosis. Since the soldier had experienced a similar situation in 1914, having been shot in the leg under enemy fire, Simmel sought to connect under hypnosis the original affect of fear (*Angstaffekt*) to the second incident:

> I let the first "film" roll and chased him into the water of the tunnel that was to protect him—memory tracks had been created. And while he describes how now the grenades explode, I suddenly interject the question "What is now the same as 1914?" and he stammers in utmost fear for his life: "No cover, no cover!" And while the utmost affect of fear shows on his face I ask: "What is now?"; and from the greatest depth actually bursts forth a roar: "The grenades."[37]

Simmel concludes that in such cases he should not wake patients up right away, but "guide them gradually into the safety of the present," pointing out "that their anxiety has now become completely unfounded." It is hardly surprising that we recognize Simmel's treatment in Dr. Larsen's therapy—not only the need for narrative but the importance of detecting the memory trace created by the affective charge of a prior incident, which in Francesca's case is the childhood caning. But in *The Seventh Veil*, it falls to sound and music to make the "film" roll.

As Muriel and Sydney Box based their allegory of war neurosis on more recent forms of hypnotic therapy, developed during the Second World War, the traumatized performer proved to be a powerful object lesson for the relation between affect and memory. Francesca's treatment could not only illustrate parallel mechanisms in psychosomatic and technological processes of memory formation and retrieval, but could also showcase music's emerging position at the intersection of the media unconscious and the cultural unconscious. The story of Francesca, Peter, and Nicholas thereby reconfigures the trauma of modernity as the loss and recovery of traditional culture, with modern popular music, the dance club, and the bandleader set against the classical canon conserved in the concert hall by the conservatory-trained performer. Half a century later, in *Little Voice*, the tables would turn. Now the popular classics are the lost object, and their recovery in disco-dominated post-Thatcher Britain becomes an ambivalent return of the repressed, whose destructive potential needs to be expelled to salvage the remnants of bourgeois romance.

Regressing into Recordings

The protagonist of Mark Herman's 1998 film *Little Voice* is Laura, an adolescent girl, nicknamed Little Voice ("LV"), played by Jane Horrocks.[38] The antagonists are her bossy mother, Mari (Brenda Blethyn), and a sleazy agent, Ray (Michael Caine), who are both eager to profit off of LV's amazing ability to imitate the voices of female stars from the classic Hollywood era, above all Judy Garland. Shy and introverted, LV spends most of her time cooped up in her room with the vinyl collection of her deceased father, Frank, the owner of a record store in a western England seaside resort. The plot has two strands. The first revolves around Ray's "discovery" of Little Voice and his attempt to stage her debut at a local establishment that has seen better times and is kept afloat as a strip club by Boo (Jim Broadbent). The second is the romance between LV and Billy (Ewan McGregor), a telecommunications technician who is equally shy and taciturn, and who devotes his off hours to looking after his flock of carrier pigeons.

Both strands offer a grim picture of a post-Thatcher Britain, whose working and lower middle classes, exhausted from neoliberal economics, seem to have lost the verve of the postwar boom, along with its business model. Despite its comic touches and happy ending, *Little Voice* is a depressing portrait of the petty trials and tribulations at the lower end of the entertainment industry, where the struggle for survival is as ruthless as the perpetual hope for even the smallest break. At the same time, it is a pointed parody about what remains at stake in the age of technical reproducibility, namely the unique aura of live performance, even when given by an impersonator. Although the parody centers on music, its cinematic dimension is not to be dismissed, not least because the film blatantly puts bodies at center stage—or, rather, center frame. In this regard, the romance between Billy and Little Voice pales against the main plot line, which pits the scrawny and wallflowerish LV against her plus-sized, man-crazy mother. The stark physical disparity is amplified by Mari's boisterous gabbiness (superbly rendered by Blethyn), while Little Voice, true to her name, barely gets a faint word across her lips—except when singing, alone.

Hence the conflict between mother and daughter plays out on another stage that involves a different contest: one between the dead father (still very much present in LV's life) and Ray, who, as Mari's new boyfriend, seeks to usurp that paternal role and exploit it for his own gain. Once he has heard LV sing and realizes that she could become a star, Ray invokes the memory of her father to coax her into appearing at Boo's nightclub "just once"—a provision that will turn out to be critical. To mount the show, Ray goes for broke. Wagering that the event will be a smashing success and LV will become a national and international sensation, he sells his red 1972 Oldsmobile Delta 88 convertible, which serves in the film as a token of Ray's unfulfilled aspirations as an impresario of American-style show-biz. The highpoint of the film is a six-minute montage of LV's grand debut, during which she brings the house down. Wearing a tight dress inspired by the glittering garment Shirley Bassey wore at a 1990 concert in Costa Del Sol, Little Voice "becomes" hip-shaking Bassey to sing "Big Spender," pursed-lipped Marilyn Monroe ("I Wanna Be Loved by You"), sultry Marlene Dietrich ("Falling in Love Again"), spunky Grace Fields ("Sing As We Go"), and the ever-so-energetic Judy Garland ("Get Happy"). Horrocks delivers impressive vocal stunts, from Bassey's belting and Monroe's quivers to Dietrich's huskiness and Garland's velvety timbre. But LV sticks to her promise to perform only once, dashing Ray and Mari's hopes to exploit the "gold mine" on which they thought they were sitting. True to the title of the original stage play by Jim Cartwright—*The Rise and Fall of Little Voice*—Herman spends the remaining third of his film fleshing out the fall, which culminates in LV's house (including her beloved record collection) going up in flames due to a short circuit in its old electrical wiring. She is rescued by Billy.

Although the film puts the Freudian facets of its story in plain view—LV is portrayed as a girl stuck in an earlier stage of her psychosexual development, and with a fixation on her father—they are not dramatized as a clinical case study but rather deployed in an ambivalent allegory about the effects of modern mass culture on live performance and musical consumption. In Freudian thought, psychosexual development has five phases, during which the sex drive (libido) seeks satisfaction by focusing on a sequence of erogenous zones, which change with age. The first three phases are the oral (years 0 to 1), anal (years 1 to 3), and phallic (years 3 to 6). Each of these phases is associated with its own forms of fixation, which manifest themselves in behaviors that express unresolved problems. In the first phase, such behavior includes aggressive chewing; in the third phase, the development of an Oedipus complex (or Electra complex), which arises from a child's unconscious desire to possess the parent of the opposite sex, and concomitant conflict with the same-sex parent.

In *Little Voice*, the conflict between LV and her mother is the central locus of dramatic tension in the plot. The flip side of Mari's hypersexuality is maternal neglect: she uses her body to gratify men, not to nurture her daughter. The dearth of food in the house points to a systemic lack of care, suggesting that Mari may not have satisfied LV's needs during the oral phase (a busty mom with little interest in breastfeeding). We learn that this deficit was made up by the father, who raised his daughter with the help of musical wet-nurses, named Garland and Monroe—surrogate mothers who provided an alternative form of nourishment that resulted in LV's fixation on a very different oral pleasure: singing their songs. So the clash between mother and daughter becomes one between voices: LV's gift as an impressionist versus Mari's quite distinct vocal prowess. Viewers of *Little Voice* typically recall the punch line from her voluble account of getting laid by Ray in his convertible: "Never had a shag in a Chevy?" Mari is the prima donna of the fisheries, whose verbal rants find their match in the pop divas that LV plays on her record player before she impersonates them at Boo's.

But LV can do such impersonations only because of her habitual listening. Her room is a shrine to the memory of her father, whose records she displays on the mantel like relics on an altar (figure 6.5, top). While the worship of pop idols is common in teenagers, the trinity of LV's inherited taste are three goddesses from the golden era of American entertainment: Billie Holiday, Judy Garland, and Marilyn Monroe. Herman pushes their quasi-religious veneration by staging LV's nighttime routine with a prayer to her father, whose photograph hangs over her bed, watching like a patron saint over his little girl (figure 6.5, bottom). The goodnight ritual is not complete without the father's spectral return from the realm of shadows, summoned by LV's incantation, an a cappella version of "Over the Rainbow," which emerges—like Wagner's prelude to *Lohengrin*—from the shimmering halo of high strings. Intended or not, this sonic allusion is apt. If Wagner's Elsa cried out to the knight in shining armor, LV conjures her father's visitation by becoming all voice. All this may seem quite overdone—even a little perverse—but Herman turns allegory into caricature to make the Freudian facets even more drastic: LV's entreaty is shown as a distinctly oral pleasure, which, however sublimated, collapses her fixation on mimicking her musical stepmothers into the desire to reunite with her record-loving father.

This moment is a first turning point in the plot. If Ray and Mari have tried in vain to cajole LV into auditioning for Boo, she gives voice to her distress and desire like Dorothy in *The Wizard of Oz*. But now that her singing penetrates into the streets, the effect is even more powerful: "That's *Judy!* You've got Judy Garland in there!" Boo's astonishment registers the impact of the acousmêtre—a voice that exercises its mysterious power by being heard while remaining unseen. Boo *knows* that voice. Even screened-off, it conjures up Judy—if not Dorothy. Above all, however, LV's voice pronounces a categorical difference between organic and mechanical reproduction. She may be a copycat, but she is no machine. In a culture of canned music, live performance still trumps technological precision with a different kind of fidelity: that of a palpably physical presence. In this respect, LV not only offers a spectacle of the here and now, but turns herself into a medium that promises the quasi-resurrection of mostly deceased singers, who serve as living connections to her beloved father.

This is why Ray positions himself as Frank's replacement. When he enters LV's darkened room at night like her daddy, the light from the hallway wedges his shadow between the daughter and the picture of her father on the wall. LV had failed the trial run at Boo's earlier that day, and Ray realizes he can only convince her to sing by paying tribute to

Figure 6.5 Little Voice's father fixation: She listens to her father's recordings during the day (*top*) and sings to his spectral presence at night (*bottom*).

her father. At her bedside, he tells her the story of the little bluebird that was reared by his aunt. When set free one day, it stopped on the window ledge to sing *once*, no less than one of England's most popular World War II tunes, "The White Cliffs of Dover" (the lyric's second line, following "There'll be bluebirds over . . ."). Of course, the bluebird also alludes to a line from Garland's most famous number: "If happy little bluebirds fly beyond the rainbow, why, oh why can't I?" As the script has it, Ray "flutters his hand like dad used to. The hand's flightpath trails wickedly up and past the photo of dad. LV follows it and stares at the photo."[39] That does the trick: the little bluebird agrees to fly and to peep.

And so, LV will make her grand entrance at Boo's by emerging from an actual cage, like a bird set free to sing at the ledge of the stage. Yet she can only begin after she makes out her father's ghost in the audience. All of this seems a little heavy-handed, but Herman develops the bird motif to bring out the link between Ray and Frank as parental objects of desire: one standing for the consumption of physical pleasures, the other for the communion of a spiritual bond. Read as a double fixation in the oral and phallic phases, song and sex are the two sides of the libidinal energy to be released in LV's public show. Nowhere is this imbrication more palpable than in the transition from trial run to gala performance. In the former, Ray pushes her onto the stage like a child prodigy reluctant to step into the limelight, revealing her skinny frame in a pink sweater; in the latter, she has blossomed into a young woman, whose long and sparkling white dress brings out the feminine attributes of her body. This transition from forced exploitation to voluntary exhibition takes place through sublimation: LV's behavior evolves from the socially unacceptable into the culturally desirable. Herman depicts that change by pointing, rather bluntly, to its psychosexual dimension. The first time LV walks on stage, she is blinded by the lights, facing the unseen audience while a pink microphone seems to rise before her—in a more than suggestive POV shot—like a phallus. Thus visually and vocally exposed (there is no backup band), LV is too shy to perform solo. It is only after Ray has the lights turned off that she begins to speak and sing isolated lines in the voices of Holiday, Garland, and Monroe. Taking Ray's coaxing words as cues she automatically retrieves such famed phrases as Monroe's "Happy *B*irthday, Mr. *P*resident," unmistakably enunciating the erotic enunciation of bilabial plosives. Since the enveloping darkness simulates the intimacy of the nighttime ritual, it secures the cover for the sublimated sexuality of song, expressing both oral and phallic pleasures.

This replay of the bedtime ritual also launches the second performance. LV still leaves her cage like a timid bird, but now, after spotting her father's ghost (called forth once again by ethereal strings), she quickly springs into action with Bassey's "Big Spender." Perched at the threshold between little girl and young woman, she now sings for two fathers—one spectral and otherworldly, the other tangible and mundane. This is why "Falling in Love Again" fits so well into her set. Following Monroe's playful "I Wanna Be Loved by You," from Billy Wilder's comedy *Some Like it Hot* (1959), Dietrich's signature song alludes to the perilous motive of the *fille*-turned-*femme fatale* in Josef von Sternberg's 1930 drama *The Blue Angel*. Now Little Voice has morphed into Big Voice—no longer a fledgling Lolita-bluebird but a full-fledged Lola-Lola. Ray watches her, incredulous, mesmerized, and pleased. The big cigar in his mouth could not be more telling. LV has turned the tables. Now it is Ray who regresses, like the other men in the audience, sitting in a strip club and gazing at "his" girl bringing to life one of the most alluring film divas of all time.

Live Impersonation and Fixation on the Fetish

Herman depicts live impersonation, not just live performance. At the crossroads of organic and mechanical reproduction, LV's mimetic feat is the outcome both of habitual listening and of habitual spectatorship. When Mari brings Ray home for the first time, LV is watching a performance of "The Man That Got Away," from the fourth episode of the *Judy Garland Show*, which aired Sunday nights on CBS during the 1963–1964 season. It is the one moment Herman sneaks into the film to show that LV's obsession with vinyl records (which seemed on the verge of extinction by the mid-1990s) is contingent on other media. LV knows her idols as icons of popular culture whose vocal presence has its visual pendant in signature performances on television and in the cinema. Yet in the plot, her character is developed vocally earlier than visually. At first, LV's impersonations are mostly heard and not seen, much helped by casting the rather skinny Horrocks—small body, big voice—in the leading role.

Figure 6.6 Little Voice's vocal-visual impersonations: at home she becomes Judy Garland from a CBS Broadcast (*top*) and at Boo's she becomes Shirley Bassey from the concert in Costa del Sol (*bottom*).

So when Mari and Ray barge into the living room on their first date, Herman sets the stage for LV's first, informal, debut. Unwilling to watch her mother get cozy with yet another man, she runs upstairs and puts on Garland's "That's Entertainment," which her mother parries downstairs with Tom Jones singing "It's Not Unusual"—as if the acoustic clash were replaying an old battle over musical tastes with her deceased husband, between American classics and the British Invasion.

But the conflict of "canned" tunes is only a prelude to a different contest, which begins after the two record players blow a fuse in the outdated electrical wiring and come to a screeching halt. As Mari throws herself onto Ray to make out with him, LV recapitulates, a cappella, "The Man That Got Away"—mimicking Garland's voice. The lyrics comment on the situation in no uncertain terms—the old trick of using songs as underscore—expressing the dismal state of a woman who suddenly feels her age after having been abandoned by such men. But the ironic gloss is only a subtext to a more serious outcome: that of sublimation. For Ray wrests himself free of Mari's advances, stunned that he is not hearing a battery-powered radio but a real voice sounding in the dark. We already know whose voice this is (and who is being impersonated), but to make the point visually Herman here cuts to LV upstairs, and we see her raising her hand, just like Garland did in the broadcast she'd watched earlier (figure 6.6, top). Later, of course, we'll see LV dressed up like Bassey at that Costa del Sol performance (see figure 6.6, bottom). Such swapping of song for sex stems from an incantation that prefigures LV's performance at Boo's, where the platform for strippers turns into the riser for a siren who lures her male listeners with the voices of divas from a bygone era.

In *Little Voice*, impersonation thus becomes a linchpin for the film's critical concern with media effects, notably the implications of mechanical reproduction for live performance. Viewers enjoy a mimetic feat by comparing the mime with the original—a double projection of sorts, especially when one voice is involved in conjuring up another. The audience must be constantly aware of the *technique* of impersonation in order to appreciate it. Hence the pleasure of LV's impressions lies in the double sense of "that's Judy Garland" and "that's Little Voice"—not to mention, "that's Jane Horrocks." The main effect of live impersonation—like LV's showcase act at Boo's—both counts on our awareness of the gap between person and persona, and relies on the physical presence of the impressionist doing all the vocal work herself (even if Horrocks lip-synced to her own prerecorded tracks, acting as both ventriloquist and dummy).

The fact that *Little Voice* was a vehicle for Horrocks not only raises the question of the difference between stage play and film, but makes the relation between actor and character—an issue in film theory since the early days of cinema—a central element of the plot. In *The Imaginary Signifier*, Christian Metz notes that spectators who identify with a character in film tend to do so "with *the actor as 'star.'*" Indeed, "if the cinematic part is fastened once and for all to its interpreter, it is because its representation involves the reflection of the actor himself, and because the reflection (the signifier) is *recorded* and is hence no longer capable of change."[40] In *Little Voice* (both as a play and film), the main protagonist first identifies with actors as stars through their recordings (including film and television appearances), and then becomes an actor impersonating those stars by replaying their recordings through the medium of her own body. *Little Voice* thus brings into focus the role of recording technology as a fetish—not just for LV as a listener and spectator, but for those watching and listening to her.

To grasp this double position, we may briefly take recourse to Adorno's notorious 1938 essay "On the Fetish-Character in Music and the Regression of Listening." Adorno, to recall, was explicitly challenging the more optimistic view of technological reproducibility in Benjamin's artwork essay. Comparing film with music, he noted, in a passage directly addressed to his friend: "One might be tempted to rescue [regressive listening] if it were something in which the 'auratic' characteristics of the work of art, its illusory elements, gave way to playful ones. However it may be with films, today's mass music shows little of such progress in disenchantment. Nothing survives in it more steadfastly than the illusion, nothing more illusory than its reality."[41] At stake was Benjamin's claim that the "withering of semblance" or "decay of aura" in the age of technological reproducibility had been "matched" by an increase in the "room for play"—and that in film, semblance had actually been "entirely displaced by the element of play."[42] In chapter 4, I invoked Miriam Hansen's argument that Benjamin effectively reconfigured aura by entering into a dialectic between semblance and play. And I proposed that one potential by-product of this dialectic is a specifically cinematic aura. What I want to suggest now is that this dialectic plays out somewhat differently in the rise and fall of *Little Voice*, for here the association between aura and semblance is more problematic in ways that align with Adorno's diagnosis of regressive listening, even as they are playfully exposed.

On one hand, Adorno's use of fetishism is Marxist: music, as a commodity, is valued independently from its means of production. On the other hand, he diagnoses the effects of commodification in quasi-Freudian terms: as a regression of listeners to a infantile state in which they constantly "demand the one dish they have once been served."[43] Key to this state is how modern recording technology and its machinery of distribution fosters the atomized consumption of musical wholes: classical compositions chopped up into culinary bits and pieces; popular music served in bite-size portions in the first place. Highlights from the classics and hit parades of pop songs are equivalent in the economy of entertainment: they rely on the same mode of listening. The premise of *Little Voice* is not only that yesterday's hit songs are the classics of today, but that they are revived as a potpourri, whose piecemeal structure is the formal paradigm of the aesthetic pseudo-whole. The critical ruse of Herman's film is to double up this revival as a form of regression. At first, we encounter LV locked up in her room, where listening to the star singers is an activity that brings her father back to life. This kind of revival, in turn, is what Ray craves for himself and his clients: bringing back a glorious past, LV promises a makeover to a club whose pleasures have been lost to mere pornography. Pertinent here is Metz's point about disavowal as a "fixation" on the moment "just before" the discovery of lack: the fetish becomes a source of pleasure precisely because it covers up what has been seen and thus turns it into an object of desire. If Metz theorized the link of disavowal and fetishism as a "lasting matrix" for "all the splittings of belief," LV's bedtime ritual and nightclub act are both instantiations of the "affective prototype" that shores up the eroticism of entertainment: it reveals and conceals.[44] The satirical side of *Little Voice* is meant to expose that matrix and make us enjoy the split.

In LV's private prayer and public tribute to her father, the eroticism of entertainment thus aligns the Freudian and Marxist conceptions of fetishism, both of which are pathologized as forms of regressive behavior. The evening prayer shows LV stuck in a quasi-oral phase, where the pleasures of vocal impersonation prevent her from facing the reality of her father's death. In turn, the nightclub performance returns Ray to a childlike mode of listening. Both prayer and performance are predicated on what Adorno calls "pseudo-activity," which is not mimesis, but mimicry—a mere imitation of sensual reality. Adorno's two types of "retarded listeners" seek (but fail) to escape "the passive status of compulsory consumers and 'activate' themselves": one is the extroverted "jitterbug," whose "ecstasy is without content"; the other, the "shy and inhibited" figure of the "radio ham," who "'occupies' himself with music in the quiet of his bedroom."[45] An uncanny portrayal of both types is the scene where Ray and Mari dance downstairs while LV counters with Garland from upstairs—forms of compulsive consumption that are two sides of the same coin. This is how closely Herman channels Adorno.

And this is why mother and daughter part ways after the big night at Boo's. On the one hand, LV generates the magic of mimesis—the expression of genuine experience that summons the star singers with utmost sensual reality. On the other hand, her live impersonations are slated to become mere mimicry—a reified rendition of this experience, impoverished under the conditions of mechanical reproduction and compulsive consumption. Mimesis and mimicry are part of a feedback loop that LV must disrupt. Mari may have counted on the get-rich scheme behind the industrial production of culture, but it turns out that her little bird holds Ray to his promise and will sing "just once." Hence the mother cannot cash in on her girl's success: LV's refusal to repeat bursts a bubble built on promiscuous reproductions. Indeed, Adorno acknowledges (with a nod to Benjamin) the temptation to "rescue" regressive listening, "if it were something in which the 'auratic' characteristics of the work of art, its illusory elements, gave way to playful ones."[46] And indeed, LV's big night at Boo's does just that, but it does so *on the very cusp* of semblance giving way to play. Her performance partakes in the auratic here and now—but just once. When apparitions of past divas turn into playful impersonations, enchantment becomes the foil for disenchantment. LV creates magic whose spell must be cast out before it can take hold. This liminal state aligns with Benjamin's idea of repetition, which, as Hansen put it so well, "oscillates" between two extremes: one is "Nietzsche's eternal return congealed in the law of the commodity"; the other—"dialectically embedded in the first"—is the Proustian pursuit of past happiness akin to the Deleuzian "*production* of that past in the very movement of repetition."[47] LV's "just once" refuses to replace her old fixation with a new one.

The singular magical turn to disenchantment carries the film's serious satire. Since LV's house is haunted by the past, her father's record collection has to go up in flames—destroying the room of regression. If radio ham and jitterbug are two sides of the same pseudo-activity, so are LV's two fathers, Frank and Ray, who fashion two sides of the same fixation. Just as LV retreats to her room to commune with her biological father, her future career would be that of a singing bird always returning to the cage. Ray, her surrogate dad, would never set her free. Things get ugly once he forces LV, curled up in her bed, into a repeat performance, attended by that big-shot agent from London. Running out of patience, Ray becomes violent: "*He grabs her. She's limp in his arms. He slaps her. Hard.*"[48] But now something strange happens: LV's defenses kick into overdrive with a rapid change from depression to mania: "*Suddenly voices begin to rush out of her. Some sung, some spoken, but all uncontrollably*":

LV (*Cilla Black, as in* Blind Date): "Hello number one, what's yer name and where d'yer come from?"

RAY: Wha . . . ?

LV: (*Judy Garland, as in* A Star Is Born): "This is Mrs. . . . Norman . . . Maine."

RAY: Hey, stop messing, LV, come on, quick we're *late!* . . .

LV (*Grace Fields*): ". . . So hurry up before they shut the gate. . . ."

RAY: Look, save it for the punters . . .

LV (*Grace Fields*): "Click clack click clack click clack click. There's music in the clatter of the clogs."[49]

With a "verbal torrent" that also quotes Monroe's "My heart belongs to Daddy" and "See what I mean? Not very bright" (a line from *Some Like It Hot*), LV forces Ray "across the room" and "out onto the landing as the verbal stream increases." It is here that LV not only utters lines from *The Wizard of Oz* but snaps into the physical action she has seen on-screen:

RAY: LV . . . please! Why . . . ?

LV (*Munchkin*): "Because because because because because because of the wonderful things he does."

Again he raises his hand to hit her.

RAY: I warned you . . .

But LV gets in first with a scratch of the Lion's face à la Wizard of Oz.

LV (*Judy Garland*): "Shame on you!!"

She scratches his nose. He topples backwards, loses his balance and crashes down the stairs, hitting the sides as he goes.[50]

What do we make of this extraordinary outburst? I noted in chapter 4 how cinematic representations of habitual spectatorship showcase specific effects of repeated viewings. In *Little Voice*, those effects are pathological—a symptom of organic mimesis becoming mechanized mimicry, which Hansen describes as the "darker vein" of the mimetic as a relational practice: "a rudiment of the once powerful compulsion to become similar and to behave accordingly."[51] Threatened by the repetitive nature of showbiz, LV jumps from the frying pan of regressive listening into the fire of uncontrollable replay, from one fixation to another. Possessed by the content of excessive media consumption, she morphs into a medium herself, emitting sound bites like a malfunctioning playback device. As lights are "popping out all over the house" and wires "flash and spark everywhere," it seems as if her explosive breakdown has also blown every last fuse in the decrepit home collapsing around her. Cued by Cartwright, Herman's LV mutates into a distressed Dorothy, hysterically ventriloquizing: "Lions and tigers and bears, oh my! Lions and tigers and bears, oh my!" and "I'm frightened, Auntie Em. I am frightened . . ." These frantic lines only betray what we seem to have known all along: LV's greatest fear may be having to leave home, but her true trauma is being trapped in it.

This is why clutching her father's records in a room surrounded by a raging fire appears to be LV's final act of regression: "This is my room . . . and I'm not going to leave here ever, ever again . . . because I love you all." Of course, these are Dorothy's last words after waking up in her own bed at the end of *The Wizard of Oz*. Recall that the Good Witch of the North transported the girl home by making Dorothy repeat the phrase, "There's no place like home," which becomes a sound bridge of sorts, whose charm seems to bring about the lap dissolve from Oz back to Kansas. But now that LV repeats those words in pure panic, the magic formula has a different effect. If Dorothy returns home from a dream, LV's retreat into her room has become a nightmare. Although the manic recollection of sound bites allows her to ward off Ray's assault, now she is locked into the compulsion to repeat. Rescue must come from outside. Using the boom lift of his truck, Billy retrieves LV before the firefighters arrive on the scene. The rescue refigures an earlier balcony scene during which Billy hauls himself up to the window of her bedroom, where she is listening to Monroe's "My Heart Belongs to Daddy." But daddy is dead.

At its dramatic climax, the film undergoes a radical reversal. Herman cuts effectively between LV's distress and a desperate Ray, who takes the stage at Boo's to sing what Greil Marcus describes as, "a horrible, self-flagellating version" of Roy Orbison's "It's Over." As Marcus puts it, "The classic song has been rubbed smooth by decades of overplay, but now it's ripped into someone else's story so violently you may never again be able to hear it as an innocent object, as a kind of toy. Now it has been brought into a play about real life—the play of life itself."[52] This phenomenon—akin to Chion's reprojection—has been ubiquitous ever since songs entered the cinema to comment on a scene, capture the gist of a situation, or allow characters to express their feelings. Moreover, what Marcus aptly describes as "old songs in new skins" are common as well in the soundtrack of life, when a hackneyed tune takes on a novel meaning that becomes its primary association. There is a bit of both in Ray's fatalistic rendition of "It's Over," giving the song a new lease on life through its interplay with LV's impulsive utterances. Falling apart, the two characters serve as each other's foil: a geeky girl-become-automaton cracking in overdrive; a phony showman delivering as his last act an authentic cover.

The contradiction inherent in such an "authentic cover" connects with the thread I have been weaving into my reading of *Little Voice* as a more or less explicit example of the parallel histories of cinema and psychoanalysis, revolving around narratives of cure from past affliction. Just as the film's furious finale culminates in LV's cathartic abreaction of her father fixation, Ray comes to give voice to his true self. Where LV abandons mimicry, Ray's cover becomes his very own. As the plot slips back into the real world, it leaves behind a farce, shattered like the pic-

Figure 6.7 Released from the fixation on her dead father's recordings, Little Voice threatens to kill her mother with a shard from one of his records (*top*), only to have her actor, Jane Horrocks, become a star in the freeze-frame from the closing credits (*bottom*).

ture of LV's father, which lies broken among the scattered shards of his records. Like a phoenix rising from the burned ruins of her house, LV grabs Mari's chin "with one hand and holds the sharp curved shard of record to her throat with the other," screaming (figure 6.7):

LV: Aaaaa! Aaaaa! Can you hear me now, mother? My dad . . . You drove him as fast as you could to an early grave with your men and your shouting and your pals and your nights, and your nights, and your nights, and your nights of *neglect*. Oh, when he had his records on . . . he sparkled, not dazzling like you, but with fine lights . . . *fine* lights! He never spoke up to you, 'cos you would never listen. . . . And I never spoke up to you . . . 'COS I COULD NEVER GET A WORD IN!!

MARI recoils from the enormous noise.

The echo of LV's scream drifts over the town. Dogs start to bark.

MARI is still reeling from the vocal gale.

MARI (*stunned*): Little Voice . . . ?
LV (*walks away and leaves her*): My name's Laura.[53]

The threat to cut her mother's throat with a shard from her father's record is no less than LV's last act to resolve her Electra complex. In a story about a contest of voices, however, there is no need for matricide: it is enough to silence Mari and turn her from the wicked witch into a wretched one. Finally freed from her father fixation, LV speaks up with a new voice to reclaim her actual name. Casting aside her nickname accords with casting out the voices she has been channeling. The exorcism that severs her bond with both parents finally readies her for real romance. Recall how Billy, too tongue-tied to address LV at first, had tested the newly hooked-up telephone to initiate a conversation. With the telephone destroyed in the fire, we know that the telecommunication technician will return to his true passion of ancient transmission: carrier pigeons. Birds with bodies, not invisible voices transmitted through electric wires. No surprise, then, that the film ends with Laura finding Billy at his loft overlooking the bay, where, as the script has it, he "hands her a pigeon which she turns and releases. As she does so, we freeze-frame on LV and the bird."

Once the fall of Little Voice leads to the rise of Laura, social satire gives way to a love story and its imperative for narrative closure. North Yorkshire is Kansas after all: there is no place like home. Although the farce has exposed musical fetishism, the romantic ending restores the film's fetish-character, and with it, the regression of spectatorship. As parodic play yields to sentimental semblance, there is something whimsically paradoxical about the freeze-frame that connects the ending of the film with the beginning of the closing credits. The frame coincides with the cadence of the carefree instrumental tune that started when Billy was setting his pigeons free for a round of exercise—including the one pigeon, Duane, that he'd feared had been lost. If such symbolism lacks all subtlety, Herman holds the frame long enough to launch Ethel Merman's vibrant rendition of "There's No Business Like Show Business," while the following script appears next to Laura: "Jane Horrocks performed all her own songs." A little star flashes over the "o" of "songs," the frame fades out, and the credits start rolling.

Why the disclosure? Why the star? We already knew that Horrocks performed her own songs—that she was, in a sense, playing herself; that she was both character and actor. Hence we might be led to think that we are hearing Horrocks and not Merman. After all, the words pop up to credit her abilities as an impersonator. If the film (like the stage play) was partly a vehicle to propel Horrock's career, it makes sense to plug her here. Yet the ambiguity of who is singing suggests once more what has been at stake throughout the film: the desire to seize and reproduce the sense of presence in a star performance. The freeze-frame points to the failure of that other fixation in technological reproducibility: even as films and other audiovisual media attach the voices of stars to their bodies, impersonators try to make up for the traumatic loss of auratic presence by replaying recorded performances through their own bodies. Here the photographic still captures the ambivalence behind such replay, for we did not just see Horrock's impersonations, we saw them in a movie. Even as *Little Voice* sought to unmask the fetishism of recording technology in spectacular moments of impersonation, the film surrenders to its disavowal and becomes complicit with this technology. The freeze-frame uncouples LV from her voice and at the same time sells Horrock's vocal skills as a commodity: she is that little star who sparkles, like her character's father, when singing those songs of old.

Ages lie between the gothic parable about the aftermath of World War II and the biting parody about the fallout from the Thatcher years. While Bennett and the Boxes came up with an earnest representation of modern trauma therapy, Herman and Cartwright offered a postmodern twist on the treatment of traumatic neurosis. Yet both drama and comedy converge in their focus on how foster daughters are fashioned into female performers by surrogate fathers who try to reclaim the lost cultural paradigm of classical music or classical entertainment. Although the stand-up impersonations in *Little Voice* appear to be a far cry from the polished performances in *The Seventh Veil*, the two films share essential scenes of cathartic abreaction in which traumatic experiences, fortified by music, are purged by turning mimetic replay into anti-mimetic narration. The two coming-of-age stories suggest different ways in which the adolescent woman can shake off her father fixation. While both perpetuate constructions of the medicalized and medialized subjectivity of the female performer, they present different conjunctions of the two.

The two films, then, reflect quite different stations in the overlapping history of psychoanalysis and cinema. *The Seventh Veil* assumes that the similarity between psychic and cinematic apparatus is scientifically valid, such that the symptoms and cure of hysteria can be accurately represented with filmic means. Scenes of writing match scenes of recall, suggesting that psychological fixation and medium fixation do not just work in similar ways, but are actually two sides of the same phenomenon, brought together by music through the woman performer. In *Little Voice*, by contrast, the hysteric musical mime becomes suspect and subject to satire, which exposes the hiatus in her psychosexual development as a consequence of regressive media consumption. Yet the comical portrayal of parental abuse and love also takes on a distinctly sinister shading. Amid the memory wars of the 1990s, the apparition of the music-loving father in his daughter's bedroom is outright disturbing. Whereas *The Seventh Veil* finally reconciles the roles of parent, lover, and therapist in the affirmation of successful psychiatric treatment, the cathartic ending of *Little Voice* appears to have exorcized not only the ghosts of the past but also the specter of Freudian psychoanalysis itself. What is left after the psychosexual fixations have been cleared is only the fixation on cinematic memory: Freud the psychoanalyst survived by the Freud the media theorist.

CHAPTER SEVEN

Affective Attachments

A few years ago I conducted an empirical study showing that film music influences how viewers relate to characters. It does so because it functions as a prime that links emotions to these characters, who are judged and remembered as more or less likeable, depending on the genre of the music: thriller music, for example, makes them less likable.[1] Music not only represents affective attachments between characters on-screen but elicits emotions that modulate the relation between these characters and viewers. The critical theorist Sara Ahmed, for example, has studied emotions by viewing them not as "psychological states" but as "social and cultural practices."[2] Moving beyond "cultural texts as repositories of feelings and emotions," she proposes a new method of "tracking how words for feeling, and objects of feeling, circulate and generate *effects*."[3] Thus the very naming of emotions has real consequences: calling someone hateful or loving designates that person as filled with hate or love, but also as someone who arouses or deserves hate or love.[4] Fear, for example, may become attached to a black man or a Muslim and thereby generate fear as an effect of encountering any black person or any practitioner of Islam. According to Ahmed, the association between objects and emotions is contingent and "sticky"—a term that resonates with Carolyn Abbate's description of how music takes on and retains associations in commercials, songs, or opera.[5]

This final chapter extends my focus on film music's contribution to cultural memory to its role in cultural politics, exploring specifically how it partakes in the formation of trust based on affective attachments. I will consider two midcentury American films in which the transition to modern society involves the creation of trust. George Stevens's *I Remember Mama* (1948) is a parable of economic trust, while Robert Mulligan's *To Kill a Mockingbird* (1962) deals with the issue of racial trust. Both films are narrated by a daughter remembering her mother or father, bringing into focus how trust emerges through affective attachments between child and parent. In both films, the formation and representation of such attachment involves music. By shaping memories of attachment, music becomes attached to these memories and thereby influences the viewer's trust in the narrator and, by extension, in film as a medium.

Why trust? As a basic element of human interaction that fulfills crucial social functions, trust is critical in human development, involving affective, cognitive, and behavioral dimensions. In a groundbreaking 1968 essay, Niklas Luhmann distinguished between personal trust and system trust. While personal trust is essential in simple societies that rely on direct interaction, complex societies require increased trust to reduce their complexity.[6] System trust is essential in establishing truth and reliability in media of communication and "symbolic media of exchange" such as money.[7] Following Luhmann, Anthony Giddens notes that one of the consequences of modernity has been the "reembedding" of "disembedded" social relations.[8] He proposes a distinction between "facework commitments" (trust established and maintained through "co-presence"); and "faceless commitments," which emerge with trust needed for "symbolic tokens or expert systems."[9] Giddens observes that the re-embedding of social relations often requires "access points" where special people, such as experts, provide the facework commitment that facilitates trust in abstract systems.[10] Just as a banker serves as the access point for the banking system or a lawyer for the legal system, a news anchor has come to do the facework that builds trust in a news organization.

Not surprisingly, parents or caregivers play a major role in the development of trust. Erik Erikson famously argued that the distinction between "basic trust" and "basic mistrust" was the first stage of social learning, and hence foundational to human relationships.[11] While "generalized trust" is the belief that people can be trusted, "particularized trust" refers to instances in which generalized trust is mitigated by in-group dynamics, whereby most people "like me" can be trusted because they share such broad attributes as class, religion, ethnicity, race, sexual orientation, or specific political goals.[12] While there is evidence that diversity drives down generalized trust, the impact is offset by the positive effects of integration.[13] Giddens links basic trust with the sense of "ontological security" formed when children can rely on a caretaker's return or on everyday routines that create a feeling of psychological security.[14] Since children form a bond with caregivers, basic trust aligns what developmental psychologists have categorized as a "secure attachment style."[15] Just as Luhmann suggested that "the emotional cathexis of the child with his family is . . . the foundation for the learning of all trust," Giddens regarded ontological security as "an emotional, rather than cognitive phenomenon . . . rooted in the unconscious."[16] This unconscious dimension of ontological security suggests that affective attachment is a central aspect of basic trust.

Why affect? The idea that trust cannot be reduced to reason goes back to Georg Simmel, who held that trust was based on "weak inductive knowledge," which requires a "leap of faith" involving a "suspension of reality"—a Jamesian "will to believe."[17] This is why the affective component of trust is essential in human relationships, explaining our strong emotional reactions in situations of betrayal. As David Lewis and Andrew Weigert put it, since trust is a "*mix* of feeling and thinking," the removal of emotional content would result in "coldblooded prediction or rationally calculated risk," while the removal of cognitive content would result in "blind faith or fixed hope."[18] Because affective trust moderates cognitive processes, it plays an important role in alternatives to purely deterministic models of trust prevalent in transaction cost economics or rational choice theory. Affective trust provides a quick heuristic for trust judgments, bypassing, for better or worse, deliberation and discernment in interpersonal trust, but also in institutional and system trust.[19] Film music, I suggest, can serve as such a powerful heuristic in cinematic representations of trustworthy caregivers with whom children—and viewers—form attachments that can last a lifetime and thereby shape the personal attitudes and actions essential for a functioning modern society.

Remembering Mama

George Stevens is remembered today for such classics as *A Place in the Sun* (1951), *Shane* (1953), and *Giant* (1956). His less well known 1948 film *I Remember Mama*, an uplifting portrait of a Norwegian immigrant family in early twentieth-century San Francisco, was based on a 1944 Broadway play that John van Druten adapted from Kathryn Forbes's fictive memoir, *Mama's Bank Account*, published the year before. The film has been seen as part of Stevens's response to his horrific task of heading a film unit in the US Army, shooting footage of D-Day and concentration camps, which led to Godard's claim about the director's postwar attempt to restore faith in cinema as a medium of representation (discussed in chapter 3). In this regard, *I Remember Mama* is a companion film of sorts to Frank Capra's *It's a Wonderful Life*. In both cases, the story is told by a trustworthy narrator whose main protagonist shores up trust in the modern banking system. Recall how, in Capra's film, George Bailey's Building & Loan survives Black Tuesday because Bailey reminds his customers that he extended their credit in time of need: "We have got to stick together, we've got to have faith in each other." Recall also how Bailey's life is "screened" for the angel Clarence, who is sent to save him from killing himself after his uncle misplaces a large deposit, and how Capra ingeniously freezes this celestial screening momentarily into a still image, allowing Clarence to see that George has a "good face" (figure 7.1). His facework not only facilitates the attachment to his customers (who will later bail him out) and thereby bolsters trust in a banking system shattered by the Great Depression; the still shot also underwrites the trust in cinema as a photographic medium that can assure viewers about the truthfulness of its representations.

I Remember Mama is less explicit about cinematic representation. Here the story is told as a flashback narrative by Katrin (Barbara Bel Geddes), an aspiring writer who has just finished her first autobiographical novel about growing up in the Hanson family:

For as long as I could remember, the house on the Larkin Street Hill had been

Figure 7.1 *It's a Wonderful Life*. The freeze-frame in the film screened for Angel Clarence secures viewers' attachment to a trustworthy person: "It's a good face. I like it. I like George Bailey."

home. Papa and Mama had both been born in Norway, but they came to San Francisco because Mama's sisters were here. All of us were born here. Nels, the oldest and the only boy . . . my sister Christine . . . and the littlest sister, Dagmar. . . . But first and foremost, I remember Mama . . ."[20]

Roy Webb, who wrote the score for *I Remember Mama*, repeats the film's title theme at this very moment so that it "becomes" not only the "I Remember Mama" theme but also the music of narrative remembrance, which will come back at similar junctures throughout the film (figure 7.2). A dissolve takes viewers back to 1910, to the family's Saturday evening ritual of going through the household budget, led by Katrin's mother, Marta (Irene Dunne). The ritual concludes, once money has been set aside for the week's expenses, when Marta says, "Is good. *We do not have to go to the bank.*" But her economic credo—not touching the family's savings—is challenged when Nels asks whether he may attend high school. After telling Katrin to fetch the "little bank," a wooden box of emergency cash, Marta adds up the family's contributions to cover the extra cost: she postpones the purchase of a coat, her husband gives up tobacco, and the children promise to work extra jobs after school. "Is good. Is enough," she says finally. "We do not have to go to the bank."

The opening scene creates a twofold frame for the film: Katrin's narration and her mother's accounting are acts of mediation (figure 7.3, top). Marta enforces fiscal discipline by invoking a trip to the bank as a last resort, thereby articulating her position between the household budget

Figure 7.2 The "I Remember Mama" theme is heard when Katrin remembers how the family gathered every Saturday for the weekly banking ritual (cue, "The Family," measures 18–22). Cue excerpts from *I Remember Mama* courtesy UCLA Special Collections, RKO Collection.

and the banking system. In Giddens's terms, she becomes an access point, providing a human face for that system. Similarly, we can trust Katrin as a narrator because she is a witness. Amid her intermittent voiceover, the film unfolds as a series of heartwarming vignettes, in which Marta takes on other roles as an intermediary: making her two priggish older sisters consent to the marriage of their youngest sister, Trina (Ellen Corby), or convincing a famed author to read her daughter's manuscripts. Stevens portrays his heroine as the paragon of the new woman at the helm of an immigrant family, who navigates the New World with character and common sense. The parallel between mother and daughter as accountants in different domains connects to another family ritual: the nightly readings of Mr. Hyde, a former actor whom Marta has taken in as a boarder to supplement the family income. When Mr. Hyde disappears one day, leaving his books and a bad check for his back rent, Marta reconciles herself with the loss by counting his readings as contributions to her family's education. Moved to tears, Katrin decides to become a writer (figure 7.3, bottom).

Here the labor of narration operates within what Ahmed calls an "affective economy," where emotions become effective not by residing in a sign, figure, or object but by circulating "sideways" through "'sticky' associations between signs, figures and objects."[21] Katrin's account of Mr. Hyde's reading is a moment of medium self-consciousness, about the transition from literature to film, suggesting how cinema enhances emotional effects by circulating affect through representational technologies,

Figure 7.3
Katrin's account of Mama's accounting (*top*) is inspired by Mr. Hyde's affecting readings to the family, creating Katrin's wish to become a writer (*bottom*).

such as the close-up of faces (what Deleuze would call the "affection image") and musical underscoring. This circulation of cinematic affect is brought out differently in Stevens's portrayal of the two main characters, Marta and her Uncle Chris, who is the head of the Hanson clan. An unkempt, gruff, and scary drunk with a heart of gold, Uncle Chris is a waning patriarch whose droll faces and bodily antics (partly the result of a limp) evoke the more vaudevillian cinema of attractions from the early twentieth century. The generational, social, and emotional gap between him and the forward-looking Marta is dramatized in two hospital scenes (figure 7.4). In the first, Uncle Chris visits his great-nephew Arne, who is recovering from a knee operation. To help Arne cope with the pain, Uncle Chris teaches him Norwegian swearwords and *sings*—a detail added in revisions of the script. First, the boisterous ditty "Ten Thousand Swedes," and then a soothing setting of the lullaby "Nu løftes Laft og Lofte."[22] Uncle Chris's singing is tender but raw, and—much to his delight and the nurse's dismay—cut short by Arne cursing away his pain.

The second hospital scene is markedly different. After her youngest daughter Dagmar has undergone emergency surgery for mastoiditis, Marta sneaks into the children's ward disguised as a cleaning woman to "croon" her daughter to sleep with "an old Norwegian lullaby"—a paradigmatic example of the caretaker's promised return to establish basic trust.[23] Webb and his music staff at RKO surely did their homework when

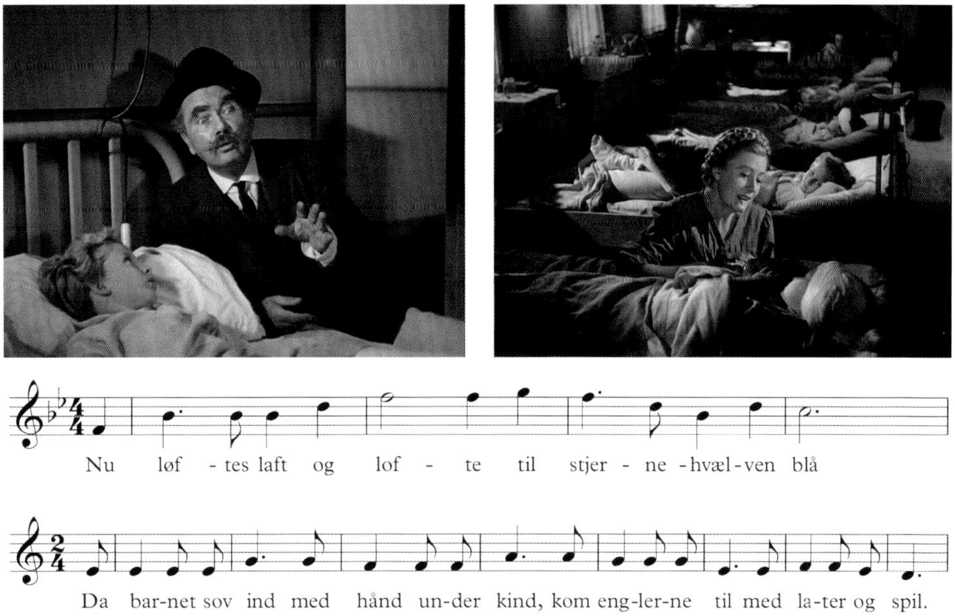

Figure 7.4 Lullabies as affective labor: "Nu løftes Laft og Lofte" (Uncle Chris) and "Sövnen" (Marta).

selecting the well-known lullaby "Sövnen," by the nineteenth-century Norwegian composer Halfdan Kjerulf.[24] Using the splendid mezzo of his top-billed lead, Stevens turns a mere three lines of description in the screenplay into one of the film's most affecting moments, warranting detailed analysis.

Marta sings the first stanza with a soft envelope of strings and harp, while the faces of mother and child appear in close-ups, along with those of other children in the ward. After all of the children have been lulled into sleep, Marta withdraws, humming a second stanza without underscore as she retreats into a dark corner to stay clear of the nurse on night duty. Special care went into the creation of this scene; production notes recommend that the strings should reenter on a close shot of the nurse walking into the ward toward the camera.[25] Once the nurse settles into her chair and dozes off, it appears that the music has lulled her to sleep, too, while a close-up of Marta's face emerges from the shadow to look over the entire ward like an "angel of sleep" (figure 7.5). As Marta withdraws, Webb "splits the cue," as indicated in the production notes, replacing the last three measures of the lullaby with a stirring harmonic progression rising to the dominant just the camera dissolves to Katrin in her attic, holding the manuscript of "I Remember Mama" in her hand and looking, with a smile, into a mirror.[26] The dissolve points to the doubling of affective attachments—as represented in the story, and as experienced in its telling. As the viewer's proxy, Katrin sees herself smile, with the implicit expectation that viewers will smile back, trusting her account.

Singing, Marta and Uncle Chris engage in what Michael Hardt has

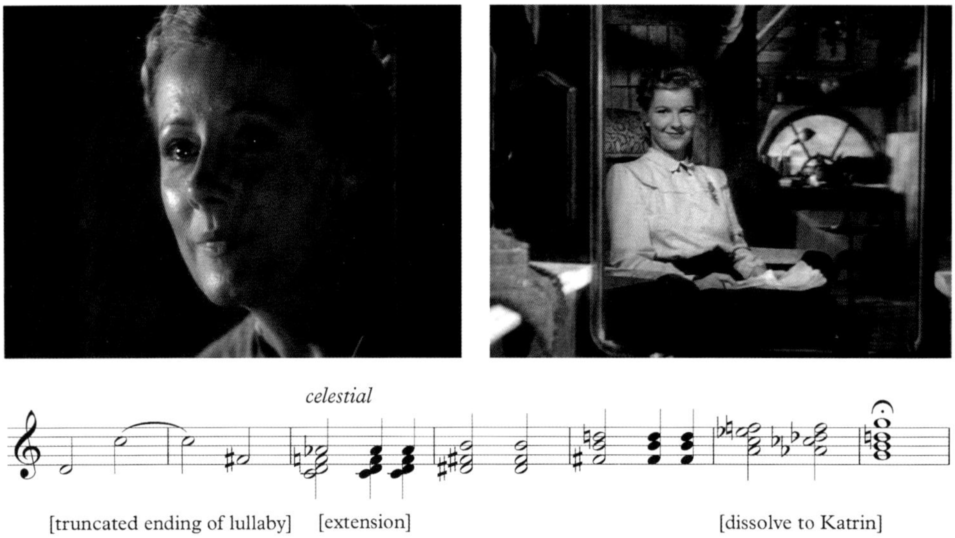

Figure 7.5 Marta's lullaby undergoes a "celestial" extension, leading to a dissolve that shows Katrin remembering Mama as the "angel of sleep" (cue "Lullaby").

called "affective labor," prevalent in the health, service, and entertainment industries today, where its "intangible" outcomes include "a feeling of ease, well-being, satisfaction, excitement, passion—even a sense of connectedness and community."[27] Sometimes associated with "women's work" or "labor in the bodily mode," affective labor resembles the emotional "sustenance" Victorian girls provided when playing the piano for fatigued fathers coming home from work at night.[28] The affective labor in *I Remember Mama*—set around 1910 and released in 1948—maintains this fantasy, where familial bonds shore up trust in social systems in an increasingly complex world. The film showcases the creation of basic trust in two variants, aligned with the distinct ways in which Marta and Uncle Chris do affective labor, and how their labor enters into Katrin's story as an emotion. Brian Massumi has described emotion as "qualified intensity," that is, intensity, inserted "into narrativizable action-reaction circuits, into function and meaning. It is intensity owned and recognized."[29] He follows the philosopher of science Gilbert Simondon, who modeled the role of affect within an emergent process of individuation, whereby unconscious or preconscious affect becomes conscious emotion.[30] Psychological models of emotion assume that affective states are categorized as emotion through cognitive appraisal, which entails reinstating prior appraisals of earlier situations. As Joseph E. LeDoux famously noted, "emotion is memory."[31] This is why Katrin's stories are affect "owned and recognized."

When Uncle Chris is dying from problems associated with too much drinking, Katrin is allowed to witness the final drink he wants to have with Marta and his housekeeper and secret wife, Jessie:

UNCLE CHRIS: Katrina. Your Mama write me you drink coffee now.

She nods; he looks at her affectionately.

UNCLE CHRIS (*cont.*): Katrina, who will be a writer. . . . You are not frightened of me now?

KATRIN: No, Uncle Chris.

UNCLE CHRIS: One day maybe you write story about Uncle Chris. If you remember.

KATRIN (*whispering*): I'll remember.[32]

If Uncle Chris represents early cinema, his death becomes his last performance. When Marta lowers the curtain on his *scena ultima*, raising her glass in a final salute, the cradle song sung to Arne earlier returns softly in the underscore—played by a solo violin and strings in a cue called "A Drink to Death." During postproduction, Webb had the ingenious idea to fade out the elegiac melody of the original E-major cue for two measures and add a muted choir of three trumpets playing the incipit of the song twice in C♯ major: first before Marta lowers the shades and then, more softly, after the shadow has fallen over Uncle Chris's face (figure 7.6). It is as if his soul is moving into the distance, off-stage.[33]

It falls to Marta to provide the epilogue to this play, revealing to her relatives that Uncle Chris has left them no money. According to the Estimating Script, she "brings forth a small notebook" to explain:

MAMA: You know how Uncle Chris was lame . . . how he walked always with limp. It was his one thought . . . lame people. He would have liked to be doctor and help them. Instead, he help them other ways. I read you the last page . . .

(*reading from notebook*)

"Joseph Spinelli. Four years old. Tubercular left leg. Three hundred thirty-seven dollars, eighteen cents."

(*pausing, then continuing*)

"Walks now. Esta Jensen. Nine years. Club-foot. Two hundred seventeen dollars, fifty cents. Walks now."

(*then, reading, very slowly*)

"*Arne* Solfeldt . . ."

SIGRID (*startled*): *My* Arne?

MAMA (*reading on*) "Nine years. Fractured kneecap. Four hundred forty-two dollars, sixteen cents."[34]

And while Arne races Katrin back to the porch at this moment, Marta suggests, "I like to write 'Walks now' . . . Maybe even . . . 'runs'?" As the script has it, "Mama writes in the book, and then closes it."[35] The poignancy of this moment cannot be overstated. When Marta takes Katrin into the

Figure 7.6 Uncle Chris's death: as Marta lowers the curtain on his final "performance," the instrumental reprise from his lullaby (cue "A Drink to Death") fades out in the underscore, with a distant call and echo of muted trumpets added later.

house to pay their last respects, the "I Remember Mama" theme returns in the underscore, leading to a dissolve to Katrin in her attic room looking into the mirror, just as she did after recounting Mama's nightly visit to the hospital.[36] Katrin remembers Uncle Chris because she remembers Mama. It is hardly surprising that Marta's visit to the hospital and Uncle Chris's death were the most highly rated scenes in previews.[37] They were effective because they made affective labor legible as moral sentiment.

Since her uncle's affective capital is all spent—expressed in the fading echo of his lullaby—it is her memory of Marta that leads to Katrin's breakthrough as a writer. After Marta convinces a famous writer to evaluate her daughter's manuscripts in exchange for recipes by her own mother, Katrin is asked to write about what she *remembers*, for example, a story about Papa. Months later, Katrin's first short story is accepted for publication and she receives a check for $500 as her first honorarium. Overjoyed, she suggests that her mother buy herself a warm coat at last and deposit the remaining sum in her bank account. But much to their surprise, the children learn that there is no such account. "Never in my life have I been inside a bank," Marta admits and goes on to explain: "It is not good for little ones to be afraid . . . to not feel secure. But now . . . with five hundred dollar . . . I think I can tell."[38]

Then, when she asks Katrin to read to the family, it is Marta's turn to be surprised, for the published story is entitled "Mama and the Hospital." The film ends with Marta, embarrassed and proud, withdrawing from the kitchen table and looking out the window, while Katrin reads to her family what had been the opening of her novel from the beginning of the film, now adding: "When I look back, 1910 seems like only yesterday. I remember that every Saturday night, Mama used to call the family together. I remember Mr. Hyde, dear Aunt Trina, and my Uncle Chris. But first and foremost, I remember Mama."[39] Although Webb was to bring back the music of the lullaby in the underscore at this point, we hear a final reprise of the "I Remember Mama" theme and, as Katrin continues, we cut to a medium close-up of Marta, seen from outside the window, pulling its sheer curtain aside and then letting it fall back to cover her face.[40] The camera pulls back and pans over the neighborhood and the city, fog horns beginning to compete with Katrin's voice until both fade into the music:

> I remember how on every Saturday night Mama would sit down at the kitchen table and count out the money that Papa had brought home in a little envelope. There would be various stacks: "For the landlord," Mama would say, piling up the big silver pieces. "For the grocer," another group of coins. At last Papa would ask, "Is all?" Mama would look up and smile. "Is good. We do not have to go to the bank."[41]

Stevens's conclusion clinches the connection between affective attachments and affective economies. Reestablishing the sense of "ontological security" that had been shattered by the monstrous destruction of livelihoods and lives in the Great Depression and two World Wars, *I Remember Mama* is a morality play. It looks back to an early twentieth-century immigrant family to promote principles that underlie a functioning social order, including the modern banking system: fiscal discipline, mutual trust, and investment in the next generation.[42] To restore and renew generalized trust, Stevens, like Capra in *It's a Wonderful Life*, replays the transition from a traditional, smaller, and simpler face-to-face society to a larger, more complex modern society—from personal trust to system trust.[43] As an intermediary, Marta takes her place between the generation of her uncle (who never adapts to the New World) and her children (who are born into it). As a parent, she effectively positions herself as the access point in the social development of her children, providing the facework commitment that fosters the trust they need to navigate their path into modern life. Marta engineers this trust as the keeper of the family's bank account. Just as George Bailey banked with parental passion, Marta is a trusted banker because she is a mother. Managing her actual little bank, she assumes the face of the big bank to shore up faith in the functioning banking system.

Hence the fact that Marta has no real bank account is not a breach of trust but an attempt to engineer trust by shielding her children from worry: "It is not good for little ones to be afraid . . . to not feel secure."

Ontological security is affect. Marta Hanson effectively links the creation of generalized trust to the creation of basic trust by cultivating affective attachments. This is why she must keep her promise to visit Dagmar at the hospital. In a striking turn, her affective labor produces capital when it inspires her daughter's story. One might say that Marta's affective attachments become attached to Katrin's affecting story which she not only reads at the kitchen table but also remembers for us as the director's proxy. In Katrin's memory, Uncle Chris becomes aligned with what Tom Gunning has called a "cinema of attraction," prominent in early film, while Marta inhabits the "cinema of narration" characteristic of classical Hollywood.[44] This difference is not only manifest in "affection images"—shots of their faces—but also in what one might call "affection sounds," where Uncle Chris's boisterous bass is eclipsed by Marta's soothing soprano. While the children must overcome their apprehension about Uncle Chris, Marta already sustains their trust. Dying, Uncle Chris exits his cinema of attraction in silence, giving way to Marta's cinema of narration, awash in sound.

Music, then, lies at the heart of this nexus between affective attachments and affective economies. If Marta's lullaby occupies the affective core of "Mama and the Hospital," the music's powerful emotional effect is "owned and recognized" in Katrin's story. It appears only logical that the honorarium uncovers her mother's secret. Using it to open a bank account redeems Marta's white lie as a form of affective labor that created a sense of economic security essential for basic trust in the financial system. What is more: just as the children believe in Mama's bank account, Katrin's readers believe her account of Mama. The slippage between her mother's story and the story of her mother shows how trust underwrites social, cultural, and economic capital. Remembering Mama, Katrin produces an authentic account of "things she knows"—which are things she remembers. Because she can be trusted as a narrator, Katrin ends up at the center of the family table taking the place of Mr. Hyde and of her mother (figure 7.7).[45] She is the new nexus of two affective economies: of media and money, and of accounts and accounting.

I Remember Mama, like *It's a Wonderful Life*, is a cinematic exercise in the "sentimental mode."[46] Central to sentiment are acts of reflection, a cognitive appraisal of an affective experience through moral analysis, from an outside point of view. Viewers trust George Bailey and Marta Hanson because the sympathetic divine screening and Katrin's flashback reassure them about the truthfulness of cinematic mediation. As accountants, George and Marta are already accounted for. If Capra and Stevens sought to restore trust in the double economy of media and money at a particular moment in postwar American history, a persistent paradox of modernity has been that its ongoing losses of security are often offset by gains in trust. Amid shifting states of trust in the booms and busts of the business cycle, trust has remained a stable human trait. Despite the

decline of generalized trust, economic trust tends to receive a lift through affect, however attenuated, ready to be converted into something we might bank for the future. Can we say the same about racial trust?

Figure 7.7 Katrin reads "Mama and the Hospital" at the family table.

Remembering Atticus

Those who grew up with Robert Mulligan's *To Kill a Mockingbird* (1962) may picture the penultimate shot with the voiceover of Jean Louise—the adult Scout—speaking the words that ended Harper Lee's book:

Ext. Finch house—Jem's window.

We can SEE *Atticus through the window, sitting by his son's bed, holding Scout.*

JEAN LOUISE (VOICEOVER): He would be in Jem's room all night and he would be there when Jem waked up in the morning.

CAMERA SLOWLY PULLS BACK as Atticus looks at the sleeping Jem.[47]

There is a detail in this shot not mentioned in the screenplay: the photograph on the mantelpiece is of Atticus's wife and the mother of his children (figure 7.8). Her presence here is a reminder of her absence in

Figure 7.8
At the end of *To Kill a Mockingbird,* Atticus holds Scout while watching Jem.

Figure 7.9
(facing, *top*) "Remember Mama" (cue 2C) begins with the main title theme (measures 1–6) interspersed with "mother chords" (measures 3 and 12–17). Cue excerpts from *To Kill a Mockingbird* courtesy USC Cinematic Arts Library, Elmer Bernstein Collection.

Figure 7.10
(facing, *bottom*) Atticus overhears how his children remember their mother.

their lives, an absence filled by others: not only by Atticus himself, but also by the family's black housekeeper, Calpurnia, their neighbor Maudie Atkinson, and of course Arthur "Boo" Radley, the reclusive member of the family next door. I begin with this final shot not merely because we see the mother's photograph. We also hear one last time the main theme music by Elmer Bernstein. This theme is introduced during the opening credits and recurs throughout the film to invoke the missing mother when others take on her role, underscoring a sense of attachment. Kevin Donnelly has suggested that musical connotations can acquire a ghostly dimension in movie soundtracks: serving as a "repository of reminders, half-memories and outbursts of emotion and the illogical . . . these 'ghosts' and 'memories' . . . can haunt a film."[48] I call it the "Remember Mama" theme because the next time it appears after the main titles is in a cue entitled "Remember Mama" (compare figures 7.9 and 7.13). The cue accompanies a poignant scene that screenwriter Horton Foote—noting that Lee "never mentions the mother"—used to "sneak in that emotional element."[49] After Atticus has tucked in Scout at night the theme is played haltingly, its phrases ending in prolonged notes, as Scout gradually remembers her mother by questioning Jem, lying awake in the adjacent room. The cue thus links their memories with the main theme, played both by piano and flutes and padded warmly with slowly shifting seventh chords in the strings, which I will call "mother chords" (figure 7.9). We feel her presence and we feel her loss for the children, and for Atticus sitting on the porch listening to them (figure 7.10).

When Lee's *Go Set a Watchman* was published in 2015, it created a furor because its image of Atticus Finch was so different.[50] Though written before *Mockingbird*, *Watchman* read like its sequel because it takes place two decades later, when the twenty-six-year-old Jean Louise "Scout"

"Remember Mama"

"mother chords"

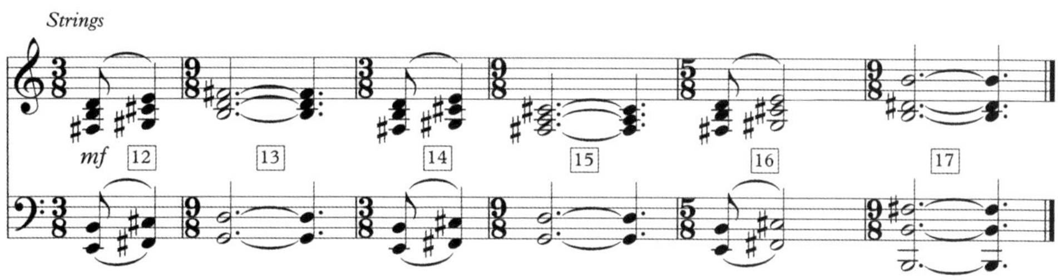

Finch, returns from New York to Maycomb, Alabama, to see her childhood sweetheart "Hank," now working for her father. Readers were dismayed to read that Atticus was no longer the man Scout remembered from her childhood: a heroic lawyer of common sense and enlightened convictions who courageously defended a black man against charges of raping a white woman. Shockingly, the Atticus of *Watchman* has become a bigot, resistant to the Supreme Court's *Brown v. Board of Education* decision, actively working against the NAACP, and holding the belief that people of color are not ready to join modern society. As Katherine Henninger puts it, the "clash of affect" between the two books shook many readers to the core.[51]

Chapter 8 of *Watchman* showcases that clash. After finding a racist pamphlet, "The Black Plague," on her father's table, Jean Louise learns from her Aunt Alexandra that Hank and Atticus have gone to a meeting of the Maycomb Citizens' Council. She follows them to the courthouse, climbs the stairs to the balcony for colored people, and observes her father introducing a segregationist speaker, who rants about saving the South, about mongrelization, about black preachers twisting the Gospel, and about the Supreme Court listening to Communists. Suddenly, Jean Louise has a flashback: "She heard her father's voice, a tiny voice talking in the warm comfortable past. *Gentlemen, if there's one slogan in this world I believe, it is this: equal rights for all, special privileges for none.*"[52] She remembers her father winning acquittal for the black man in the rape trial by proving consent, recalling how he "pursued the case to its conclusion with every spark of his ability."[53] Sickened by what she observes now, she stumbles outside and wanders aimlessly through the streets of Maycomb to the site of her former home, now occupied by an ice cream shop. After eating a scoop of vanilla, her stomach turns over: "The one human being she had ever fully and wholeheartedly trusted had failed her."[54]

Tay Hohoff, an editor at the J. B. Lippincott Company, had helped the young author rework *Watchman*, essentially fashioning a new novel with new characters and new plot lines, including the mysterious Boo Radley, who is sequestered in the neighboring house and does not come out until the very end, when he rescues Scout and her brother Jem from their nemesis, Bob Ewell—another new character—who is the father of the girl allegedly raped by Tom Robinson. Jem is no longer alive at the time of *Watchman*, having died from the same heart condition that killed his mother. But he turns up in brief flashbacks, along with their childhood friend Charles Baker "Dill" Harris, long recognized as a Truman Capote character. (Lee and Capote were childhood friends.) Lee expanded Jean Louise's flashbacks into the main story of *Mockingbird*, which starts at the time she enters grade school, in 1932, at the age of six. The new novel also became a first-person narrative, assuming the dually focalized perspective of child and reminiscing adult. Its nostalgic tone seemed untroubled by any critical hindsight and detached from the contemporary struggle of the civil rights movement, which had served, in *Watchman*, as a background for the heated exchanges Jean Louise had with Hank, with her Uncle Jack, and with her father. Although the Atticus Finch of *Mockingbird* loses the trial, he appears as a white-savior figure and a wise parent whose civility and moral compass guide his children. After Scout gets into a brawl with a classmate who taunts her because her father has black clients, Atticus teaches her what would become Lee's most memorable expression of moral sentiment: "You never really understand a person until you consider things from his point of view . . . until you climb into his skin and walk around in it."[55]

The unsettling relation between *Watchman* and *Mockingbird* invites a fresh look at Mulligan's film, which had helped to cement the memory of the morally upright Atticus in the popular imagination. Atticus was played by a kind and dignified Gregory Peck, while the role of the spunky Scout fell to Mary Badham. They remained lifelong friends, and Badham continued to call Peck "Atticus." Shooting in black and white, Mulligan captured the combination of childhood adventure, courtroom drama, and nostalgia for an earlier rural south, adopting what Henninger describes as Lee's "familiar technique of addressing contemporary racial anxieties in a setting safely past."[56] To reinforce this focalizing distance, the film begins and ends with, and occasionally inserts, the narration of the adult Jean Louise, a voiceover role cast with the theater and television actress Kim Stanley. Unlike the rebellious Jean Louise of *Watchman*, who returns to Maycomb to find the treasured memory of her father shattered, Stanley's mature voice sounded reassuring and trustworthy.

This trust was both underwritten and undermined by elements of the film, including the music, which added an ambiguous subtext to the seemingly straightforward story. Bernstein later recalled having struggled with the score, eventually deciding on music that could conjure "the magic of the child's world" in a "definitely American ambience" while expressing a grown-up view of this world.[57] Using a chamber orchestra, he expanded the timbral palette with percussion, piano, harp, celeste, and accordion to create two stylistic poles: a simpler idiom, evocative of folk songs, a rural setting, and a sense of home; and a more extravagant, occasionally high modernist, idiom, which conveyed the children's fantasies and fears.[58]

The music for the main title sequence was to introduce this combination, but in the final version of the film, an important section is missing—measures 9–19. This changed the overall effect of the opening credit sequence significantly.[59] The film begins with a simple unaccompanied melody against a black screen and the Universal logo, played in the upper register of the piano, like a motto (figure 7.11, "simple melody"). But when the main title starts to roll, the music stops, replaced by a child humming to herself. We first see a high angle shot of an old cigar box, which the child opens to reveal an array of things, including a broken pocket watch, crayons, marbles, pennies, and two soap dolls (figure 7.12). Originally, the opening of the lid was to coincide with a rising harp arpeggio that introduced an undulating line in the minor mode played by the flute and accompanied by arpeggiated chords in both harp and

"simple melody"

"magic objects" (not used in the film)

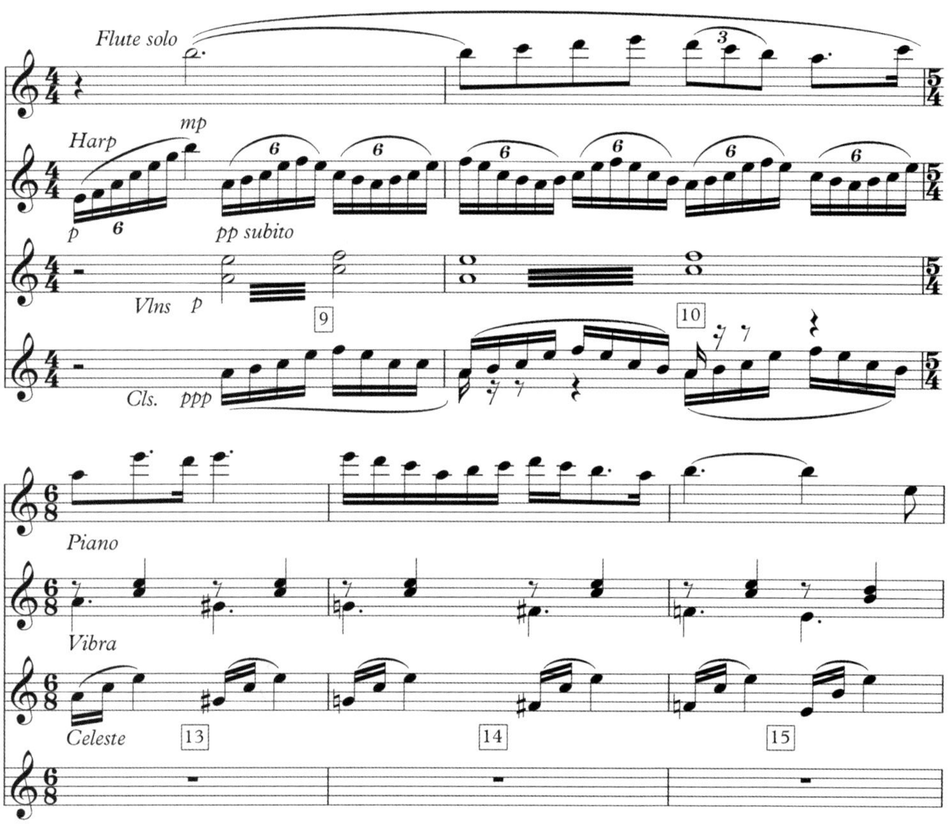

Figure 7.11 Opening of "Main Title" for *To Kill a Mockingbird*: a "simple melody" is followed by an evocation of "magic objects" from childhood (descriptors added).

clarinet, then switching to an enchanting waltzlike melody in the piano, accompanied by accordion and celeste (figure 7.11, "magic objects"). Why was this "magical" music cut from the title sequence?

The deleted measures originated with a multisection cue entitled "Tree Treasure."[60] When Jem, in a later scene, opens the cigar box to show Scout the things he has found in the knothole of a tree near the Radley house, we hear the rising harp arpeggio and flute melody. Then, before continuing with the enchanting piano waltz, we hear a section of five bizarre measures in 9/8 time, which Bernstein withheld from the main titles, "invariably" written last as a "compilation and distillation of all of the music in the film."[61] As Jem takes out a spelling medal ("they

Figure 7.12 Cigar box of things left by Boo in the knot-hole, which will become memory objects.

used to award these in school to spelling winners before we were born") and the pocket watch, a short, two-measure melody in the piano's right hand is punctuated by two flutes playing thirds with *flatterzunge* and a truncated, hiccup-ish accompaniment in the piano's left hand, accordion, and clarinets. Since this melody is associated with Boo it connects the contents of the cigar box with his enigmatic existence in the Radley house. Although the credit sequence was likely inspired by this later scene, the filmmakers may have decided to save the five striking measures for the scene itself, where they heighten the sense of mystery around the cigar box and help "explain" its contents as coming from Boo. Without "magical" music, the credit sequence exudes a greater sense of realism and presence, enhanced by the diegetic sounds of a humming child: the box is not yet seen to contain memory objects but merely a collection of ordinary things.

If the credit sequence introduces viewers into a carefree children's world, this feeling gradually disappears in the remaining sections (figure 7.13). We next hear a full version of the main theme—the "Remember Mama" theme—no longer a freely floating fragment in the piano but aired by the flute with harp accompaniment. With its Lydian beginning, this simple melody is now grounded in a tonic drone indigenous to the folk idiom, still evoking the topos of innocence and naiveté, accompanying tracking shots of the spilled-out contents of the box in extreme close-up and following the hands of the child drawing a bird—perhaps a mockingbird. But the following "adult" version of the theme moves into the middle register with full-bodied strings leading the entire chamber ensemble, the harmony expands into a mix of major and minor chords, and the accelerating harmonic rhythm increases the expressive range. A secondary melodic line suggests a second perspective, and the number

"childlike"

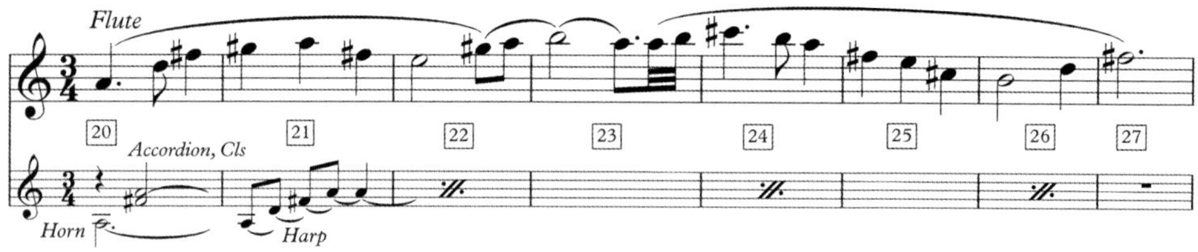

"nostalgic"

Figure 7.13a–b (*top, and facing, top*) The three versions of the main theme in the main title for *To Kill a Mockingbird*.

"unsettling"

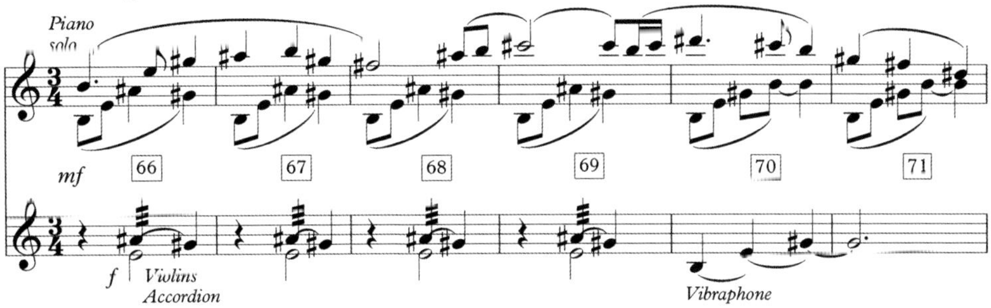

of voices increases, as if providing a broader vision of life. The greater emotional range becomes palpable in the extension of the melody by a repeated four-measure phrase (measures 50–57), whose Tchaikovskian sighs give voice to a sense of nostalgia.

If this wistful version anticipates Jean Louise's reminiscing voiceover, the coda reverts to the main theme in the piano, with the accordion changing the bittersweet sighs into off-beat tritone appoggiaturas, sending troubling signals to the musical surface. Thus the three statements of the main title theme—naive first, sentimental second, unsettling third—follow a rising trajectory (D, A, E). Yet the characteristic raised fourth of the Lydian mode in the melody, which creates a tritone that clashes with the major triad on the Lydian tonic, is most grating in the third statement. Now, having finished the drawing of the mockingbird, the child tears it apart, and the resulting gap dissolves into the tree-lined streets of Maycomb with a sense of ambivalence (figure 7.14).[62] Inasmuch as the music leads us to "the warm comfortable past," it also casts a shadow over the memory.

Figure 7.14 The torn drawing of the mockingbird opens to Maycomb's past.

Remembering Calpurnia

This unease points to the film's hidden meanings, which have become more apparent since the publication of *Watchman*. For Henninger, Jean Louise's flashbacks are no less than a "return of the repressed."[63] In chapter 12, when she learns that Calpurnia's grandson Frank has been charged with manslaughter after running over a white man in a drunk driving accident, Atticus decides to take his case to keep NAACP lawyers from challenging jury selection, making the judge step down, and moving the trial into a federal court—all strategies the organization pursued at the time to combat the racial bias baked into the legal system. Jean Louise is appalled by her father's ulterior motifs. But most telling is Calpurnia's reaction. When Jean Louise visits her, she senses the chasm that separates her from her former caretaker:

> "Cal," she cried, "Cal, Cal, Cal, what are you doing to me? What's the matter? I'm your baby, have you forgotten me? Why are you shutting me out? What are you doing to me?"
>
> Calpurnia lifted her hands and brought them down softly on the arms of the rocker. Her face was a million tiny wrinkles, and her eyes were dim behind thick lenses.
>
> "What are you doing to us?" she said.
>
> "Us?"
>
> "Yessum. Us." . . .
>
> She looked into the old woman's face and she knew it was hopeless. Calpurnia was watching her, and in Calpurnia's eyes was no hint of compassion.
>
> Jean Louise rose to go. "Tell me one thing, Cal," she said, "just one thing before I go—please, I've got to know. Did you hate us?"
>
> The old woman sat silent, bearing the burden of her years. Jean Louise waited.
>
> Finally, Calpurnia shook her head.[64]

In his review for the *New Yorker*, Adam Gopnik wrote that this exchange is the "toughest scene" of *Watchman*, amounting to "a genuine dramatic climax, worthy of the writer's gifts, offered and then evaded." Yet if Calpurnia's reaction, shaking her head in response to Jean Louise's question, was "credible," "the scene, and the book," he concluded, "would have been stronger if she hadn't."[65] For Lee, the formation of basic trust rested on Scout's attachment not only to her father but to her black caregiver. This is why the chapter is so devastating: in short order, the affective bond to both of her parental figures is destroyed. Convinced that Calpurnia loved her, Jean Louise laments that "people used to trust each other."[66] But the Maycomb she remembers in *Mockingbird* is hardly a place where social and racial trust flourished. The reworked novel dramatized this failure most vividly in the trial. After the verdict, Tom Robinson tries to escape because he has no faith in a successful appeal. Although her father appears as a trustworthy access point to the legal system—much helped by Peck's facework—his defense falters.

Atticus's attempt to overcome particularized trust in the trial has its corollary in another episode that did not make it from the novel into the screenplay, although it is essential to the evolution of Scout's racial consciousness. In chapter 12 of *Mockingbird*, Calpurnia takes the children to her church, where they see her for the first time within her own community, singing:

> Zeebo cleared his throat and read in a voice like the rumble of distant artillery:
>
> "There's a land beyond the river."
>
> Miraculously on pitch, a hundred voices sang out Zeebo's words. The last syllable, held to a husky hum, was followed by Zeebo saying,
>
> "That we call the sweet forever."
>
> Music again swelled around us; the last note lingered and Zeebo met it with the next line: "And we only reach that shore by faith's decree."
>
> The congregation hesitated, Zeebo repeated the line carefully, and it was sung. At the chorus Zeebo closed the book, a signal for the congregation to proceed without his help.
>
> On the dying notes of "Jubilee," Zeebo said, "In that far-off sweet forever, just beyond the shining river."
>
> Line for line, voices followed in simple harmony until the hymn ended in a melancholy murmur.
>
> I looked at Jem, who was looking at Zeebo from the corners of his eyes. I didn't believe it either, but we had both heard it.[67]

The children are incredulous about the lack of hymnals, and when Calpurnia explains "linin'" as a result of illiteracy, Scout suddenly realizes what Lee had set up as the point of the excursion: "That Calpurnia led a modest double life never dawned on me. The idea that she had a separate existence outside our household was a novel one, to say nothing of her having command of two languages." When Scout goes on to ask, "Why do you talk nigger-talk to the—to your folks when you know it's not right?" Calpurnia answers, "Well, in the first place, I'm black—."[68]

The reality of double consciousness puts an end to the color-blindness that Atticus had instilled in his children, dismantling their racial innocence and his legal idealism. Since the visit to Calpurnia's church did not make it into Mulligan's film, the issue of race—including the problem of trust and mistrust—tilted toward the trial. This exacerbated the attrition of agency for black characters, shown in the film as passive subjects: Tom responding on the stand, Reverend Sykes observing the trial from the courthouse balcony, Tom's wife Helen breaking down after the news of his death.[69] Despite the novel's more nuanced portrayal of Maycomb's black community, it also drew on stereotypes that excluded African-American characters who were successful, professional, and educated. Lee's ideas about racial equality were high-minded, but her views on racial politics were hardly radical. Amid the white liberal humanism of postwar Hollywood, the cinematic adaptation by Foote and Mulligan treaded carefully on the subject of race, largely following the "deadcentrism" of television drama.[70] Imagine how Bernstein might have approached the church scene and how the calls and responses would have provided Calpurnia's community with a voice of their own, as source music in a score dominated by underscoring. But the vernacular black voice in the score of *Mockingbird* remains muted.

Where Bernstein could have composed cues that gave black characters their own voice, he decided to score racial encounters differently. The first case is embedded in a longer cue entitled "Ewell's Hatred," written for a visit Atticus pays to Helen Robinson to speak with her about her husband's upcoming trial.[71] Since his children come along, the cue begins with an upbeat version of the "Remember Mama" theme, leading to the gently shifting "mother chords" once we see Scout asleep on the backseat upon their arrival. The music changes after Atticus enters the house, and David, a boy Jem's age (Tom Robinson's son, in the screenplay), approaches the car: now a pseudo-imitative counterpoint in oboe and clarinet gives way to slowly shifting celeste-cued chords for three flutes, before returning to oboe and clarinet, coming together just as Jem waves at David from inside the car and David waves back (figure 7.15). No words are spoken, but the woodwind duo intimates that some connection between the boys has been made.

Bernstein's decision to score the encounter between Jem and David with the strange idiom of contrapuntal Americana—sparse and restrained, bucolic and melancholic—appears peculiar. The "diaphanous linear texture," with its mixture of neoclassical learnedness and folklike simplicity in a modal environment, is evocative of what Wilfrid Mellers identified early on as the "American features" in Aaron Copland's music.[72] Bernstein, who credited Copland with having "invented American music," clearly had in his ear the up-tempo numbers in the composer's ballets from the 1940s when writing such cues as "Atticus Accepts the Case" and "Roll in the Tire."[73] His use of Americana reveals a specific musical point of view on the film's racial conflict, also born out in the remaining sections of "Ewell's Hatred." The delicate counterpoint for the meeting between Jem and David gives way to ominous octaves in the bass, whose tritone heralds Bob Ewell approaching the car, seething with hate, ogling the sleeping Scout, and denouncing Atticus as a "nigger-lover." If the slur is the strongest verbal expression of racial resentment in the film, its use in the novel shows how Lee struggled to confront white racism with white humanism. When Scout later asks her father why people in Maycomb decry him that way, Atticus owns up to Ewell's insult: "I certainly am. I do my best to love everybody."[74] Bernstein's expressive choice for this stance appears to have been in line with the way Mulligan and his producer Alan Pakula envisioned Atticus as a quieter character.

As Atticus comes out of Helen's house, Bob Ewell's tritones are countered by a stately motif of octaves in the lower strings (figure 7.16). What one might call the "Atticus Hero" motif was first to be heard at the beginning of the cues "Atticus Accepts the Case" and in "Crack Shot," which was to accompany his marksmanship when killing a mad dog—an ep-

Figure 7.15 David meets Jem amid a duet of austere Americana counterpoint in clarinet and oboe ("Ewell's Hatred," cue 5C, measures 22–32).

isode that leaves a deep impression on Jem. But both instances of the motif were cut from the score—"Crack Shot" was never used at all—in an effort to attenuate Atticus's image as a heroic figure. Even during his confrontation with Ewell, Atticus sounds less courageous than undaunted. Indeed, when he gets into the car and tells Jem not to be afraid of a man who is "all bluff," we hear a counterpoint between the cellos and basses against flutes and clarinets playing rising and falling fourths. Neil Lerner has shown how rising fourths—prevalent in the music of

Figure 7.18 Reverend Sykes holds his hands around Scout: "Miss Jean Louise, stand up, Your Father's passin'" (*top*); and when Atticus leaves the court house (*bottom*), the members of the black community rise to their feet ("Guilty Verdict Pt. 1," cue 11B, measures 15–18).

the oboe paired with a falling chromatic line in the clarinet and a pedal in bassoon, harp, and muted horn. This response underscores a brief exchange between Jem and Reverend Sykes about the jury's deliberation time—almost banal compared to the longer conversation in the novel where the Reverend dampens Jem's confidence about Tom's acquittal.[78] The painful knowledge of what will happen is folded into the anguish of the chromatic descent while showing the children's attachment to the Reverend as a parental figure who has taken them under his wings on the "colored balcony"—holding his hands around Dill and Scout (figure 7.18).

Then, following the reading of the jury's decision, the cue "Guilty Verdict Pt. 1" begins after Tom is escorted out of the courtroom. Atticus attempts to reassure him about an appeal, but Tom, as the screenplay has it, "looks at him with a kind of mute hopelessness on his face."[79] Slow-moving chords in the strings cede to a muted horn call while Atticus packs his briefcase, and a mournful melody sounds in the solo clarinet three times—the second time with a counterpoint in the bassoon—while the black community on the balcony slowly rises to its feet. Amid a brief interjection in oboe and flute, Reverend Sykes tells Scout, "Miss Jean Louise, stand up. Your father's passin'." Clarinet and bassoon return when Atticus leaves the courthouse, the whole balcony standing.

Rachel Watson has noted that the visual equivalent of Atticus's belief in perspective-taking, the point-of-view shot, is mitigated in the film by the many porches and balconies, which are indicative of "the proper limits of sympathetic access."[80] These limits, she argues, were already inherent in a well-known passage from Adam Smith's *Theory of Moral Sentiments*, where he claimed that the sympathizer's compassion could never be exactly the same as the sufferer's original sorrow: "Though they will never be unisons, they can be concords, and that is all that is wanted or required."[81] Smith's musical analogy resonates with the way Bernstein's score evolves from the unison of the simple motto—a sonic metaphor for the children's social and racial innocence—into music expressing the fraught vibrations of sympathy. In this regard, the cue sounds woefully ambivalent. The genuine show of respect by the people on the "colored balcony" is undercut by a context wherein a black person who did not step aside on the sidewalk to let a white person pass would risk severe punishment, even death. The Reverend's paternal role, expressed in the hand he puts around Scout's shoulder, is at odds with formally addressing her as "Miss Jean Louise." Inasmuch as the plaintive music might give voice to the profound sorrow on his face, it clashes with the color of his skin. Foregoing the black vernacular, Bernstein focalized interracial conflict through a seemingly catholic musical idiom that appeared white.

According to Jodi Melamed, postwar race novels such as *To Kill a Mockingbird* not only sought "to concretize racial liberalism's ideologemes, including the power of sympathy, liberal whites as heroic agents of reform, and the moral hazards of racial prejudice"; they also "stabilized a field of social and moral value that made it possible for white Americans to comprehend the act of reading a novel as (and as a substitute for) an active politics of social transformation."[82] Gregory Jay has suggested that *Mockingbird*'s focus on the moral dimension of racial injustice can also be seen as part of shoring up the underlying "racial conversion narrative"—a concept Fred Hobson has put forward to describe "works in which the authors, all products of and willing participants in a harsh, segregated society, confess racial wrongdoings and are 'converted,' in varying degrees, from racism to something approaching racial enlightenment."[83] The cinematic adaptation of *Mockingbird* provided a complement to the growing momentum of the civil rights movement, raising awareness in an environment where changing attitudes eventually contributed to catalyzing action. However, by addressing the issue of color-blindness, Lee's novel and Mulligan's film grappled not only with the difficulty of understanding racial differences but also the problem of seeing one's whiteness at work.[84] Writing to Pakula and Mulligan, Foote noted, regarding Atticus's address to the jury:

> I think it should perhaps be kept in mind that particularly at this period a Southerner like Atticus is not an unprejudiced man speaking to a group of prejudiced ones. He is surely a man that has had to fight the prejudice in himself, so in a measure one might say he is addressing the speech to a part of himself as a "noble man" explaining the obvious facts to a man who has shared their prejudices, struggled with them at all costs. And, too, he knows the depth of the complexity of the prejudice that he is trying to get them to renounce in themselves.[85]

While contemporary reviews of Mulligan's film typically focused on racial injustice, one reviewer wrote not only that "fantasy and illusion are the cause of the town's prejudice against Boo (a Caucasian)," but that "a corollary story also points out the idea that illusion and imagination contribute to suspicion and fear, for prejudice takes the more familiar appearance of racial antipathy."[86] Arguably, Bernstein's melancholic Americana was not musically whitewashing the wretched conditions of Maycomb's black community, but it may have been composer's way of conveying his own cultural limitations. Instead of giving a voice to that community, he opted for mourning the insurmountable barriers that separated Atticus, Jem, and Scout from Tom, Reverend Sykes, and Calpurnia.

Remembering Boo

Reworking *Watchman* into *Mockingbird*, Lee created a new plot line by introducing the mysterious character of Boo, whose whiteness complicates her portrayal of otherness, framing the drama of racial conflict with an allegory of the closet. Boo Radley becomes a white stand-in of sorts for the black boy and the black man. Hidden next door, the man-child vindicates Tom Robinson by killing Bob Ewell, who tries to harm Jem and Scout on their way home from a Thanksgiving pageant. The legal conundrum of *Mockingbird* is that Tom dies running from the law, while Boo's life is spared by the law. Sheriff Tate refuses to investigate Boo, justifying his assessment that Ewell fell on Boo's knife by saying, "There's a black man dead for no reason."[87] Atticus's reluctant acceptance of this scenario is less surprising than Scout's interpretation of it, suggesting that indicting Boo would be tantamount to "shootin' a mockingbird." Earlier, when Atticus told Jem—eager to have his own gun—that he can kill all the blue jays he wants but that it is "a sin to kill a mockingbird," Miss Maudie explained to the children, "Mockingbirds don't do one thing but make music for us to enjoy. They don't eat up people's gardens, don't nest in corncribs, they don't do one thing but sing their hearts out for us."[88] As Boo and Tom become the novel's titular "mockingbirds," the simile echoes the Kantian affinity between aesthetic judgment and moral judgment. They are unsung heroes—Tom helping Mayella Ewell and Boo rescuing Atticus's children are acts of pity and care—whose disinterested moral actions clash with the interested judgments of the world around them. Although Atticus, committed to the values of the founding fathers, holds up the courts as the "great levelers," where "all men are created equal," he knows all too well that the ideal of the Constitution clashes with the "working reality" of a jury system marred by racial prejudice.[89] When reworking *Watchman*, Lee put her didactic treatment of racial injustice in the courtroom drama but tied her subliminal and more subversive critique of such injustice to the portrayal of people coded as strange and beautiful others—as mockingbirds.

Boo is black at first—shown as a shadow. When Jem steps onto the neighbors' porch one night to "get a look at Boo Radley" through the windows, Scout suddenly sees the "shadow of a man" who "stopped a foot beyond Jem" and whose "arm came out from his side, dropped, and was still. Then it turned and moved back across Jem, walked along the porch and off the side of the house, returning as it had come." In the film, the shadow reaches out to Jem, stopping just short of "touching him" with his ghostly hand (figure 7.19).[90]

Bernstein wrote two cues for the night adventure: "Creepy Caper," for the children sneaking up to the Radley house, and "Peek-a-Boo," for the encounter on the porch, as well as the children's frantic retreat, during which Jem is caught in the fence and leaves behind his pants. (He finds those pants carefully folded when retrieving them later.) Both cues belong to the most flamboyant music of the entire score: a high modernist idiom with atonal dissonances, occasional free meter, and colorful timbres. This idiom emerges early on when the children look at the Radley house for the first time from across the street. The cue "The Meanest Man" accompanies Jem's description of Boo as a monster whose father keeps him "chained to a bed," who "only comes out at night," who eats squirrels and cats, who has "a jagged scar running across his face," whose "teeth are yellow and rotten," whose "eyes popped," and who "drools most of the time."[91]

But mixed into these cues are two little melodies, one of which becomes closely associated with Boo himself. Amid the modernist estrangement, these melodies are not dissonant. Played by piano or flute (or both), they borrow gestures and rhythms from the main title music—a distant relative of the "Remember Mama" theme (see figure 7.20). Bernstein seems to have intuited that in Lee's new gothic plot line of *Mockingbird*, Boo is an incarnation of the uncanny—actualizing the two meanings of *heimlich* that caught Freud's attention: on the one hand, "belonging to the house," invoking what is familiar, comfortable, and friendly; on the other hand, what is hidden, kept from sight, as, for example, in "the

Figure 7.19 Amid music in a modernist idiom, the children approach the Radley porch, where the dark hand of Boo's shadow reaches for Jem's face ("Creepy Caper," cue 3B, measures 1–4).

heimlich art" of magic.[92] Freud had been struck that *heimlich* is "a word whose meaning develops in the direction of ambivalence, until it finally coincides with its opposite, *unheimlich*"—the uncanny.[93] As repressed emotional impulses turn into anxiety, he argued, we are frightened by what may have been familiar things, which have become alien in the process of repression. Scary things that are repressed but recur are uncanny. Here Freud invokes Schelling's definition of the uncanny as something that "ought to have remained secret and hidden but has come to light," and singles out as an archetypal case the haunted house, where the dead return as spirits and ghosts, epitomizing the persistent, yet repressed, fear of death.[94] Let us note that the German word *vertraut* (familiar) has the same root as *Vertrauen* (trust). The uncanny is a phenomenon, a thing, or a person that was once trusted, that could be trusted again.

As a narrative frame and as a narrative thread, Boo's uncanny appearances are attempts to understand his otherness. Dill's plan of "making Boo Radley come out" is no less than a return of the repressed, revealing its origin in the familiar, the homey, and the trustworthy. The black shadow that appears on the Radley porch will later emerge as a white man from the corner of Jem's bedroom. The mysterious figure Scout identifies as the person who saved Jem from Bob Ewell has "white hands, sickly white hands that had never seen the sun, so white they stood out garishly against the dull cream wall in the dim light of Jem's room. . . . His face was as white as his hands . . . and his grey eyes were so colorless, I thought he was blind."[95] Scout notices Boo's whiteness just as she discerns "soft black velvet" of Tom's skin.[96] Her attention to the aesthetic attributes of Boo's and Tom's bodies affirms their status as mockingbirds. Tom's blackness is beautiful while Boo's whiteness is garish; yet Tom is pronounced guilty while Boo is pronounced innocent. Amid such reversals, both share their otherness as social outcasts with disabled bodies or deranged minds. While Tom has a limp left arm, which he had caught in a cotton gin as a boy, Boo's mental illness includes an episode when he drove a pair of scissors into his father's leg while scrapbooking. Being both abject and appealing is key to their marginal positions, from which they emerge to do good, only to vanish again into the actual or apparent realm of the dead.

Writing in the late 1950s, Lee necessarily treated Scout's awakening to racial and sexual knowledge differently. Race could be in plain sight, but sexual orientation had to be hidden. While Tom's trial replaces Jean Louise's acrimonious academic debates with her father and uncle in *Watchman* with a straightforward tale of good and evil, Lee develops the uncanny queerness of Boo Radley into the children's plot under the coded veneer of the Victorian gothic.[97] Dill's desire to make Boo come out parallels his own running away from home to escape parental pressures to be a boy like other boys. Asking Scout why Boo has remained sequestered in the Radley house for all those years, Dill surmises that "maybe he doesn't have anywhere to run off to . . ."[98] When the children's summer activities include acting out their own little dramatic scenes of the Radley clan—Dill, who saw the 1931 movie *Dracula*, shining in Gothic performances as a "villain's villain"—they conjure up a Boo believed to be undead next door.[99] As Holly Blackford has suggested, *Mockingbird* is "truly remarkable" because it shows "the interconnectedness of those confined to the closet, those racially persecuted, and the perspective of a girl resisting Maycomb femininity."[100] Where the novel conflated race and sexuality, innuendo is often concealed behind the children's seemingly innocuous play. Its most campy example is the "nigger snowman" that Jem and Scout build from layers of dirt and snow, which dons Miss Maudie's sun hat—an emblem of drag that prompts her and Atticus to muse about such an "absolute morphodite."[101] Yet the attribute "morphodite" belongs not only to the snowman but also to the britches-wearing Scout, who dreads donning a dress on her first day to school.

Lee found a model for rendering queerness in Capote's 1948 novel

Other Voices, Other Rooms, whose semiautobiographical plot includes a tomboyish character, Idabell, inspired by the young Lee, and Joel Knox, a girlish boy like Dill, who not only pursues the "voyeuristic activity of peering into windows" but is fascinated by apparitions of a "phantom lady"—a sort of drag queen—in his father's house.[102] Indeed, both Jem and Scout wonder whether Boo, whose eyes they believe to have "popped," is watching them through their windows at night. Mulligan works this fear into Scout's bedtime scene with Atticus, which begins with the camera pushing in on her room from outside. If this shot is *unheimlich*, the corresponding one that pulls back from Jem's bedroom at the end of the film has surely become *heimlich*. Boo exemplifies what Blackford describes as "the 'everywhere and nowhere' invisibility of gays after the release of Kinsey's report and in the perpetual suspicion of McCarthy era hunts for them."[103] However, as Lee taps into sensibilities simmering under the cultural surface of the cold war and the civil rights struggle, the subtext of Boo's hidden monstrosity becomes readable in racial terms. The shot heard when the children retreat from the their night jaunt to the Radley house is explained by Dill's aunt as Mr. Radley having taken aim "at a Negro in his collard patch."[104] Later that night, when Scout has trouble falling asleep in her cot on the back porch, "every scratch of feet on gravel was Boo Radley seeking revenge, every passing Negro laughing in the night was Boo Radley loose and after us."[105]

There are other links between Boo and blackness. When Calpurnia returns with the children from the visit to her church, she responds to Scout's asking whether they can visit it again:

> "Any time you want to," she said. "We'd be glad to have you."
>
> We were on the sidewalk by the Radley Place.
>
> "Look on the porch yonder," Jem said.
>
> I looked over to the Radley Place, expecting to see its phantom occupant sunning himself in the swing. The swing was empty.[106]

If Calpurnia has just become visible to the children as a black person, the invisible Boo belongs to the empty swing on the Radley porch—a recurring shot in the film that Bernstein paired with a characteristic melody that is like a faint echo of the "Remember Mama" theme, suggesting that Boo is watching the children with whom he communicates through objects left in the knothole of the oak tree (figure 7.20). He is one of those "'ghosts' and 'memories' that can haunt a film" as "half-remembered sounds."[107]

The motif of youth seduced by a homosexual was not uncommon in midcentury literature, but here it is overlaid with a more momentous trope—the association between monster and mother.[108] The most perplexing objects the children retrieve from the knothole are a pair of soap dolls, which Scout immediately recognizes as "almost perfect miniatures

Figure 7.20 Invisible Boo: the empty swing on the Radley porch is accompanied by a little theme with "magic" timbres ("Jem's Discovery," cue 5D-6A, measures 49–52).

of two children," carved by Boo to resemble her bangs and the shock of hair falling to her brother's eyebrows.[109] Although Mr. Radley plugs the knothole with cement as a remedy for the dying tree and thus cuts Boo off from secretly communicating with his neighbors, Scout later finds that "the trunk was swelling around its cement patch."[110] The passing of dolls through the orifice in the oak tree is legible as an act of symbolic procreation, which foreshadows Boo saving Jem and Scout's lives. Striking, in this regard, is the color of the soap figures in the film—they are dark, as if dark-skinned (see figure 7.12).

As the children discover their miniature selves, we hear an oboe motif embedded into a mysterious tapestry of flutes, harp, and celeste—music that returns later in the cue when Jem looks at the figures on his windowsill before hiding them in the cigar box. One can hear this motif as a distant echo to the oboe line heard when Tom's son David approached Jem and Scout in the car. The allusion links David and Boo: invisible children living on the dark side.

Figure 7.21 Tom and Boo as black and white Mockingbirds.

Mulligan returns to the theme of unseen others when Scout detects Boo in the corner of Jem's bedroom, where he has taken her unconscious brother after Bob Ewell's assault. As Boo emerges from behind the door, the light falling on him still casts his shadow against the wall to reveal someone wholly white from leading a life in darkness—a reverse image of Tom, whose blackness was in the spotlight throughout the trial (figure 7.21). For his screen debut, Robert Duvall had stayed out of the sun for weeks, also dying his hair to accentuate the effect, rendered even more uncanny by Bernstein's music for a monster coming out as a mother. The cue "Boo Who?" begins with two flutes, recalling the unsettling appoggiaturas that first signaled the unseen at the end of the main titles. But when Sheriff Tate pulls the door back, the accordion resolves to an E-minor triad as if to uncover Boo's secret and break its spell. A little duet ensues. The flute's descending E-minor triad (shot of Scout looking at Boo) is answered by a D-major triad (Boo looking at Scout). The sense of otherness gives way to the recognition of likeness (figure 7.22). The duet's counterpoint is no longer austere but has turned into a sweet twosome between Boo's solo violin (marked "gentle") and Scout's flute, both accompanied by the harp. Taking up Boo's little theme, the violin even adds pickup notes to its head to change its countenance, as if to give an answer to the cue's title. "Boo Who?" is "Boo Mama!"

"Hey Boo," says Scout. While the queer characters exchange glances, the strings swell toward a reprise of their little duet to seal their secret bond. Now Scout walks into an extraordinary shot with Boo in the shadow standing next to the brightly lit photograph of Scout's mother

Figure 7.22
"Hey Boo"—queer encounter and recognition, with a sweet duet between solo violin and flute expressing a deeper attachment ("Boo Who?" cue 13A, measures 11–15).

on the mantelpiece, itself sitting above the shadow of her daughter's dark double (figure 7.23). The reprise of the duet ties them together: black and white, shadow and light, dead and living. As if cued by the mother chords, she comes alive in the friendly monster, now visible and demystified. Then, to the strains of the "Remember Mama" theme, Scout leads Boo to Jem's bed and invites him to "pet" her brother (figure 7.24). Reaching out to the sleeping boy, Boo does not touch Jem's head with his hand—only his shadow does, as if to show that the *unheimlich* monster from the Radley porch was already a *heimlich* mother. The "Remember Mama" theme has long prepared us for this moment, suggesting that the mother's ghost has always been behind the closeted monster: watching through the window when Scout was reading to her father; neatly folding Jem's pants the night he had left them by the fence after running from Boo's shadow; protecting the children from Ewell's assault. True, there are other occurrences of the "Remember Mama" theme associated with parental care: the lively one that accompanies Atticus taking the children along to Helen; the one with the shot of him putting Scout to bed that evening;[111] the one that accompanies Miss Maudie's attempt to console Jem after the jury's guilty verdict; even the one heard when Jem starts walking Scout home from the Thanksgiving pageant. But none of these amounts to the homecoming of the theme now, with Boo having come out of the shadows.

In Foote's screenplay, this scene had come *after* the conversation between Tate and Atticus about Boo's role in the death of Bob Ewell. But in the final version of the film, Mulligan switched the order to create

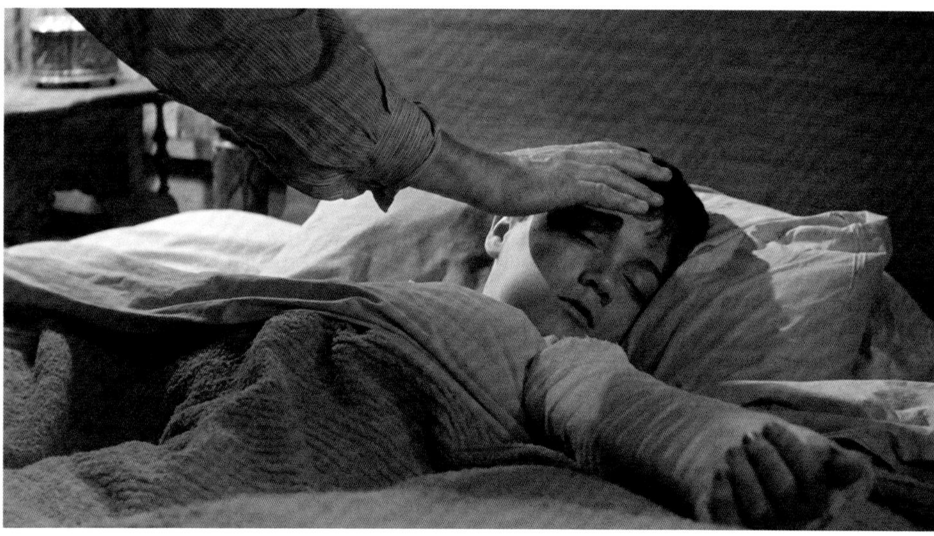

Figure 7.23 Boo and the Mother; Scout and her shadow.

Figure 7.24 The shadow of Boo's hand "touches" Jem's head.

a different sense of closure. Now Boo and Scout come out to the front porch, so that Scout can say that prosecuting Boo "would be sort of like shootin' a mockingbird," and Atticus can respond by embracing his daughter and walking over to Boo to shake his hand: "Thank you for my children, Arthur."

They are Boo's children, too.[112] The revised ending reimagines the Finch family by including Boo as a surrogate mother, seen and unseen. Mulligan divides the final sequence into three parts—moving from the Finch porch to the Radley porch and back to the Finch porch—unified by Bernstein's "End Title." The cue first recapitulates Boo's theme with its motherly physiognomy, now played by the piano, as Boo looks at Jem through his bedroom window—the very point of view of the penultimate

shot showing Scout on her father's lap (compare figures 7.8 and 7.25). The two shots of a father-daughter embrace appear to be tied to two shots of Boo looking, first visible and then invisible. Between those shots, Atticus will thank Boo for his children (accompanied by the mother chords); Scout will walk with Boo to the Radley place and stand with him on the porch until he enters his house (accompanied by an extended reprise of the "Remember Mama" theme from the main title sequence); and Scout will run back home to climb on Atticus's lap (accompanied by the nostalgic version of the theme from the main title sequence). Having seen Boo look through Jem's window while standing on the Finch porch, how would we know that he is later looking through that window from the point of view of an invisible ghost?

Figure 7.25 From the porch Boo looks at Jem through his bedroom window.

Consider Jean Louise's final voiceover, reproduced here from the screenplay with the lines later deleted for the film:

Neighbors bring food with death, and flowers with sickness, and little things in between. Boo was our neighbor. He gave us two soap dolls, a broken watch and chain,	*Scout walks with Boo to the Radley house where they stand on the porch*
a knife and our lives. One time Atticus said you never really knew a man until you stood in his shoes	*Boo enters the house*
and walked around in them. Just standing on the Radley porch was enough.	*Scout alone on the porch*

[. . .]

~~Well~~, the summer that had begun so long ago had ended, and another summer had taken its place, and a fall, and Boo Radley had come out and Jem was to live. I was to think	*Scout walks back home*
of these days many times, of Jem, and Dill and Boo Radley and Tom Robinson ~~and the Ewells~~	*Scout starts running*
and Atticus—~~his fairness, his stubbornness, his devotion, his courage, his love.~~	*Scout climbing on Atticus's lap*
[. . .]	
He would be in Jem's room all night and he would be there when Jem waked up in the morning.[113]	*camera pulls back from window*

The reprise of the "Remember Mama" theme imbues Jean Louise's closing voiceover with a sense of wistful gratitude for those "little things" in the cigar box and for the gift of life, no less. Her story has turned into the story of Boo Radley: saving his children, epitomizing the other, coming out. Although the middle paragraph was Foote's own, it reworked a sentence from an earlier chapter: "If Mr. Ewell was as forgotten as Tom Robinson, Tom Robinson was as forgotten as Boo Radley."[114] Jean Louise did not forget. As the story about racial injustice is framed by an allegory of the closet, the odd neighbor becomes the main bearer of its moral: that to know others, we need to walk around in their shoes.

As the acousmatic narrator of the film, the adult Jean Louise conjures the ghosts of her past: we never see her, we only see what she remembers, eventually through Boo's eyes. Their queerness converges in the last shot, where she seems to stand in his shoes on the Finch porch as a woman looking at her younger self. Might not her mature voice *sound* like that of her mother? Heard that way, the "Remember Mama" theme blends with that voice to tell the story of childhood. Mama remembered. The ending of Mulligan's film is not unlike that of Stevens's, which harks back to its opening, where Katrin reads the story of her mother, who looks out of the window and hears herself, in her daughter's voice, recount the weekly accounting ritual. Zooming out from the family scene, both films close by affirming the secure attachment between child and parent as the foundation of basic trust, while the returning title music reassures viewers that cinema is a trustworthy medium of reminiscence. Moreover, both films are parables of assimilation where ontological security is grounded in affective attachments that sustain the nexus of liberal economics and liberal politics. In *I Remember Mama*, Uncle Chris, dis-

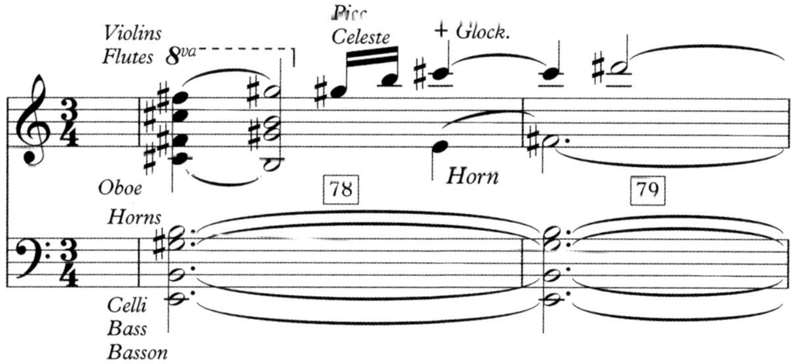

Figure 7.26 Sweet resolution to ninth and seventh at the end of "End Title."

paraged by Aunt Jenny as "black," ultimately fails the test of social and economic integration that Marta passes with, and for, her children. In *To Kill a Mockingbird*, the solution to racial conflict shifts from the economic problem of poverty to the need for accepting marginalized others.

If the racial conflict of *To Kill a Mockingbird* points to the problem of particularized trust in the 1930s, recalled during a time of rising social tensions over civil rights in the early 1960s, the film ends on a hopeful note by seeking to mend a rift manifest in the torn drawing of the mockingbird. After the camera retreats from Jem's window, Mulligan closes with a dissolve to a static shot of the Finch house from a higher angle, with the light from its rooms illuminating the night. As the closing shot lingers over "The End" and the production credits, Bernstein adds eight measures to replace what would have otherwise been a return of the unsettling version of the "Remember Mama" theme from the main title, whose tritone appoggiaturas in the accordion had become a recurring sonic signature of Boo Radley's unseen existence. But the "End Title" lands on a sustained E-major ninth chord, which leads the Lydian melody to a diatonic close that assures Scout/Jean Louise's secure attachments: strings resolving the ninth up to a tenth; horns "resolving" the tonic up to the ninth; piccolo, celeste, and glockenspiel finishing on the major seventh (see figure 7.26). Concluding the sentimental and nostalgic version of the "Remember Mama" theme one last time, the cadential dissonance is no longer disturbing. If this affecting music has secured the attachment of so many viewers to their memory of Atticus Finch, it might also have shaped unconsciously how they remembered him, through the eyes of a grown-up tomboy who had become the child of a queer neighbor. Having walked around in his shoes, the adult Scout had come to share his point of view, now ours: standing out on the porch, looking in from the dark.

Coda

In the first chapter of *The World Viewed*, Stanley Cavell writes that going to the movies created for him "hours and days of awe; momentous, but only for the moment; unrecapturable fully except in memory and evocation; gone."[1] This experience of cinema was of course shaped by the time Cavell came of age as a moviegoer. With films not yet available on VHS or DVD for repeated viewings and close analysis, much hinged on the first encounter in the movie theater. Hence Cavell's rhetoric is a little melodramatic, with the word "gone"—set apart by a semicolon—creating an emphatic sense of finality. Yet his sentence also harbors a paradox: cinematic experience may be gone but not lost. It can be fully recaptured "in memory and evocation."

Throughout this book I have sought to show how music can be evocative of cinematic experience. Since mnemonic powers are part of music's presence effects, cinematic memories called up by film music are not merely retrieved but can be relived. The main title music of a film can take us back to the movie theater just as, within the film, a song triggers the flashback of a character. What is more, when the main title theme is based on that very song, the viewer's recollection aligns with that of a character. Since music can belong both to the real and the represented world, it can create a mimetic—auratic—slippage between life and cinema. We can share Annie's experience of meeting Sam at the top of the Empire State Building at the end of *Sleepless in Seattle* because the main theme from her favorite movie, *An Affair to Remember*, replays in her head and ours.

One of the ongoing attractions of moving pictures has come from their ability to render a piece of reality as a slice of time. A central concern in this book has been to provide evidence for Bernard Stiegler's claim that the fixation of temporal objects through recording technologies created a major shift in cultural history—a shift that remains as pivotal and potent now as it was for listeners of the first recordings and viewers of the early films. Ever since, film music has been a principal point of reference for the way audiovisual media affect audiovisual memory.

As recording technology and playback devices have evolved rapidly in recent decades, audiovisual objects have become ubiquitous. Yet in the age of smartphones, many of the phenomena and concepts put forward in this book remain pertinent, even relevant, for understanding how music partakes in the storage, retrieval, and affect of visual memories. Although the digital age may have attenuated our sense of recordings as material objects, digital artifacts, changing resolutions, and the shaky footage of handheld devices evince a sense of thingness in the apparatus. Even with the most casual and contingent clip stored in the digital cloud, the tip of Bergson's memory cone still pierces the plane of the present to offer through sound and music a sense of life-giving "warmth."

In the spring of 2018, I ended my course "Listening to Movies" with a section called "beyond cinema." It included a screening of Asif Kapadia's 2015 *Amy*, which had won an Academy Award for Best Documentary Feature. Kapadia follows the life and early death of the British singer Amy Winehouse, drawing heavily on personal videos made by family, friends, and colleagues as well as interviews and concerts produced for public consumption. Some of the most powerful and disquieting moments of the film are song montages that juxtapose Winehouse's riveting performances (bootlegged or produced) with raw and random footage of her physical and mental problems. As I was putting the finishing touches on my monograph, I was struck by how *Amy* rehearsed and reimagined cinema's impact on audiovisual memory.

The use of preexisting clips turns *Amy* into a rememory service of sorts, but without the sanitized sentimentalism Omar Naïm chastised in *The Final Cut* or the magic conjuring cherished in Fellini's *Intervista*. Instead, the film is an unsettling account of how omnipresent recording devices mercilessly tracked Winehouse's meteoric rise to stardom and her simultaneous decline through a troubled relationship marred by excessive use of drugs and alcohol. Kapadia's unvarnished rememory is agonizing, intensifying Barthes's sense of a future anterior that relegates the moment of capture "inexorably to the past." Perhaps the most uncanny example comes during the closing credits, a collage of short clips from those personal videos: some of these clips, already in slow-motion, stop in a freeze-frame—as if to remind us that film is photography after all, and that even moving pictures cannot undo death.

Watching *Amy* creates a dizzying assemblage of double projections with viewers' recollections of Winehouse's live performances, television appearances, or recordings shared on YouTube—most starkly, perhaps, with her devastating song "Love Is a Losing Game." Kapadia creates a protagonist whose songs are painfully prescient, giving the singer an authentic sense of her fatal predicament, akin to the knowledge imparted in the synoptic review of panoramic memory. But here the film blurs the line between documentary and fiction, alluding not only to the melodrama of the unknown woman but also to that of the female musician whose body serves as a medium for the storage and transmission of childhood trauma, to be cured by cathartic abreactions in performance. Although Winehouse failed to deliver the cure for herself, her voice remains so evocative of the unrecapturable. Amid the flood of images that her songs now call up when I hear them, I trust her telling some truth.

Acknowledgments

Support for this book was provided by a Humboldt Research Fellowship, a Mellon New Directions Fellowship, and a Residential Fellowship at the Franke Institute of the Humanities at the University of Chicago. I am most grateful to James Chandler, director of the Franke Institute, whose encouragement and guidance throughout the main gestation of the manuscript were essential for its completion, and who suggested the University of Chicago Press as a publisher. I am deeply honored that Tom Gunning welcomed the book into his Cinema and Modernity series. Special thanks to Susan Bielstein, the acquiring editor of the series, for her wisdom and patience; to James Toftness, for providing logistical assistance; to Kevin Quach, for working on the figures and examples; to Joel Score, for meticulously copyediting the manuscript; and to Josh Rutner, who vetted a much longer earlier version and who created the index for the final one. Publication has been made possible with generous support from Martha Roth, former dean of the Humanities Division, and John Boyer, dean of the College at the University of Chicago.

This book was partly inspired by two monographs written by my esteemed late colleagues Alison Winter and Miriam Hansen. While Winter's *Memory: Fragments of a Modern History* (2012) offered a model for focusing on facets of memory in specific case studies, Hansen's *Cinema and Experience: Siegfried Kracauer, Walter Benjamin, and Theodor W. Adorno* (2013) provided the lasting critical impetus for my own historical imaginary. The Mellon New Directions Fellowship was instrumental in laying the groundwork for my research on film by funding practical training in film music, a year of academic coursework in cinema and media studies, and subsequent empirical research on audiovisual memory. Special thanks go to Ilya Levinson for suggesting that I enroll in a film-scoring course at Columbia College, and to Andy Hill, former music supervisor at Disney, for leading that course during the 2006 summer semester in Studio City, where he shared invaluable perspectives from inside the industry regarding the production of Hollywood film music. At Chicago, my colleagues James Lastra, Yuri Tsivian, and Miriam Hansen welcomed me into their graduate courses and research seminars, and I greatly benefited from collaborative research on the psychology of audiovisual memory with Howard Nusbaum and his postdoctoral researchers Stephen van Hedger and Shannon Heald.

Research assistance for this book was provided by Warren Sherk, Louise Hilton, and Kristine Krueger at the Margaret Herrick Library of the Academy; Ned Comstock at the Cinematic Arts Library Special Collections of the University of Southern California; Kristen Castellana at the Music Library of the University of Michigan; Jonny Davies at the British Film Institute; Mary K. Huelsbeck at the Wisconsin Center for Film and Theater Research; David K. Frasier and Zach Downey at the Lilly Library, Indiana University, Bloomington; James Wintle at the Music Division, Library of Congress; Michelle May and Julia Graham at the Special Collections at the University of California, Los Angeles; Eduard Strauss at the Wiener Institut für Strauss-Forschung; Stan Howell at the Chicago Public Library; Scott Landvatter and Nancy Spiegel at the University of Chicago Library; Julia Gibbs at the University of Chicago's Film Studies Center; and the Musikarchiv der Akademie der Künste, Berlin.

I am immensely indebted to numerous colleagues and friends who have kept the project moving forward by allowing me try out ideas in seminars, offering opportunities to present portions of the book for feedback in workshops and lectures, and providing assistance, large and small, direct and indirect, emotional and intellectual: Gillian Anderson, Jason Beaster-Jones, Aaronson Bell, Robert Bird, Seth Brodsky, James Buhler, Matti Bunzl, Todd Decker, Martha Feldman, Caryl Flinn, Maria Fuchs, Doron Galili, Michael Gallope, Peter Gillette, Daniel Goldmark, Marcus Gräser, Roger Hillman, Gerhard Höckner, Rembert Hüser, Thomas Irvine, Travis Jackson, Maria Kaoutzani, Sarah Keller, Lawrence Kramer, Richard Kurth, Robert Kendrick, David Neumeyer, Sherry Lee, Trent Leipert, Michael Long, Sandy Lu, Richard Leppert, Martin Miller Marks, Arnulf Christian Mattes, Steven McClatchie, Marilynn Miller, Ryan Minor, Daniel Morgan, Mitchell Morris, Scott Murphy, Nathan Platte, Tobias Plebuch, Andrew Poulos, Tobias Pontara, Don Randel, Art Reblitz, Eric Rentschler, William Rosar, Benjamin Ruder, Robert Ryder, Martin Scherzinger, Jordan Schonig, Martha Sprigge, Jürg Stenzl, Robynn Stilwell, Ursula Storch, Sui-Lan Tan, Marta Tonegutti, Tim Trager, Claudio Vellutini, Neil Verma, Holly Watkins, Ståle Wikshåland, Amy Wlodarski, and Lawrence Zbikowski. A special thanks goes to the Reading Group of doctoral students who have been brilliant interlocutors over the past few years: Liz Hopkins, Chaz Lee, Zach Loeffler, Brad Spiers, Dan Wang, Lindsay Wright, and Tien Tien Zhang. Our Pasta & Pictures gatherings have been the highlights of academic sociality.

Last but not least, I am profoundly grateful to my wife Eva, my daughter Julia, and my son Markus for their unwavering support, encouragement, and love throughout this seemingly never-ending undertaking. You made it all worthwhile.

Notes

INTRODUCTION

1 Bernard Stiegler, *Technics and Time* (Stanford, CA: Stanford University Press, 1998), 3:16.

2 James Buhler, "Ontological, Formal, and Critical Theories of Film Music and Sound," in *The Oxford Handbook of Film Music Studies*, ed. David Neumeyer (Oxford: Oxford University Press, 2014), 188.

3 See Claudia Gorbman, *Unheard Melodies: Narrative Film Music* (Bloomington: Indiana University Press, 1987); Michel Chion, *Film: A Sound Art*, trans. Claudia Gorbman (New York: Columbia University Press, 2009); David Neumeyer and James Buhler, *Meaning and Interpretation of Music in Cinema* (Bloomington: Indiana University Press, 2015); Ben Winters, *Music, Performance, and the Realities of Film: Shared Concert Experiences in Screen Fiction* (New York: Routledge, 2014); Guido Heldt, *Music and Levels of Narration in Film: Steps across the Border* (Bristol: Intellect, 2013); Kevin J. Donnelly, *Occult Aesthetics: Synchronization in Sound Film* (New York, Oxford University Press, 2014); Kathryn Marie Kalinak, *Sound: Dialogue, Music, and Effects* (New Brunswick, NJ: Rutgers University Press, 2015); Giorgio Biancorosso, *Situated Listening: The Sound of Absorption in Classical Cinema* (New York: Oxford University Press, 2016).

4 Recent examples include Heather Laing, *The Gendered Score: Music in 1940s Melodrama and the Woman's Film* (Aldershot: Ashgate, 2007); Michael Long, *Beautiful Monsters: Imagining the Classic in Musical Media* (Berkeley: University of California Press, 2008); Jürg Stenzl, *Jean-Luc Godard—Musicien: Die Musik in Den Filmen von Jean-Luc Godard* (Munich: Edition Text + Kritik, 2010); Todd Decker, *Music Makes Me: Fred Astaire and Jazz* (Berkeley: University of California Press, 2011); Peter Franklin, *Seeing through Music: Gender and Modernism in Classic Hollywood Film Scores* (Oxford: Oxford University Press, 2011); Katherine Spring, *Saying It with Songs: Popular Music and the Coming of Sound to Hollywood Cinema* (Oxford: Oxford University Press, 2013); Arved Ashby, *Popular Music and the New Auteur: Visionary Filmmakers after MTV* (New York: Oxford University Press, 2013); Michael Slowik, *After the Silents: Hollywood Film Music in the Early Sound Era, 1926–1934* (New York: Columbia University Press, 2014); Richard Leppert, *Aesthetic Technologies of Modernity, Subjectivity, and Nature: Opera, Orchestra, Phonograph, Film* (Berkeley: University of California Press, 2015); Michael Dwyer, *Back to the Fifties: Nostalgia, Hollywood Film, and Popular Music of the Seventies and Eighties* (New York: Oxford University Press, 2015).

5 See Maureen Turim's pathbreaking study *Flashbacks in Film: Memory and History* (New York: Routledge, 1989).

6 Peter Burke, *What Is Cultural History?* (Cambridge: Polity Press, 2008), 79;

Susannah Radstone and Katharine Hodgkin, "Regimes of Memory," in *Memory Cultures: Memory, Subjectivity, and Recognition* (New Brunswick, NJ: Transaction, 2006), 1–22.

7 Walter Benjamin, *Gesammelte Schriften*, ed. Rolf Tiedemann and Hermann Schweppenhäuser (Frankfurt: Suhrkamp, 1987), 2:1064; translation from Miriam Bratu Hansen, "Benjamin's Aura," *Critical Inquiry* 34, no. 2 (2008): 348; see also Miriam Hansen, *Cinema and Experience: Siegfried Kracauer, Walter Benjamin, and Theodor W. Adorno* (Berkeley: University of California Press, 2012): 111–12.

8 Walter Benjamin, "Little History of Photography," in *Selected Writings*, ed. Michael W. Jennings (Cambridge, MA: Belknap, 1996–2006), 2:511–12. See Hansen, *Cinema and Experience*, 155–62.

9 Hansen, *Cinema and Experience*, 156.

10 Benjamin, *Selected Writings*, 4:265.

11 Robert G. Ryder, "Walter Benjamin's Shell-Shock: Sounding the Acoustical Unconscious," *New Review of Film and Television Studies* 5, no. 2 (2007): 135–55. See also Veit Erlmann, "Acoustic Space: Marshall McLuhan Defended against Himself," *Senses and Society* 11, no. 1 (2016): 42; Julie Beth Napolin, "The Fact of Resonance: An Acoustics of Determination in Faulkner and Benjamin," *symplokē* 24, nos. 1–2 (2016): 178–82.

12 Michel Chion, *Audio-Vision: Sound on Screen*, trans. Claudia Gorbman (New York: Columbia University Press, 1994), 63–64.

13 See James Buhler, "Psychoanalysis, Apparatus Theory, and Subjectivity," in Neumeyer, *Oxford Handbook of Film Music Studies*, 385–92, drawing on Jean Louis Baudry and Jean-Louis Comolli.

14 See the first chapter, "Inscriptions and Simulations: The Imagination of Technology," in James Lastra, *Sound Technology and the American Cinema: Perception, Representation, Modernity* (New York: Columbia University Press, 2000), 5–15; Mary Ann Doane, "The Voice in the Cinema: The Articulation of Body and Space," *Yale French Studies* 60 (1980): 35.

15 The juxtaposition in figure 0.2 is illustrated here with the fourth still, which is taken from the same position as the shot in which the woman opens her eyes. There is already a hint of animation through the transition from the fifth to the sixth still in that it appears as if the woman opens her mouth.

16 Roland Barthes, *Camera Lucida: Reflections on Photography* (New York: Hill and Wang, 1981), 79; see also 94–96.

17 For a close reading of *12 Monkeys*, see Julie McQuinn, "Strange Recognitions and Endless Loops: Music, Media, and Memory in Terry Gilliam's *12 Monkeys*," in *The Oxford Handbook of Film Music Studies*, ed. David Neumeyer (Oxford: Oxford University Press, 2014), 445–67, esp. 458–62.

18 Barthes, *Camera Lucida*, 79.

19 Slavoj Žižek, "'I Hear You with My Eyes'; or, the Invisible Master," in *Gaze and Voice as Love Objects*, ed. Renata Salecl and Slavoj Žižek (Durham, NC: Duke University Press, 1996), 94. See Buhler, "Psychoanalysis, Apparatus Theory, and Subjectivity," 405.

20 Hansen, *Cinema and Experience*, 195 (emphasis in original).

21 See Chion, *Film: A Sound Art*, 266–74. See also Wolfgang Ernst, *Im Medium*

erklingt die Zeit: Technologische Tempor(e)alitäten und das Sonische als ihre privilegierte Erkenntnisform (Berlin: Kulturverlag Kadmos, 2015).

CHAPTER ONE

1 Klaus Theweleit, "Three Steps aus 31 Jahren mit Miles," in "In a Silent Way: Miles Davis," special issue of *Du: die Zeitschrift der Kultur* 49, no. 8 (1989): 82–83.

2 Quoted in Friedrich Kittler, *Gramophone, Film, Typewriter*, trans. Geoffrey Winthrop-Young and Michael Wutz (1986; Stanford, CA: Stanford University Press, 1999), 30–31.

3 William Howland Kenney, *Recorded Music in American Life: The Phonograph and Popular Memory, 1890–1945* (Oxford: Oxford University Press, 1999), 5.

4 Kenney, *Recorded Music in American Life*, 8. A little over 2,600 responses are held at the University of Michigan School of Music Library.

5 Kenney, *Recorded Music in American Life*, 6.

6 Giuseppe Tornatore, *La leggenda del pianista sull'oceano* (Milan: Leonardo International, 1999); Alessandro Baricco, *Novecento: un monologo* (Milan: Feltrinelli, 1994).

7 Tornatore, *La leggenda*, 21.

8 Walter Benjamin, *Gesammelte Schriften*, ed. Rolf Tiedemann and Hermann Schweppenhäuser (Frankfurt: Suhrkamp, 1987), 2:1064; translation from Miriam Bratu Hansen, "Benjamin's Aura," *Critical Inquiry* 34, no. 2 (2008): 348; see also Miriam Hansen, *Cinema and Experience: Siegfried Kracauer, Walter Benjamin, and Theodor W. Adorno* (Berkeley: University of California Press, 2012): 111–12.

9 "Produce un suono che, in un sorriso, Novecento, sembra aver riconosciuto." Tornatore, *La Leggenda*, 45. In the longer version of *The Legend of 1900*—issued on Bluray—this transition is less direct because of an intervening scene in which the police search for Novecento to take him off the ship. Unless otherwise noted, English translations are drawn from the DVD release of the film.

10 Edith Lang and George West, *Musical Accompaniment of Moving Pictures* (New York: Arno Press, 1920), 5.

11 Tornatore, *La Leggenda*, 70.

12 Tornatore, *La Leggenda*, 83–85 (translation by Claudio Vellutini).

13 See Michael V. Pisani, *Music for the Melodramatic Theatre in Nineteenth-Century London and New York* (Iowa City: University of Iowa Press, 2014). The original soundtrack issued by Sony (SK 60790 37-060790-10), published in Italy, actually has *five* portraits, inserting a bluesy refrain between and after the five pieces. These refrains and the last portrait (with its more advanced chromaticism) may not have been used in the film in order to keep the musical characterizations stylistically more unified in line with the romantic character piece.

14 Tornatore, *La Leggenda*, 99 (translation by Claudio Vellutini).

15 Tornatore, *La Leggenda*, 107: "sue musiche più sincere." In the English version of the film, Max calls it Novecento's most "passionate music."

16 Tornatore, *La Leggenda*, 108–9 (translation by Claudio Vellutini). While the DVD chapter is called "Recorded with Love," the piece itself is called "Playing Love" on the soundtrack.

17 Walter Benjamin and Michael W. Jennings, "The Work of Art in the Age of Its Technological Reproducibility [First Version]," *Grey Room*, no. 39 (2010), 13. In the second and third version the last two sentences read, "*Around 1900, technological reproduction not only had reached a standard that permitted it to reproduce all known works of art, profoundly modifying their effect, but it also had captured a place of its own among the artistic processes. In gauging this standard, we would do well to study the impact which its two different manifestations—the reproduction of artworks and the art of film—are having on art in its traditional form.*" In the third version the whole passage comes at the end of the first section and the last sentence is not italicized. See *Walter Benjamin: Selected Writings*, ed. Michael W. Jennings (Cambridge, MA: Belknap, 1996–2006), 3:102, 4:253.

18 Benjamin, *Selected Writings*, 2:103.

19 Robynn J. Stilwell, "The Fantastical Gap between Diegetic and Non-Diegetic," in *Beyond the Soundtrack: Representing Music in Cinema*, ed. Daniel Goldmark, Lawrence Kramer, and Richard D. Leppert (Berkeley: University of California Press, 2007), 186.

20 For a detailed account of *Dangerous Moonlight*, see Heather Laing, *The Gendered Score: Music in 1940s Melodrama and the Woman's Film* (Aldershot: Ashgate, 2007), 147–78.

21 Miriam Bratu Hansen, *Cinema and Experience: Siegfried Kracauer, Walter Benjamin, and Theodor W. Adorno* (Berkeley: University of California Press, 2012), 107, quoting Benjamin, "Little History of Photography," in *Selected Writings*, 2:510, including modifications by Hansen.

22 Hansen, *Cinema and Experience*, 107.

23 Roland Barthes, *Camera Lucida: Reflections on Photography* (New York: Hill and Wang, 1981), 96.

24 "Will you remember the day?" Amazon review of *Maytime* (VHS) by Rick D. Barszcz, September 19, 2002, accessed February 10, 2016, https://www.amazon.com/review/RRMS4LNMI2R53.

25 "Wonerbar!" Amazon review of *The Producers* by Rick D. Barszcz, January 2, 2007, accessed December 22, 2018, https://www.amazon.com/gp/customer-reviews/R3UZBYFY4RH12J.

26 Svetlana Boym, *The Future of Nostalgia* (New York: Basic Books, 2001), xviii, 41–48; Annette Kuhn, *Dreaming of Fred and Ginger: Cinema and Cultural Memory* (New York: New York University Press, 2002), chap. 8, "All My Life and Beyond . . ."

27 Kuhn, *Dreaming of Fred and Ginger*, 211.

28 Bill Brown, "Thing Theory," *Critical Inquiry* 28, no. 1 (2001): 4.

29 Jean Epstein, "On Certain Characteristics of Photogénie," in Epstein, *Critical Essays and New Translations*, ed. Sarah Keller and Jason N. Paul (Amsterdam: Amsterdam University Press, 2012), 295.

30 Allan Megill, Steven Shepard, and Phillip Honenberger, *Historical Knowledge, Historical Error: A Contemporary Guide to Practice* (Chicago: University of Chicago Press, 2007), 25. The distinction goes back to Johann Gustav Droysen but was formulated by Ernst Bernheim, who in *Einleitung in die*

Geschichtswissenschaft (Leipzig: Göschen, 1905), 79–80, compares "reports" against *Überreste* (remains, remnants, residues).

31 Benjamin, "Little History of Photography," in *Selected Writings*, 2:510–12.

32 Henri Bergson, *Matter and Memory*, trans. Nancy Margaret Paul and W. Scott Palmer (New York: Macmillan, 1911), 92.

33 Bergson, *Matter and Memory*, 197 (emphasis in original).

34 Brown, "Thing Theory," 5.

35 See Elodie A. Roy, *Media, Materiality and Memory: Grounding the Groove* (Farnham: Ashgate, 2015), 13–27. 181–92.

36 Theodor W. Adorno, *Essays on Music*, ed. Richard Leppert, trans. Susan H. Gillespie (Berkeley: University of California Press, 2002), 445.

37 Theodor W. Adorno, "The Form of the Phonograph Record," trans. Thomas Y. Levin, *October*, no. 55 (1990), 57; Adorno, "The Curves of the Needle," trans. Thomas Y. Levin, *October*, no. 55 (1990), 54

38 See Neil Verma, *Theater of the Mind: Imagination, Aesthetics, and American Radio Drama* (Chicago: University of Chicago Press, 2012).

39 Rick Altman, *The American Film Musical* (Bloomington: Indiana University Press, 1987), 62, 74.

CHAPTER TWO

1 Bernard Stiegler, *Technics and Time* (Stanford, CA: Stanford University Press, 1998), 3:16.

2 Bernard Stiegler, "Time of Cinema," trans. G. Collins, *Tekhnema* 4 (1998): 106.

3 Stiegler, *Technics and Time*, 3:11, 16.

4 Stiegler, *Technics and Time*, 2:4.

5 Stiegler, *Technics and Time*, 2: 232–33, quoting Husserl: "Memory is the re-presentation of something itself in the sense of the past. The present memory is a phenomenon wholly analogous to perception. It has the appearance of the object in common with the corresponding perception, except that the appearance has a modified character, in consequence of which the object does not stand before me as present but has having been present." See Edmund Husserl, *On the Phenomenology of the Consciousness of Internal Time (1893–1917)* (Dordrecht: Kluwer Academic Publishers, 1991), 61.

6 Stiegler, *Technics and Time*, 3:27.

7 Stiegler, *Technics and Time*, 3:28.

8 Stiegler, *Technics and Time*, 3:19–20.

9 Stiegler, *Technics and Time*, 2:10–11.

10 Garrett Stewart, *Framed Time: Toward a Postfilmic Cinema* (Chicago: University of Chicago Press, 2007), 190.

11 Stiegler, *Technics and Time*, 2:4 (see also1:17, where Stiegler speaks of "inorganic organized beings" that have their "own dynamic when compared with that of either physical or biological beings"). See Ulrik Ekman, "Of Transductive Speed—Stiegler," *Parallax* 13, no. 4 (2007): 52.

12 Mark B. N. Hansen, *New Philosophy for New Media* (Cambridge, MA: MIT Press, 2004), 255.

13 Stiegler, *Technics and Time*, 2:100.

14 Stiegler, *Technics and Time*, 2:229.

15 Stiegler, *Technics and Time*, 2:229, citing Husserl, *On the Phenomenology of the Consciousness of Internal Time*, 45.

16 *The Final Cut*, directed by Omar Naïm (2004; Santa Monica, CA: Lions Gate Entertainment, 2005), DVD.

17 Stiegler, *Technics and Time*, 2:230, citing Paul Ricoeur, *Temps et Récit* (Paris: Seuil, 1983–1985), 3:55; cf. *Time and Narrative*, trans. Kathleen McLaughlin and David Pellauer (Chicago: University of Chicago Press, 1984–1988), 3:34–35 (emphasis added).

18 Stiegler, *Technics and Time*, 3:12, 13.

19 Ben Roberts, "Cinema as Mnemotechnics," *Angelaki: Journal of the Theoretical Humanities* 11, no. 1 (2006): 59.

20 Stiegler, *Technics and Time*, 3:20–21.

21 Merriam Webster Online Dictionary, accessed October 22, 2018, https://www.merriam-webster.com/dictionary/hackwork.

22 This is part of the conversation with the anti-implant activist Fletcher about obtaining Bannister's implant. Strikingly, the music enters at the very moment Hakman explains the ancient tradition.

23 One could hear this music as belonging to a long sound advance that begins with Hakman's look at his bloody hand, continues during Fletcher's POV shot (arguably Fletcher's own recollection when looking at Hakman's implant video), and then appears to have been "scored" by Hakman when looking at his own implant and "hearing" music along with it.

24 Stiegler, *Technics and Time*, 3:28.

25 Stiegler, *Technics and Time*, 3:28.

26 Walter Benjamin, *Gesammelte Schriften*, ed. Rolf Tiedemann and Hermann Schweppenhäuser (Frankfurt am Main: Suhrkamp, 1989), 2:1064, translated in Miriam Bratu Hansen, "Benjamin's Aura," *Critical Inquiry* 34, no. 2 (2008): 348; see also Miriam Hansen, *Cinema and Experience: Siegfried Kracauer, Walter Benjamin, and Theodor W. Adorno* (Berkeley: University of California Press, 2012): 111–12.

27 Stiegler, *Technics and Time*, 3:12.

28 James Chandler, "The Affection-Image and the Movement-Image," in *Afterimages of Gilles Deleuze's Film Philosophy*, ed. David Norman Rodowick (Minneapolis: University of Minnesota Press, 2009), 236–38. See also James Chandler, *An Archaeology of Sympathy: The Sentimental Mode in Literature and Cinema* (Chicago: University of Chicago Press, 2013): 119–28.

29 Chandler, "Affection-Image," 236.

30 Stiegler, *Technics and Time*, 3:23, quoting Roland Barthes, *Camera Lucida: Reflections on Photography* (New York: Hill and Wang, 1981), 96 (emphasis added).

31 Stiegler, *Technics and Time*, 3:23.

32 Stiegler, *Technics and Time*, 3:23. See also *Technics and Time*, 2:21, where Stiegler has already discussed this scene: "Seeing her past self, in the present—in this present in which she says to herself: 'I passed'; where she re-sees a past present, a present in the past, she sees the present passing, in the present and ineluctably."

33 Translation by Claudio Vellutini. See also scene 69, entitled "Casa di Anita,"

in the Block Notes for *Intervista*, Lilly Library, University of Indiana, Bloomington, Fellini Manuscript Collection.

34 Cristina Degli-Esposti, "Federico Fellini's Intervista or the Neo-Baroque Creativity of the Analysand on Screen," *Italica* 73, no. 2 (Summer 1996): 163.

35 Stiegler, *Technics and Time*, 3:23.

36 See Peter Bondanella, *The Films of Federico Fellini* (Cambridge: Cambridge University Press, 2002), 159: "In an important BBC documentary on his entire career, Fellini employed not the image of the *Deus artifex* but a more mundane one, describing his profession as 'precisely a total, cynical vocation of puppet master.'" See also *Fellini on Fellini*, trans. Isable Quigley (New York: Da Capo, 1976), 146, where Fellini speaks of "the besotted selfishness of a puppet-master in relation to his puppets."

37 Stiegler, *Technics and Time*, 3:8. Stiegler's first subheading is, "Desire for Stories/Stories of Desire."

38 Stiegler, *Technics and Time*, 3:24. See also *Technics and Time*, 2:23.

CHAPTER THREE

1 George W. Beynon, *Musical Presentation of Motion Pictures* (New York: G. Schirmer, 1921), 32–33.

2 Frank Edson, "A Moving Picture Score by Victor Herbert," *Metronome* 32, no. 6 (1916): 16; Julia Bess Hubbert, *Celluloid Symphonies: Texts and Contexts in Film Music History* (Berkeley: University of California Press, 2011), 15. Herbert's complaint was first reported in "Herbert Composes Setting for Film: Writes Original Score to Accompany Showing of 'Fall of a Nation,'" *Musical America* 24, no. 2 (1916): 43.

3 Gilles Deleuze and Félix Guattari, *A Thousand Plateaus: Capitalism and Schizophrenia*, trans. Brian Massumi (Minneapolis: University of Minnesota Press, 1987): 348.

4 Andrew P. Yonelinas, "The Nature of Recollection and Familiarity: A Review of 30 Years of Research," *Journal of Memory & Language* 46 (2002): 441–517.

5 Michel Chion, *Audio-Vision: Sound on Screen*, trans. Claudia Gorbman (New York: Columbia University Press, 1994), 21–22; on "synchresis," see 63–64.

6 Deleuze and Guattari, *A Thousand Plateaus*, 348.

7 Rick Altman, *Silent Film Sound* (New York: Columbia University Press, 2004), 318.

8 Hans Erdmann, *Allgemeines Handbuch Der Film-Musik, von Hans Erdmann und Giuseppe Becce, Unter Mitarbeit von Ludwig Brav* (Berlin-Lichterfelde, Leipzig: Schlesinger, 1927). For a thorough study of the *Allgemeines Handbuch*, see Maria Fuchs, *Stummfilmmusik: Theorie und Praxis im Allgemeinen Handbuch der Film-Musik' (1927)* (Marburg: Schüren, 2017).

9 Erdmann, *Allgemeines Handbuch Der Film-Musik*, 1:59.

10 Erdmann, *Allgemeines Handbuch*, 1:4.

11 Scott Simmon et al., *More Treasures from American Film Archives, 1894–1931: 50 Films* (United States: Image Entertainment, 2004).

12 Martin Miller Marks, *More Treasures from American Film Archives 1894–1931* (booklet), 147–48.

13 Peter C. Lutze, *Alexander Kluge: The Last Modernist* (Detroit, MI: Wayne State University Press, 1998).

14 "Interview von Ulrich Gregor" (1976), in Alexander Kluge, *In Gefahr und grösster Not bringt der Mittelweg den Tod: Texte zu Kino, Film, Politik*, ed. Christian Schulte (Berlin: Vorwerk 8, 1999), 227.

15 Alexander Kluge, "On Film and the Public Sphere," *New German Critique* 24, no. 25 (1981–1982): 209.

16 Kluge, "Die realistische Methode und das sogenannte 'Filmische,'" in *In Gefahr und grösster Not*, 121.

17 Miriam Bratu Hansen, "Introduction to Adorno, 'Transparencies on Film' (1966)," *New German Critique*, nos. 24–25 (1981–1982): 197 (emphasis added).

18 Miriam Bratu Hansen, "Alexander Kluge, Cinema and the Public Sphere: The Construction Site of Counter-History," *Discourse* 6 (1983): 60.

19 Miriam Bratu Hansen, "Cooperative Auteur Cinema and Oppositional Public Sphere: Alexander Kluge's Contribution to *Germany in Autumn*," in *Alexander Kluge Raw Materials for the Imagination*, ed. Tara Forrest (Amsterdam: Amsterdam University Press, 2011), 52 and 62–63.

20 Caryl Flinn, *The New German Cinema: Music, History, and the Matter of Style*, (Berkeley: University of California Press, 2004), 107–37; Roger Hillman, *Unsettling Scores: German Film, Music, and Ideology* (Indianapolis: Indiana University Press, 2005), 89–109.

21 Alexander Kluge, *Die Patriotin: Texte, Bilder 1–6* (Frankfurt am Main: Zweitausendeins, 1980), 50 (emphasis added).

22 Hillman, *Unsettling Scores*, 98–99. Special thanks to Eric Rentschler for making a copy of this film available to me.

23 See Robert Hughes, *Film Book 2: Films of Peace and War* (New York: Grove Press, 1962), 154, 189.

24 Albrecht Dümling, "Eisler's Music for Resnais' 'Night and Fog' (1955): A Musical Counterpoint to the Cinematic Portrayal of Terror," *Historical Journal of Film, Radio and Television* 18, no. 4 (1998): 579-80. See also Amy Lynn Wlodarski, "Excavating Eisler: Relocating the Memorial Voice in Nuit Et Brouillard," in *Kompositionen Für Den Film: Zu Theorie Und Praxis Von Hanns Eislers Filmmusik*, ed. Peter Schweinhardt (Wiesbaden: Breitkopf & Härtel, 2008), 163–84, and an expanded version in Amy Lynn Wlodarski, *Musical Witness and Holocaust Representation* (Cambridge: Cambridge University Press, 2015), 57–91.

25 Manfred Wekwerth, "Musikalische Merkwürdigkeiten auf dem Theater," *Musik und Gesellschaft* 8, no. 6 (1958): 38.

26 In Eisler's autograph housed in the Archive of the Akademie der Künste, Berlin, this part of the prelude is written on 24-staff paper (unlike the remainder of the score, which is written on French 20-staff paper made by Durand). This suggests that Eisler might have added the music later or chose it as his point of departure. Strikingly, he eventually decided to frame the film with the prelude, by bringing back the entire number (with slight modifications) for Cayrol's closing reflections, merely adding the remaining section on French paper at the end. For the final number of *Night and Fog*, Eisler originally planned a composite of the first part of the prelude, followed by the first measures (1–18) of the second number, followed

by the second part of the prelude. In the final version of film, this insert is omitted, such that we hear a version quite close to the original prelude of *Winterschlacht*. See Hanns Eisler, *Filmmusik Zu Nuit Et Brouillard*, ed. Knud Breyer and Oliver Dahin (Wiesbaden: Breitkopf & Härtel, 2014), xxxiv.

27 See Manfred Grabs, "Über Berührungspunkte Zwischen Der Vokal- Und Instrumentalmusik Hanns Eislers," *Arbeitshefte der Akademie der Künste der Deutschen Demokratischen Republik* 19 (1974): 124–28; *Hanns Eisler: Lieder für eine Singstimme und Klavier* (Leipzig: VEB 1976), 188–89, 258–59.

28 Alain Resnais, "Für Hanns Eisler" (Alain Resnais in Conversation with Edouard Pfrimmer), in *Sinn und Form: Beiträge zur Literatur—Sonderheft Hanns Eisler*, 373 (Berlin: Rütten & Loening, 1964); translation (modified) from Sylvie Lindeperg, *Night and Fog: A Film in History*, trans. Tom Mes (Minneapolis: University of Minnesota Press, 2014), 131.

29 Johannes Robert Becher, *Winterschlacht (Schlacht Um Moskau). Ein Deutsche Tragödie in Fünf Akten Mit Einem Vorspiel* (Berlin: Aufbau-Verlag, 1961), 7.

30 Peter Schweinhardt and Johannes C. Gall, "Composing for Film: Hanns Eisler's Lifelong Film Music Project," in *The Oxford Handbook of Film Music Studies*, ed. David Neumeyer (Oxford: Oxford University Press, 2014), 157–58. Grabs surmises that Eisler may not have adapted Shakespeare's text to the music from *Night and Fog* until early 1956. A detail that speaks for the composition of the song after *Night and Fog* is that the distinct incipit is in half notes (as it is in the film score) and not in quarter notes (as it is in *Winterschlacht*).

31 Kluge's script remains deliberately indefinite: "It is either the time of the Seven Years' War or during the Wars of Liberation, but now we see an anti-aircraft cannon of 1943." Kluge, *Die Patriotin*, 51.

32 Eric Rentschler, "Remembering Not to Forget: A Retrospective Reading of Kluge's Brutality in Stone," *New German Critique* 49, no. 1 (1990): 39. See also Anton Kaes, "In Search of Germany: Alexander Kluge's *The Patriot*," in *From Hitler to Heimat: The Return of History as Film* (Cambridge, MA: Harvard University Press, 1989), 105–36.

33 Thomas Elsaesser, "New German Cinema and History: The Case of Alexander Kluge," in *The German Cinema Book*, ed. Tim Bergfelder, Erica Carter, and Deniz Göktürk (London: British Film Institute, 2002), 189.

34 Elsaesser, "New German Cinema and History," 184–85.

35 Letter from the West German Embassy cited in Richard Raskin, Sacha Vierny, and Alain Resnais, *Nuit et Brouillard by Alain Resnais: On the Making, Reception and Functions of a Major Documentary Film* (Aarhus: Aarhus University Press, 1987), 35; see Wlodarski, *Musical Witness*, 86. See also Ewout van der Knaap, *Uncovering the Holocaust: The International Reception of Night and Fog* (London: Wallflower Press, 2006), 49–54.

36 Elsaesser, "New German Cinema and History," 185.

37 This portion of the *Winterschlacht* prelude extends nineteen measures beyond the first seventeen measures Kluge used for the opening credits, until after the downbeat of measure 36, which is six measures beyond the twenty-nine measures Eisler reused for the opening credits of *Night and Fog*, but stops short of the full version recycled for the ending of the film. With the start of his voiceover, Kluge adjusts the volume in measure 17, making the internal reprise of the prelude very explicit.

38 Kluge, *Die Patriotin*, 154.

39 Hillman, *Unsettling Scores*, 100.

40 Daniel Morgan, "The Afterlife of Superimposition," in *Opening Bazin Postwar Film Theory and Its Afterlife*, ed. Dudley Andrew and Herve Joubert-Laurencin (Oxford: Oxford University Press, 2011), 133.

41 Daniel Morgan, *Late Godard and the Possibilities of Cinema* (Berkeley: University of California Press, 2013), 180.

42 Morgan, *Late Godard*, 180–81. See also Céline Scemama, "Jean-Luc Godard's *Histoire(s) du cinéma* Brings the Dead Back to the Screen," in *The Legacies of Jean-Luc Godard*, ed. Douglas Morrey, Christina Stojanova, and Nicole Côté (Waterloo, Ontario: Wilfrid Laurier University Press, 2013), 99–124; Michael Temple, "Elizabeth Taylor at Auschwitz: JLG and the Real Object of Montage," in *The Cinema Alone: Essays on the Work of Jean-Luc Godard 1985–2000* (Amsterdam: Amsterdam University Press, 2000), 51–60; and James S. Williams, *Encounters with Godard: Ethics, Aesthetics, Politics* (Albany: State University of New York Press, 2016), 72–81. For the complete soundtrack and script, see Jean-Luc Godard et al., *Histoire(s) du cinéma* (Munich: ECM, 1999); a list of visual, textual, and musical sources is given in Céline Scemama, *Histoire(s) du cinéma de Jean-Luc Godard: La force faible d'un art* (Paris: Harmattan, 2006). For a wide-ranging account of Godard's use of music, see Jürg Stenzl, *Jean-Luc Godard—Musicien: Die Musik in den Filmen von Jean-Luc Godard* (Munich: Edition Text + Kritik, 2010).

43 Morgan, *Late Godard*, 182.

44 Quoted in Morgan, *Late Godard*, 182.

45 Morgan, *Late Godard*, 232; Christopher Pavsek, *The Utopia of Film: Cinema and Its Futures in Godard, Kluge, and Tahimik* (New York: Columbia University Press, 2013), 39. The poem was the first published in the March 1918 issue of *Nord-Sud: Révue littéraire*: "L'image est une création pure de l'esprit. /Elle ne peut naître d'une comparaison mais du rapprochement de deux réalités plus ou moins éloignées. Plus les rapports des deux réalités rapprochées seront lointains et justes, plus l'image sera forte—plus elle aura de puissance émotive et de réalité poétique."

46 Jacques Rancière, *Film Fables*, trans. Emiliano Battista (Oxford: Berg, 2006), 18; Scemama, "Jean-Luc Godard's *Histoire(s) du cinéma*," 102.

47 Williams, *Encounters with Godard*, 136; see also 78.

48 "Ce qui est grand ce n'est pas l'image—mais l'émotion qu'elle provoque; si cette dernière est grande on estimera l'image à sa mesure. L'émotion ainsi provoquée est pure, poétiquement, parce qu'elle est née en dehors de toute imitation, de toute évocation, de toute comparaison." *Nord-Sud: Révue littéraire*, March 1918. See Williams, *Encounters with Godard*, 144.

49 Quoted in Richard Neer, "Godard Counts," *Critical Inquiry* 34, no. 1 (2007): 140–41 (emphasis in original).

50 Neer, "Godard Counts," 149.

51 Pavsek, *Utopia of Film*, 166–67.

52 The Swiss psychoanalyst Carl Gustav Jung famously defined "synchronicity" as "sinngemäße Koinzidenz," which is often translated as "*meaningful* coincidence," but *sinnvoll* (meaningful) is not the same as *sinngemäß* (corresponding, analogous). The latter implies that coinciding events are characterized at first by a formal similarity that may suggest an objective

relation between events. See Carl Gustav Jung, *Synchronicity: An Acausal Connecting Principle*, in *The Collected Works of C. G. Jung*, vol. 8, trans. R. F. C. Hull (Princeton, NJ: Princeton University Press, 2012), 22; and Wolfgang Giegerich, "A Serious Misunderstanding: Synchronicity and the Generation of Meaning," *Journal of Analytical Psychology* 57, no. 4 (2012): 501–2. See also "Synchronicity and Space-time Transgression in Film and Video," chapter 8 in Gregory Matthew Singh, *Film after Jung: Post-Jungian Approach es to Film Theory* (London: Routledge, 2009), 175–96.

53 Williams, *Encounters with Godard*, 78.

54 Godard used the very slow 1951 version by Bruno Walter and the New York Philharmonic. See Stenzl, *Jean-Luc Godard—Musicien*, 287–92. Godard's tendency to use music as a "floating signifier" is incipient in the *nouvelle vague* phase; see Giorgio Biancorosso, "Melodrama, Anti-Melodrama and Performance: Rereading *Le mépris*," in *Il Melodramma*, ed. Lucilla Albano and Elena Dagrada (Rome: Bulzoni, 2007), 282.

55 Deleuze and Guattari, *A Thousand Plateaus*, 319.

56 Deleuze and Guattari, *A Thousand Plateaus*, 185–86, 319.

57 Deleuze and Guattari, *A Thousand Plateaus*, 319, 548, quoting Proust, *The Captive*, vol. 3 of *Remembrance of Things Past*, trans. C. K. Scott Moncrief, Terence Kilmartin, and Andreas Mayor (New York: Random House, 1981), 156. Deleuze later notes how Pierre Boulez learned from Proust "the manner in which noises and sounds detach themselves from the characters, places, and names to which they are first attached in order to form autonomous 'motives' that ceaselessly transform themselves in time" and thus become "individuations without identity." Gilles Deleuze, "Boulez, Proust and Time: 'Occupying without Counting,'" *Angelaki: Journal of the Theoretical Humanities* 3, no. 2 (1998): 70.

58 Deleuze and Guattari, *A Thousand Plateaus*, 349.

59 Miriam Heywood, *Modernist Visions: Marcel Proust's 'À la recherche du temps perdu' and Jean-Luc Godard's 'Histoire(s) du cinéma'* (Oxford: Peter Lang, 2012), 153, 159.

60 Jean-Jacques Nattiez, *Proust as Musician* (Cambridge: Cambridge University Press, 1989), 61.

61 Heywood, *Modernist Visions*, 153, 166.

62 Heywood, *Modernist Visions*, 160.

63 Jean-Luc Douin, *Jean-Luc Godard* (Paris: Rivages, 1989), 98; translation from Williams, *Encounters with Godard*, 130.

64 Benjamin, *Selected Writings*, 2:510. See chapter 1.

65 Marcel Proust, *La prisonnière*, vol. 5 of *À la recherche du temps perdu* (Paris: Gallimard, 1961), 250; Heywood, *Modernist Visions*, 152.

CHAPTER FOUR

1 Gérard Genette, *Palimpsests: Literature in the Second Degree*, trans. Channa Newman and Claude Doublinsky (Lincoln: University of Nebraska Press, 1997), 156–57.

2 Serge Lacasse, "Intertextuality and Hypertextuality in Recorded Popular Music," in *The Musical Work: Reality or Invention?* ed. Michael Talbot (Liver-

pool: Liverpool University Press, 2000), 35–58. See also Andrew Horton and Stuart Y. McDougal, eds., *Play It Again, Sam: Retakes on Remakes* (Berkeley: University of California Press, 1998).

3 For an overview of these evolving uses of Samuel Barber's *Adagio*, see Julie McQuinn, "Listening Again to Barber's *Adagio for Strings* as Film Music," *American Music* 27, no. 4 (2009): 461–99.

4 While Allan wrote the screenplay for *Play It Again, Sam*, the film was actually directed by Herbert Ross.

5 Miriam Bratu Hansen, *Cinema and Experience: Siegfried Kracauer, Walter Benjamin, and Theodor W. Adorno* (Berkeley: University of California Press, 2012).

6 Hansen, *Cinema and Experience*, 150.

7 Richard Dyer, *Heavenly Bodies: Film Stars and Society*, 2nd ed. (London: Routledge, 2004), 2–3.

8 John Biguenet, "Double Takes: The Role of Allusion in Cinema," in Horton and McDougal, *Play It Again, Sam*, 131–43.

9 Umberto Eco, "'Casablanca': Cult Movies and Intertextual Collage," *Sub-Stance* 14, no. 2 (1985): 5.

10 Berthold Hoeckner, "Transport and Transportation in Audiovisual Memory," in *Beyond the Soundtrack: Representing Music in Cinema*, ed. Daniel Goldmark, Lawrence Kramer, and Richard D. Leppert (Berkeley: University of California Press, 2007), 168–73. Chapters 3 to 5 of David Neumeyer and James Buhler, *Meaning and Interpretation of Music in Cinema* (Bloomington: Indiana University Press, 2015), offer the most thorough and insightful analysis of Steiner's score for *Casablanca* to date.

11 Genette, *Palimpsests*, 158.

12 See Noah Isenberg, *We'll Always Have Casablanca: The Life, Legend, and Afterlife of Hollywood's Most Beloved Movie* (New York: Norton, 2017).

13 Siegfried Kracauer, "The Little Shopgirls Go to the Movies," in *The Mass Ornament: Weimar Essays*, trans. Thomas Y. Levin (Cambridge, MA: Harvard University Press, 1995), 291–306.

14 Hansen, *Cinema and Experience*, 59.

15 Woody Allen, *Three Films of Woody Allen* (New York: Vintage Books, 1987), 432–34. The contents page notes that "the italicized passages that describe the action have been provided by the publisher," but the dialogue appears to be transcribed from the film. Note that the description of the action includes what Cecilia does with the ukulele.

16 Hansen, *Cinema and Experience*, 147. See Walter Benjamin, "On the Mimetic Faculty," in *Selected Writings*, ed. Michael W. Jennings (Cambridge, MA: Belknap Press, 1996–2006), 2:720-22.

17 Hansen, *Cinema and Experience*, 88, 140.

18 Benjamin, *Selected Writings*, 3:127.

19 See Benjamin, *Selected Writings*, 4:264, 4:282; Hansen, *Cinema and Experience*, 93.

20 Hansen, *Cinema and Experience*, 164–65.

21 Benjamin, *Selected Writings*, 2:734–35.

22 Benjamin, *Selected Writings*, 3:119.

23 Benjamin, *Selected Writings*, 3:120.

24 Benjamin, *Selected Writings*, 3:112. Benjamin quotes Pirandello as invoked

by Léon Pierre-Quint, "Signifiation du Cinema," in *L'art cinématographique* (Paris: Librairie Félix Alcan, 1927), 14. The original passage stems from Pirandello's novel *Il gira: Quadernie die Serafino Gubbio operatore* (1915); see *The Notebooks of Serafino Guibbio, Cinematograph Operator*, trans. C. K. Scott Moncrieff (Chicago: University of Chicago Press, 2005), 68.

25 Benjamin, *Selected Writings*, 3:112.

26 Benjamin, *Selected Writings*, 3:113.

27 See also Hansen, *Cinema and Experience*, 106n4. Walter Benjamin, "Little History of Photography," in *Selected Writings*, 2:518 (a nearly identical version appears in the artwork essay, 3:104); Benjamin, "On Some Motifs in Baudelaire," in *Selected Writings*, 4:338.

28 See Hansen, *Cinema and Experience*, 124–25, on Benjamin's appropriation of this polarity from the philosopher and psychologist Ludwig Klages.

29 See Todd R. Decker, *Music Makes Me: Fred Astaire and Jazz* (Berkeley: University of California Press, 2011), 75: Berlin "built 'Cheek to Cheek' on an especially generous scale, one reason Astaire could shape the dance so directly on the song."

30 After the two quatrains of the opening section and the first quatrain of the B section, Allen connects to the transition that leads over the bridge to the pure dance portion in D major. Using only the first eight bars of the A section, he skips directly to the extended melodic anacrusis (C-D-E♭-F-G-A♭) that leads to the final return of the A section in E♭ major.

31 Hansen, *Cinema and Experience*, 166; Theodor W. Adorno, Henri Lonitz, and Walter Benjamin, *The Complete Correspondence, 1928–1940* (Cambridge, MA: Harvard University Press, 1999), 130.

32 Hansen sums up Adorno's stance this way: "In the dancers' relation to the music, this submission corresponds to a stubborn refusal to really dance the 'break' . . . the syncope which is jazz's futile assertion of difference." It is these very "breaks," she adds, that, in Adorno's own formulation, Mickey Mouse "alone translates . . . into precise visual equivalents." Hansen, *Cinema and Experience*, 166–67.

33 Hansen, *Cinema and Experience*, 162.

34 Transcription from *Sleepless in Seattle* DVD (Sony Pictures Home Entertainment, 2003). Cf. *Sleepless in Seattle*, screenplay by Jeff Arch, rewritten by Nora Ephron and Delia Ephron, May 10, 1992, accessed October 10, 2018, https://www.imsdb.com/scripts/Sleepless-in-Seattle.html.

35 Jeff Arch, interview with Matt Ryan, "Script to Screen" interview series, produced by DRTV, accessed October 10, 2018, ttps://www.youtube.com/watch?v=YY5kE5Nsepw.

36 *Sleepless in Seattle*, screenplay. These lines actually belong to the dialogue from the night before, and Ephron presents them out of order for greater effect, also cutting music from the film's original underscore to the words to heighten that effect. After Nickie says, "It's now or never," Terry responds "Never is a frightening word," and then—just as the melody enters—continues, "We'd be fools to let happiness pass us by." In *An Affair*, this portion of the dialogue was preceded by Terry's anxious line, "Winter must be cold for those with no warm memories," and was originally scored with the strikingly Tristanesque opening of Friedhofer's cue. This opening was not used in *Sleepless*, where Friedhofer's soft entry of Warren's melody

in the stings is used for all fragments from *An Affair*—even Nickie's suggestion to meet on the top of the Empire State Building (which has no music in the original).

37 Transcription from *Sleepless in Seattle* DVD.

38 James George Frazer, *The Golden Bough: A Study in Magic and Religion* (Oxford: Oxford University Press, 1998), 27.

39 Frazer, *Golden Bough*, 26. For a creative and provocative discussion of Frazer's idea of sympathetic magic, see Michael T. Taussig, *Mimesis and Alterity: A Particular History of the Senses* (New York: Routledge, 1993). See also Gary Tomlinson, *Music in Renaissance Magic: Toward a Historiography of Others* (Chicago: University of Chicago Press, 1993); and the persistence of beliefs in magic in contemporary discourse, Zachary John Loeffler "Speaking of magic: enchantment and disenchantment in music's modernist ordinary," (PhD diss., University of Chicago, 2018).

40 Michel Chion, "The Acousmêtre," in *The Voice in Cinema*, trans. Claudia Gorbman (New York: Columbia University Press, 1999), 23.

41 On *You've Got Mail*, see Dan Wang, "The Structure of Romantic Affect: Soundtracks and the Intimate Event," chap. 3 in "Scenes of Feeling: Music and the Imagination of the Liberal Subject" (PhD diss., University of Chicago, 2017), 114–79.

42 Terence Davies, too, had Cole's cover open his autobiographical *The Long Day Closes* (1992): here the camera slowly travels down a dilapidated rainy street (shot in black and white), and then makes a turn to traverse the threshold to his childhood house, dissolving to the past, shown in color, where a young boy sits on the stairs, calling out, "Mom, can I go to the pictures?" See Hoeckner, "Transport and Transportation," 175–82, for a discussion of similar strategies in Davies's *Distant Voices, Still Lives* (1988).

43 Eco, "'Casablanca,'" 5.

44 The song was also used by Aaron Copland to connect the two main protagonists in William Wyler's 1947 film, *The Heiress*, but it is most familiar today through Elvis Presley's "Can't Help Falling in Love."

45 Kerr was dubbed by Marni Nixon, whose voice expressed both modern flair and domestic warmth. See Elizabeth Hopkins, "Science Fiction, Lounge Music, and Mid-Century Domestic Utopia," unpublished paper, presented at the 2015 annual meeting of the American Musicological Society in Louisville, KY.

46 Wang, "Scenes of Feeling," 153.

47 For an analysis of the scene's soundtrack, see James Buhler and David Neumeyer, *Hearing the Movies: Music and Sound in Film History*, 2nd ed. (New York: Oxford University Press, 2015), 19–24.

48 Benjamin, "On the Mimetic Faculty," in *Selected Writings*, 2:721.

49 Hansen, *Cinema and Experience*, 147.

CHAPTER FIVE

1 S. A. Kinnier Wilson, *Modern Problems in Neurology* (London: Arnold, 1928), 55–57, 70–75. Wilson notes the similarity to near-death incidents from drowning.

2 For this and the other quotes in this paragraph, see Thomas De Quincey, *Confessions of an English Opium-Eater and Suspiria de Profundis* (Boston: Ticknor, Reed and Fields, 1851), 234–35. De Quincey refers here to an earlier passage from his *Confessions of an Opium Eater* (110–11), which he had first published anonymously in *London Magazine* 4 (1821): 273. "I was once told by a near relative of mine, that having in her childhood fallen into a river, and being on the very verge of death but for the critical assistance which reached her, she saw in a moment her whole life, in its minutest incidents, arrayed before her simultaneously as in a mirror; and she had a faculty developed as suddenly for comprehending the whole and every part."

3 Douwe Draaisma, "I Saw My Life Flash before Me," in *Why Life Speeds Up As You Get Older: How Memory Shapes Our Past*, trans. Arnold and Erica Pomerans (Cambridge: Cambridge University Press, 2004), 255–56.

4 Draaisma, "I Saw My Life Flash before Me," 257.

5 Maureen Turim, *Flashbacks in Film: Memory and History* (New York: Routledge, 1989), 2, 109.

6 James Chandler, *An Archaeology of Sympathy: The Sentimental Mode in Literature and Cinema* (Chicago: University of Chicago Press, 2013), 12.

7 Roger Brown and James Kulik, "Flashbulb Memories," *Cognition* 5, no. 1 (1977): 73–99. For a more recent overview and critique, see "Flashbulb Memories," in Alison Winter, *Memory: Fragments of a Modern History* (Chicago: University of Chicago Press, 2012), 157–78.

8 Draaisma, "I Saw My Life Flash before Me," 249, 263–64.

9 Robin Wood, "Ewig hin der Liebe Glück," in *Personal Views: Exploration in Film* (London: Gordon Fraser Gallery, 1976), 116–32 (reprinted in Virginia Wright Wexman, *Letter from an Unknown Woman* [New Brunswick, NJ: Rutgers University Press, 1986], 220–36); Stephen Heath, "The Question Oshima," *Wide Angle* 2, no. 1 (1978): 48–57; George Wilson, "Max Ophüls' *Letter from an Unknown Woman*," *MLN* 98, no. 5 (December 1983): 1121–42; Tania Modleski, "Time and Desire in the Woman's Film," *Cinema Journal* 23, no. 3 (Spring 1984): 19–30; Gaylyn Studlar, "Masochistic Performance and Female Subjectivity in 'Letter from an Unknown Woman.'" *Cinema Journal* 33, no. 3 (Spring 1994): 35–57; Karl Sierek, "Emblems of Modernism in the Early Films of Max Ophüls," *Arizona Quarterly* 60, no. 5 (2004): 211–22; Steve Neale, "Narration, Point of View, and Patterns in the Soundtrack of 'Letter from an Unknown Woman,'" in *Style and Meaning: Studies in the Detailed Analysis of Film*, ed. John Gibbs and Douglas Pye (Manchester: Manchester University Press 2005), 98–107; Laura Mulvey, "Max Ophüls's Auteurist Adaptations," in *True to the Spirit: Film Adaptation and the Question of Fidelity*, ed. Colin MacCabe, Rick Warner, and Kathleen Murray (Oxford: Oxford University Press, 2011), 75–89; Pansy Duncan, "Tears, Melodrama and 'Heterosensibility' in *Letter from an Unknown Woman*," *Screen* 52, no. 2 (2011): 173–92; Laura Mulvey, "Love, History, and Max Ophüls: Repetition and Difference in Three Films of Doomed Romance," *Film & History* 43, no. 1 (2013): 7–29.

10 Susan M. White, *The Cinema of Max Ophüls: Magisterial Vision and the Figure of Woman* (New York: Columbia University Press, 1995); Lutz Bacher, *Max Ophüls in the Hollywood Studios* (New Brunswick, NJ: Rutgers University Press, 1996).

11 Heather Laing, *The Gendered Score: Music in 1940s Melodrama and the Woman's Film* (Aldershot: Ashgate, 2007), 67–98. See also Alexander Dhoest, "Ophüls Conducting: Music and Musicality in *Letter from an Unknown Woman*," *Senses of Cinema* 28 (October 2003).

12 Turim, *Flashbacks in Film*, 69–74, discusses early examples of "obsessive memory," such as Louis Delluc's *Silence*—a tradition that persists in contemporary examples, notably Michel Gondry's *Eternal Sunshine of the Spotless Mind* (2004) and Spike Jonze's *Her* (2013).

13 Bacher, *Max Ophüls in the Hollywood Studios*, 194.

14 Tony Pipolo, "The Aptness of Terminology: Point of View, Consciousness and *Letter from an Unknown Woman*," *Film Reader* 4 (1979): 166–79; Robin Wood, "Letter from an Unknown Woman: The Double Narrative," *cineACTION* 31 (1993): 5; Edward Branigan, *Narrative Comprehension and Film* (New York: Routledge, 1992), 177–90.

15 Wood, "Ewig hin der Liebe Glück," 231.

16 Wexman, *Letter from an Unknown Woman*, 136.

17 Here I differ from the prevailing view of Lisa. See, among others, Wood, "Ewig hin der Liebe Glück," 231, and Wilson, "Ophüls' *Letter from an Unknown Woman*," 1123–24. Immensely useful has been Guido Heldt, "The Conceptual Toolkit: Music and Levels of Narration," chap. 2 in *Music and Levels of Narration in Film: Steps across the Border* (Bristol: Intellect, 2013), 57–69, in particular Heldt's discussion of the homodiegetic narrator—a term adopted from Genette. For other flexible and productive conceptions of the blurred line between diegetic and nondiegetic music, see Robynn J. Stilwell, "The Fantastical Gap between Diegetic and Non-Diegetic," in *Beyond the Soundtrack: Representing Music in Cinema*, ed. Daniel Goldmark, Lawrence Kramer, and Richard D. Leppert (Berkeley: University of California Press, 2007), 184–202; Ben Winters, "The Non-Diegetic Fallacy: Film, Music, and Narrative Space," *Music & Letters* 91, no. 2 (2010): 224–44; Daniel Yacavone, "Spaces, Gaps, and Levels: From the Diegetic to the Aesthetic in Film Theory," *Music, Sound, and the Moving Image* 6, no. 1 (2012): 21–37; and Nick Davis, "Inside/Outside the Klein Bottle: Music in Narrative Film, Intrusive and Integral," *Music, Sound, and the Moving Image* 6, no. 1 (2012): 9–19.

18 Here it is useful to consult Koch's Final Shooting Script (see Bacher, *Max Ophüls in the Hollywood Studios*, 334), which reinforces the visual connection by specifying that this last photo was to be from a concession stand Stefan and Lisa had visited in the Prater. See Howard Koch Papers, *Wisconsin Center for Film & Theater Research*, box 2, *Letter from an Unknown Woman*, Final Shooting Script, 82.

19 Wexman, *Letter from an Unknown Woman*, 131.

20 Stefan Zweig, *The Royal Game, Amok, Letter from an Unknown Woman* (New York: Viking Press, 1944), 187. See also Bacher, *Max Ophüls in the Hollywood Studios*, 188.

21 Laing, *Gendered Score*, 83.

22 Wexman, *Letter from an Unknown Woman*, 41.

23 Wexman, *Letter from an Unknown Woman*, 87.

24 Bacher, *Max Ophüls in the Hollywood Studios*, 190.

25 *Letter from an Unknown Woman*, Final Shooting Script, 16.

26 *Letter from an Unknown Woman*, Final Shooting Script, 16. After Stefan says, "Thanks so much," the screenplay notes, "Almost as quickly as he appeared, he moves toward the front entrance and out of the SHOT. Lisa is left speechless and breathless. Marie, who has appeared from behind Lisa, has absorbed the whole encounter and its effect on her friend."

27 *Letter from an Unknown Woman*, Final Shooting Script, 17; Wexman, *Letter from an Unknown Woman*, 142. This portion is missing in the final film.

28 Wexman, *Letter from an Unknown Woman*, 73 (shot information omitted). The Final Shooting Script already went to considerable lengths to describe the musicians, noting that they were to play a "sentimental Viennese song." (49)

29 For an extensive analysis of the Linz sequence, see Victor F. Perkins, "Letter from an Unknown Woman," *Movie* 29/30 (Summer 1982): 61–72.

30 White, *Cinema of Max Ophüls*, 193, notes the unusual avoidance of Mozart's German original as a sign of the exiled Jewish director seeking to suppress his mother tongue. See also Wexman, "The Transfiguration of History: Ophüls, Vienna, and *Letter from an Unknown Woman*," in *Letter from an Unknown Woman*, 12.

31 Jerrold Levinson, "Film Music and Narrative Agency," in *Post-Theory: Reconstructing Film Studies*, ed. David Bordwell and Noel Carroll (Madison: University of Wisconsin Press, 1996), 248–82. For a nuanced critique and on the idea of "unlikely coincidence" of source music, see Heldt, *Music and Levels of Narration*, 77–89.

32 Already described this way in *Letter from an Unknown Woman*, Final Shooting Script, which specifies: "An ORCHESTRA plays softly OFF SCENE." (55)

33 Wexman, *Letter from an Unknown Woman*, 79 (shot information omitted)

34 *Letter from an Unknown Woman*, Final Shooting Script, 59.

35 Chandler, *Archaeology of Sympathy*, 198–99.

36 While the final version of the film has considerably more music for the Prater scene, the Final Shooting Script does specify that the dance music from the Pavilion can be heard, "OFF SCENE," in various spatial constellations, first from a distance, then "more clearly" and "very faintly" from the train. See *Letter from an Unknown Woman*, Final Shooting Script, 63–64. For the Venice trip, the "appropriate music" was to be "O sole mio." (69)

37 Quoted in Ursula Storch, *Die Welt in Reichweite. Imaginäre Reisen im 19. Jahrhundert* (Vienna: Czernin Verlag 2009),89. A photo of the train concession from Vienna to Constantinople—circa 1930—can be found in Ursula Storch, *Zauber Der Ferne: Imaginäre Reisen Im 19. Jahrhundert*, Ausstellung Des Wien Museums (Weitra: Verlag Bibliothek der Provinz, 2008), 159.

38 Wexman, *Letter from an Unknown Woman*, 128, 149.

39 Stanley Cavell, "Psychoanalysis and Cinema: Moments of *Letter from an Unknown Woman*," in *Contesting Tears: The Hollywood Melodrama of the Unknown Woman* (Chicago: University of Chicago Press, 1996), 108.

40 Wexman, *Letter from an Unknown Woman*, 95–97 (shot information omitted).

41 *Letter from an Unknown Woman*, Final Shooting Script, 108.

42 See Kaja Silverman, *The Acoustic Mirror: The Female Voice in Psychoanalysis and Cinema* (Bloomington: Indiana University Press, 1988), 57–58.

43 Wexman, *Letter from an Unknown Woman*, 89.

44 Miriam Bratu Hansen, *Cinema and Experience: Siegfried Kracauer, Walter*

Benjamin, and Theodor W. Adorno (Berkeley: University of California Press, 2012), 112.

45 Cavell, *Contesting Tears*, 81 (emphasis in original).

46 Cavell, *Contesting Tears*, 105.

47 Modleski, "Time and Desire in the Woman's Film," 20, 26.

48 Stanley Cavell, "Postscript (1989): To Whom it May Concern," *Critical Inquiry* 16, no. 2 (1990): 275.

49 Cavell, *Contesting Tears*, 111.

50 Cavell, *Contesting Tears*, 81, 108; Cavell, "Postscript," 275.

51 Cavell, "Postscript," 267.

52 Wexman, *Letter from an Unknown Woman*, 124, 129.

53 *Letter from an Unknown Woman*, Final Shooting Script, 125–26.

54 Wexman, *Letter from an Unknown Woman*, 134.

55 *Letter from an Unknown Woman*, Final Shooting Script, 126–27.

56 Bacher, *Max Ophüls in the Hollywood Studios*, 190.

57 Cavell, "Postscript," 265.

58 Cavell, "Postscript," 280.

59 Bacher, *Max Ophüls in the Hollywood Studios*, 194.

60 Bacher, *Max Ophüls in the Hollywood Studios*, 190.

61 Cavell, "Postscript," 265.

62 *Letter from an Unknown Woman*, Final Shooting Script, 127.

63 *Letter from an Unknown Woman*, Final Shooting Script, 127.

64 Mulvey, "Love, History, and Max Ophüls," 28–29.

65 Mulvey, "Love, History, and Max Ophüls," 29.

66 Wexman, *Letter from an Unknown Woman*, 111–12 (shot information omitted).

67 *Letter from an Unknown Woman*, Final Shooting Script, 116.

68 Bacher, *Max Ophüls in the Hollywood Studios*, 166–67.

CHAPTER SIX

1 Sigmund Freud and Nandor Fodor, *Freud: Dictionary of Psychoanalysis* (New York: Philosophical Library, 1950), 75, taken from Freud's *Psycho-Analytic Notes upon an Autobiographical Account of a Case of Paranoia*.

2 See in Sigmund Freud, *A General Introduction to Psychoanalysis*, part 3, "General Theory of the Neurosis," chap. 18, "Traumatic Fixation—The Unconscious" (New York: Boni and Liveright, 1920), 236 (emphasis in original).

3 Freud, *General Introduction*, 237–38.

4 Mary Ann Doane, *The Desire to Desire: The Woman's Film of the 1940s* (Bloomington: Indiana University Press, 1987), 21.

5 Doane, *Desire to Desire*, 37.

6 Thomas Elsaesser, "Freud and the Technical Media: The Enduring Magic of the Wunderblock," in *Media Archaeology: Approaches, Applications, and Implications*, ed. Erkki Huhtamo and Jussi Parikka (Berkeley: University of California Press, 2011), 100. See also Thomas Elsaesser, "Freud as Media Theorist," *Screen* 50, no. 1 (2009): 100–113; Thomas Elsaesser, "The New Film History as Media Archaeology," *Cinémas: Revue d'études cinématographiques* 14, nos. 2–3 (2004): 75–117.

7 Sigmund Freud, "The Mystic Writing Pad," in *The Standard Edition of the Complete Psychological Works of Sigmund Freud*, vol. 19, ed. and trans. James Strachey (London: Hogarth Press, 1955), 228.

8 Freud, "Mystic Writing Pad," 230.

9 Freud, "Mystic Writing Pad," 230–31 (translation modified).

10 Elsaesser, "Freud and the Technical Media," 109.

11 Elsaesser, "Freud and the Technical Media," 110 (emphasis added).

12 Janet Bergstrom, "Alternation, Segmentation, Hypnosis: Interview with Raymond Bellour," *Camera Obscura* 1–2, no. 3 (1979): 101.

13 *The Seventh Veil*, Third Script, 16 (British Film Institute Archives, Muriel and Sydney Box Collection, Fonds–N-37231 ITM-2342).

14 Freud, "Mystic Writing Pad," 232.

15 Sydney Box, *The Lion That Lost Its Way and Other Cautionary Tales of the Show Business Jungle*, ed. Andrew Spicer (Lanham, MD: Scarecrow Press, 2005), 49. In early 1940, Box had founded Verity Films to produce propaganda films for the British government and other agencies. See Andrew Spicer, *Sydney Box* (Manchester: Manchester University Press, 2006), 18 and 51.

16 William Brown, Charles Myers, and William McDougall, "The Revival of Emotional Memories and Its Therapeutic Value," *British Journal of Medical Psychology* 1, nos. 20–22 (1920):16–33. See also Ruth Leys, *Trauma: A Genealogy* (Chicago: University of Chicago Press, 2000), 83–87.

17 Leys, *Trauma*, 199. See John Stephen Horsley, *Narco-Analysis, a New Technique in Short-Cut Psychotherapy: A Comparison with Other Methods, and Notes on the Barbituates*. (London: Oxford University Press/H. Milford, 1943). For an overview on the treatment of war trauma, see Alison Winter, *Memory: Fragments of a Modern History* (Chicago: University of Chicago Press, 2013), 53–73.

18 Leys, *Trauma*, 87. See also Janice Haaken, "The Seventh Veil: Feminism, Recovered Memory, and the Politics of the Unconscious," in *Memory: Histories, Theories, Debates*, ed. Susannah Radstone and Bill Schwarz (New York: Fordham University Press, 2010), 428–41. For the larger cultural history of the memory wars, see Alison Winter, *Memory: Fragments of a Modern History* (Chicago: University of Chicago Press, 2012), 225–55, and Ian Hacking, *Rewriting the Soul: Multiple Personality and the Sciences of Memory* (Princeton, NJ: Princeton University Press, 1995).

19 Abram Kardiner, *The Traumatic Neuroses of War* (Washington, DC: National Research Council, 1941), 87.

20 Kardiner, *Traumatic Neuroses*, 88 (emphasis added).

21 Sándor Ferenczi, "Psycho-Analytical Observations on Tic [1921]," in *Further Contributions to the Theory and Technique of Psycho-analysis* (New York: Boni and Liveright, 1927), 156. See Leys, *Trauma*, 149.

22 Leys, *Trauma*, 8.

23 Leys, *Trauma*, 9.

24 Tony Williams, *Structures of Desire: British Cinema, 1939–1955* (Albany: State University of New York Press, 2000), 49.

25 Williams, *Structures of Desire*, 49.

26 Williams, *Structures of Desire*, 50, points to such contemporary manuals as *Living Together Again*, as discussed in Raynes Minns, *Bombers and Mash: The Domestic Front, 1939–45* (London: Virago, 1980), 187–200.

27 *The Seventh Veil*, Third Script, 17–19.

28 Freud, *Introductory Lectures on Psycho-Analysis*, in *The Standard Edition of the Complete Psychological Works of Sigmund Freud*, vol. 14, ed. and trans. James Strachey (London: Hogarth Press, 1955), 442–43.

29 Muriel Box and Sydney Box, *The Seventh Veil; a Play in Three Acts* (London: Rylee, 1952), 53.

30 Spicer, *Sydney Box*, 53; *The Seventh Veil*, Third Script, 78–79.

31 Box and Box, *The Seventh Veil,* 60–61. In the film, Beethoven's Adagio overlaps with the dialogue, so the moment where Francesca stopped is not as exposed.

32 Ann Todd, *The Eighth Veil* (New York: Putnam, 1981), 19–20. Alan Wood, *Mr. Rank: A Study of J. Arthur Rank and British Films* (London: Hodder and Stoughton, 1952), 151–52: "It was remarkable in that the final ending was decided by a card vote taken at sneak previews; the script was so written that Ann Todd could have married any one, or none, of three men; but audiences, showing a sound knowledge of psychology, were empathic that she was bound to fall for James Mason, the one who had treated her worst."

33 Box and Box, *The Seventh Veil*, 61.

34 Anton Kaes, *Shell Shock Cinema: Weimar Culture and the Wounds of War* (Princeton, NJ: Princeton University Press, 2009).

35 See Fred H. Frankel, "The Concept of Flashbacks in Historical Perspective," *Journal of Clinical and Experimental Hypnosis* 42, no. 4 (1994): 326. Note the evolution of the use of the term in the *Diagnostic and Statistical Manual of Mental Disorders*, published by the American Psychiatric Association: *DSM*-III (1987) refers to instances of "sudden acting or feeling as if the traumatic event were recurring (includes a sense of reliving the experience, illusions, hallucinations, and dissociative [flashback] episodes, even those that occur upon awakening or when intoxicated)" (250). *DSM*-IV (1994) has the same phrase but drops the brackets around "flashback" (428). In *DSM*-V (2013), the term is the only one specified: "Dissociative reactions (e.g., flashbacks) in which the individual feels or acts as if the traumatic event(s) were recurring" (271). While *DSM*-IV adds a note stating that in "young children trauma-specific reenactment may occur," *DSM*-V specifies in this note that with children under six years old, such reenactment may occur "in play."

36 See Kaes, *Shell Shock Cinema*, 49; Ernst Simmel, *Kriegs-Neurosen und "Psychisches Trauma": Ihre Gegenseitigen Beziehungen Dargestellt Auf Grund Psycho-Analytischer, Hypnotischer Studien* (Leipzig: Otto Nemnich Verlag, 1918), 25.

37 Simmel, *Kriegs-Neurosen*, 27.

38 Mark Herman and Jim Cartwright, *Little Voice* (London: Methuen Film, 1999).

39 Herman and Cartwright, *Little Voice*, 57.

40 Christian Metz, *The Imaginary Signifier: Psychoanalysis and the Cinema*, trans. Celia Britton (Bloomington: Indiana University Press, 1982), 67 (emphasis in original).

41 Theodor W. Adorno, "On the Fetish-Character in Music and the Regression of Listening," in *Essays on Music*, ed. Richard Leppert, trans. Susan H. Gillespie (Berkeley: University of California Press, 2002), 312.

42 See Miriam Bratu Hansen, *Cinema and Experience: Siegfried Kracauer, Walter Benjamin, and Theodor W. Adorno* (Berkeley: University of California Press,

2012), 190; Walter Benjamin, *Selected Writings*, ed. Michael W. Jennings (Cambridge, MA: Belknap Press, 1996–2006), 3:127.

43 Adorno, "On the Fetish-Character," 307.

44 Metz, *Imaginary Signifier*, 70.

45 Adorno, "On the Fetish-Character," 308–9.

46 Adorno, "On the Fetish-Character," 312.

47 Hansen, *Cinema and Experience*, 195.

48 Herman and Cartwright, *Little Voice*, 83.

49 Herman and Cartwright, *Little Voice*, 83–84.

50 Herman and Cartwright, *Little Voice*, 84–85.

51 Hansen, *Cinema and Experience*, 147.

52 Greil Marcus, "Old Songs in New Skins," in *Da Capo Best Music Writing 2000*, ed. Peter Guralnick (New York: Da Capo Press, 2000), 374.

53 Herman and Cartwright, *Little Voice*, 94.

CHAPTER SEVEN

1 Berthold Hoeckner et al., "Film Music Influences How Viewers Relate to Movie Characters," *Psychology of Aesthetics, Creativity, and the Arts* 5, no. 2 (2011): 1–8.

2 Sara Ahmed, *The Cultural Politics of Emotion* (Edinburgh: Edinburgh University Press, 2014), 9.

3 Ahmed, *Cultural Politics of Emotion*, 14 (emphasis added).

4 Ahmed, *Cultural Politics of Emotion*, 13.

5 Ahmed, *Cultural Politics of Emotion*, 18n13; Carolyn Abbate, "Music: Drastic or Gnostic," *Critical Inquiry* 30, no. 3 (2004): 523.

6 Niklas Luhmann, *Vertrauen; Ein Mechanismus Der Reduktion Sozialer Komplexität* (Stuttgart: Enke, 1968), 37–57, 21–29, 85; Niklas Luhmann, *Trust and Power: Two Works* (New York: Wiley, 1979), 39–60, 24–31, 84.

7 See J. David Lewis and Andrew Weigert, "Trust as a Social Reality," *Social Forces* 63, no. 4 (1985): 974, 970.

8 Anthony Giddens, *The Consequences of Modernity* (Stanford, CA: Stanford University Press, 1990), 79.

9 Giddens, *Consequences of Modernity*, 80.

10 Giddens, *Consequences of Modernity*, 83–88.

11 Erik Erikson, *Childhood and Society* (New York: Norton, 1963), 247–51.

12 The social psychologist Julian Rotter defined trust as "a generalized expectancy held by an individual that the word, promise, oral or written statement of another individual or group can be relied on." Julian B. Rotter, "Interpersonal Trust, Trustworthiness, and Gullibility," *American Psychologist* 35, no. 1 (1980): 1. The General Social Survey, which has tracked generalized trust for over four decades in the United States, shows a decline between 1972 and 2014 from 46 percent to 30 percent. See http://www.gss.norc.org/, data extracted on November 29, 2016; and Sandra Susan Smith, "Race and Trust," *Annual Review of Sociology* 36 (2010): 455, 463.

13 Robert D. Putnam, *Bowling Alone: The Collapse and Revival of American Community* (New York: Simon & Schuster2000), 140. While the phenomenon is observable in Australia, France, and Britain, other counties, like

Sweden, the Netherlands, Japan, and Canada have seen increases in trust. See Laura Nishikawa and Dietland Stolle, "Do Not Trust Strangers: How Parents Shape the Generalized Trust of Their Children," in *Trust: Comparative Perspectives*, ed. Masamichi Sasaki and Robert M. Marsh (Leiden: Brill, 2012), 133–34; Eric M. Uslaner, *Segregation and Mistrust: Diversity, Isolation, and Social Cohesion* (Cambridge: Cambridge University Press, 2012).

14 Giddens, *Consequences of Modernity*, 92, 97–98.

15 John Bowlby, *Attachment and Loss* (London: Hogarth Press/Institute of Psycho-Analysis, 1969–1973); John Bowlby, *The Making and Breaking of Affectional Bonds* (London: Tavistock, 1979); Mary D. Salter Ainsworth et al., *Patterns of Attachment: A Psychological Study of the Strange Situation* (London: Routledge, 2015).

16 Luhmann, *Vertrauen*, 81; Luhmann, *Trust and Power*, 81; Giddens, *Consequences of Modernity*, 92.

17 Guido Möllering, "The Nature of Trust: From Georg Simmel to a Theory of Expectation, Interpretation and Suspension," *Sociology* 35 (2001): 412, 416; Guido Möllering, *Trust: Reason, Routine, Reflexivity* (Amsterdam: Elsevier, 2006), 105–21. See also William James et al., *The Will to Believe and Other Essays in Popular Philosophy* (Cambridge, MA: Harvard University Press, 1979).

18 Lewis and Weigert, "Trust as a Social Reality," 972.

19 Stephan Alexander Rompf, *Trust and Rationality: An Integrative Framework for Trust Research* (Wiesbaden: Springer VS, 2015), 56–63, 76–77.

20 Before the sentence "But first and foremost, I remember Mama," the following lines had been cut from the script for the final version of the film: "Besides us, there was our boarder, Mr. Hyde. Mr. Hyde was an Englishman who had once been an actor, and Mama was very impressed by his flowery talk and courtly manners. He used to read aloud to us in the evenings." DeWitt Bodeen, *I Remember Mama*, Estimating Script, December 9, 1946, 2, UCLA Special Collections (RKO Studio Records, Boxes 959S and 960S). While DeWitt Bodeen, a script writer at RKO, had produced an adaptation of Forbes's episodic book after its publication in 1943, van Druten's successful Broadway adaptation in 1944–1946 (with Marlon Brando making his debut) led to a revised screenplay in 1946 that followed the play's tight structure and its new title.

21 Ahmed, *Cultural Politics of Emotion*, 44–45.

22 The former is about a single Norwegian holding up a whole Swedish army, while the latter is sung by Queen Margrethe to her little son Håkon in Ibsen's *Kongsemnerne*. Edward Grieg had set "Nu løftes Laft og Lofte" as the first of four songs published as op. 15, but Webb composed or used a different melody for the film. (It is announced in the underscore during the dissolve to the hospital scene.)

23 *I Remember Mama*, Estimating Script, 75. Dagmar's mention of being "worried" in the film is not in the script, but it matters later when Marta says, "It is not good for little ones to be afraid . . . to not feel secure" (148).

24 "Søvnens engler" ("The Angels of Sleep"), by the Norwegian poet Bjørnstjerne Bjørnson (1832–1910). "Sövnen" is the second song of Kjerulf op. 14.

25 Notes for the music, sound, and dubbing during postproduction indicate that the "full string section comes in at finish of lullaby sequence" (November 20, 1947); that the underscore should start "on the last note of

the humming—the Nurse returns to the Ward. She falls asleep and Mama leaves—dissolve to Katrin in her Room (November 20, 1947), that Stevens "wants music under Mama's song" (February 3, 1948); and that the music initially was "too loud" when the nurse enters (February 20, 1948). George Stevens Papers, box 227.f–2652, Margaret Herrick Library, Academy of Motion Picture Arts and Sciences.

26 Cue M75A (originally M82), "Lullaby," UCLA Special Collections (RKO Collection, box 799, folder 19), including score, parts, and conductor score. Originally only the last measure of the lullaby was to be replaced by the "celestial" extension.

27 Michael Hardt, "Affective Labor," *Boundary* 2 (1999): 96. See also Michael Hardt and Antonio Negri, *Empire* (Cambridge, MA: Harvard University Press, 2000), 289–94 ("The Sociology of Immaterial Labor").

28 Hardt, "Affective Labor," 96. Ruth A. Solie, "'Girling' at the Piano," in *Music in Other Words: Victorian Conversations* (Berkeley: University of California Press, 2004), 100.

29 Brian Massumi, *Parables for the Virtual: Movement, Affect, Sensation* (Durham, NC: Duke University Press, 2002), 28.

30 Massumi, *Parables for the Virtual*, 34–39. Although Massumi has been variously criticized for reinstating a mind-body dualism, his description of the relationship between affect and emotion has some validity. See Ruth Leys, "The Turn to Affect: A Critique," *Critical Inquiry* 37, no. 3 (2011): 434–72; Margaret Wetherell, *Affect and Emotion: A New Social Science Understanding* (London: SAGE, 2012), 62–67.

31 Gerald L. Clore and Andrew Ortony, "Appraisal Theories: How Cognition Shapes Affect into Emotion," in *Handbook of Emotions*, ed. Michael Lewis, Jeannette M. Haviland-Jones, and Lisa Feldman Barrett (New York: Guilford Press, 2008), 633. Joseph E. LeDoux, *The Emotional Brain: The Mysterious Underpinnings of Emotional Life* (New York: Simon & Schuster, 1996), 249.

32 *I Remember Mama*, Estimating Script, 122.

33 The music notes from postproduction suggest that "have Roy Webb catch melodies Uncle Chris sings in the hospital" (October 18, 1947) and the notes on the Preview suggest that Webb was not only "to do something over [Marta's] 'farvell Uncle Chris,'" but also mention the "New Trumpets" after Mama's and Uncle Chris's "Skoal" (February 20, 1948). George Stevens Papers, box 227.f–2652, Margaret Herrick Library, Academy of Motion Picture Arts and Sciences. The additional three muted trumpets can be found on separate sheets for Cue M:121A, which is part of the music for the film that is preserved in the UCLA Special Collections (RKO Studio Records, Box 402M).

34 *I Remember Mama*, Estimating Script, 126.

35 *I Remember Mama*, Estimating Script, 127.

36 Not in the Estimating Script, this return to Katrin was apparently an afterthought.

37 In the breakdown of preview comments from February 10, 1948, the hospital scenes were liked best, a staggering 143 times, with the death scene following at 37. On February 28, the numbers were 212 and 60, respectively. George Stevens Papers, box 227.f–2654, Margaret Herrick Library, Academy of Motion Picture Arts and Sciences.

38 *I Remember Mama*, Estimating Script, 148.

39 Text transcribed from the final version of the film. Cf. *I Remember Mama*, Estimating Script, 1–2, 151–52.

40 "Improvise lullaby music for Katrin reading story," music notes (February 3, 1948). George Stevens Papers, box 227.f–2652, Margaret Herrick Library, Academy of Motion Picture Arts and Sciences.

41 Text transcribed from the final version of the film. Cf. *I Remember Mama*, Estimating Script, 1–2, 151–52.

42 According to Joanna Rapf, the film rejected consumer culture but embraced capitalism. See Joanna Rapf, "1948 Movies and the Family, " in Wheeler W. Dixon, *American Cinema of the 1940s: Themes and Variations* (New Brunswick, NJ: Rutgers University Press, 2006), 215–16.

43 See Barbara A. Misztal, *Trust in Modern Societies: The Search for the Bases of Social Order* (Cambridge: Polity Press, 1996), 73–77. System trust is built on the belief that others also trust—something Luhmann called "trust in trust" (see Luhmann, *Trust and Power*, 66–70).

44 Tom Gunning, "The Cinema of Attractions: Early Film, Its Spectator and the Avant-Garde," in *Early Cinema: Space, Frame, Narrative*, ed. Thomas Elsaesser and Adam Barker (London: BFI, 1990), 56–62.

45 *I Remember Mama*, Estimating Script, 150: "The group around the table is now a duplicate of the grouping around Mr. Hyde when it had been his wont to read, only now Katrin is in his place as the reader."

46 Chandler, *Archaeology of Sympathy*, 1–36.

47 Horton Foote, *To Kill a Mockingbird*, Final Screenplay, February 8, 1962 (Los Angeles: Script Collectors Service [1962]), 146.

48 Kevin Donnelly, *The Spectre of Sound: Music in Film and Television* (London: BFI, 2005), 21.

49 Charles J. Shields, *Mockingbird: A Portrait of Harper Lee, from Scout to "Go Set a Watchman"* (New York: Henry Holt, 2016), 175.

50 Harper Lee, *Go Set a Watchman* (New York: Harper Collins Publishers, 2015).

51 Katherine Henninger, "'My Childhood Is Ruined!' Harper Lee and Racial Innocence," *American Literature* 88, no. 3 (2016): 598; Robin Bernstein, *Racial Innocence: Performing American Childhood from Slavery to Civil Rights* (New York: New York University Press, 2011).

52 Lee, *Watchman*, 108 (emphasis in original).

53 Lee, *Watchman*, 109.

54 Lee, *Watchman*, 113.

55 Lee, *Mockingbird*, 33.

56 Henninger, "My Childhood Is Ruined!," 605.

57 Quoted by Kevin Mulhall in Elmer Bernstein, *To Kill a Mockingbird*, Varèse Sarabande VSC 5754, 1997, compact disc, liner notes.

58 Bernstein, *To Kill a Mockingbird*, liner notes.

59 For a useful first take on the title sequence as it appears in the film, see James Buhler, David Neumeyer, and Rob Deemer, *Hearing the Movies: Music and Sound in Film History*, 1st ed. (Oxford: Oxford University Press, 2010), 172–75.

60 "Tree Treasure" (cue 6B) begins earlier, when Jem and Scout discover the two soap dolls in the tree hole. Bernstein revised the cue for the part when

Mr. Radley closes the hole with cement, creating an insert (measure numbers A–U) that replaced measures 13–33 with less threatening music. The harp arpeggio starts measure 59 of the original cue.

61 See the interview with David Spear in Ron Sadoff, "Elmer Bernstein's Orchestrators," *Music and the Moving Image* 6, no. 3 (2013): 43.

62 A sense of mystery comes with the nondiegetic ticking of the broken pocket watch, which also recurs within the music of "Tree Treasure." The ticking seems to give voice to the passing of time—almost calling forth the "Remember Mama" theme in both cases.

63 See Henninger, "'My Childhood Is Ruined!'," 612.

64 Lee, *Watchman*, 159–60.

65 Adam Gopnik, "Sweet Home Alabama: Harper Lee's 'Go Set a Watchman,'" *New Yorker* 91, no. 21 (July 27, 2015): 71.

66 Lee, *Watchman*, 161.

67 Lee, *Mockingbird*, 138.

68 Lee, *Mockingbird*, 143.

69 For a broad and detailed overview of such stereotypes, see Donald Bogle, *Toms, Coons, Mulattoes, Mammies, and Bucks: An Interpretive History of Blacks in American Films* (New York: Bloomsbury, 2016).

70 Barton Palmer, *Harper Lee's To Kill a Mockingbird: The Relationship between Text and Film* (London: Methuen Drama, 2008), 137.

71 "Ewell's Hatred" (5C) is a multisection cue preceded by measures 5–15 from the cue "Atticus Accepts the Case" (2D–3A), which was likely so named because its first four measures (not used in the film) were to accompany the end of Atticus's conversation with Judge Taylor, who had asked him to serve as Tom Robinson's defense lawyer. The Coplandesque jauntiness of the remainder of the cue is evocative of children's play and returns in various places of the score. Since "Atticus Accepts the Case" runs on into the cue "Roll in the Tire" (3B), recordings that combine both cues omit these first four measures. Running into "Ewell's Hatred," the ten measures from "Atticus Accepts the Case" accompany the children's general excitement when Atticus drives off after having shot a rabid dog near his house, and then the scene dissolves to him driving to the Robinsons that evening. As I will note later, the omission of the first four measures from "Atticus Accepts the Case," as well as the entire cue "Crack Shot" (5B) from the rabid dog scene (which originally came later in the screenplay), serves to tone down Atticus's musical characterization as "heroic."

72 Wilfrid H. Mellers, "American Music (an English Perspective)," *Kenyon Review* 5, no. 3 (1943): 370–71.

73 Donald C. Meyer, "Music Cue Archetypes in the Film Scores of Elmer Bernstein," *Journal of Film Music* 5, nos. 1–2 (2012): 160–61.

74 Lee, *Mockingbird*, 124.

75 Neil Lerner, "Copland's Music of Wide Open Spaces: Surveying the Pastoral Trope in Hollywood," *Musical Quarterly* 85, no. 3 (2001): 502–3. See Mellers, "American Music," 370.

76 "I don't understand this approach"; "the result is mild and flat"; "Atticus was tamed down considerably." Cutting notes to George Chasin, June 18, 1962. "This scene [Atticus guarding jail] should go to Atticus. . . . Mulligan perhaps bending over backwards to avoid having Atticus do anything

heroic." Note to Mel Tucker, July 6, 1962. Gregory Peck Papers (70.f–689), Margaret Herrick Library, Academy of Motion Picture Arts and Sciences.

77 The filmmakers must have felt that this moment made for an effective dramatic subdivision because they eliminated the next shot, which was to show Atticus getting Scout ready for bed. Dropping that shot also meant deleting the next segment of the cue, which recapitulated the "Remember Mama" theme to accompany Atticus's motherly care. Other passages that were cut include the chorale-like phrase in the strings ("Jem's Discovery," measures 20–23), which is marked "strong" in the score and would have served for Atticus's departure with Calpurnia, and measures 24–30, which are more "spooky," with a rocking accordion figure and the imitation of a bird call. The remainder of the cue, starting with muted strings in measure 31, was left intact.

78 Lee, *Mockingbird*, 238.

79 Foote, Final Screenplay, 123.

80 Rachel Watson, "The View from the Porch: Race and the Limits of Empathy in the Film To Kill a Mockingbird," *Mississippi Quarterly* 63, nos. 3/4 (2010): 438.

81 Adam Smith, *The Theory of Moral Sentiments* (Cambridge: Cambridge University Press, 2002), 27. See Watson, "View from the Porch," 439.

82 Jodi Melamed, *Represent and Destroy: Rationalizing Violence in the New Racial Capitalism* (Minneapolis: University of Minnesota Press, 2011), 23–24.

83 Fred Hobson, *But Now I See: The White Southern Racial Conversion Narrative* (Baton Rouge: Louisiana State University Press, 1999), 2. See also Gregory Jay, "Queer Children and Representative Men: Harper Lee, Racial Liberalism, and the Dilemma of *To Kill a Mockingbird*," *American Literary History* 27, no. 3 (2015): 490, 500–501.

84 On this point, see Henninger, "My Childhood Is Ruined!," 618.

85 Horton Foote, letter to Alan Pakula and Robert Mulligan (March 28, 1962), Alan Pakula Papers, Script Notes 1962 (115.f–791), Margaret Herrick Library, Academy of Motion Picture Arts and Sciences.

86 Michael Thorpe, "'Mockingbird' Interlocks Illusions and Prejudice," *Daily Trojan*, January 4, 1963, Gregory Peck Papers, Reviews 1962–63 (71.f–699), Margaret Herrick Library, Academy of Motion Picture Arts and Sciences.

87 Foote replaced "boy" with "man." See Lee, *Mockingbird*, 316: "There's a black boy dead for no reason." Foote, Final Screenplay, 143.

88 Lee, *Mockingbird*, 317, 103.

89 Lee, *Mockingbird*, 233.

90 Lee, *Mockingbird*, 58–60.

91 Foote, Final Screenplay, 11; see Lee, *Mockingbird*, 13–15.

92 Sigmund Freud, "The 'Uncanny,'" in *The Standard Edition of the Complete Psychological Works of Sigmund Freud*, vol. 17 (1917–1919), *An Infantile Neurosis and Other Works* (London: Hogarth Press, 1955), 224, 226.

93 Freud, "Uncanny," 226.

94 Freud, "Uncanny," 225, 241.

95 Lee, *Mockingbird*, 310.

96 Lee, *Mockingbird*, 219.

97 Holly Virginia Blackford, *Mockingbird Passing: Closeted Traditions and Sexual Curiosities in Harper Lee's Novel* (Knoxville: University of Tennessee Press,

2011), 214–16. See George E. Haggerty, *Queer Gothic* (Urbana: University of Illinois Press, 2006); Paulina Palmer, *The Queer Uncanny: New Perspectives on the Gothic* (Cardiff: University of Wales Press, 2012).

98 Lee, *Mockingbird*, 163.

99 Lee, *Mockingbird*, 8. On *Dracula*, see also Blackford, *Mockingbird Passing*, 214–16.

100 Blackford, *Mockingbird Passing*, 34.

101 Lee, *Mockingbird*, 75, 77. See Blackford, *Mockingbird Passing*, 30–31; Gerald Early, "The Madness in the American Haunted House: The New Southern Gothic, and the Young Adult Novel of the 1960s: A Personal Reflection," in *On Harper Lee: Essays and Reflections*, ed. Alice Hall Petry, (Knoxville: University of Tennessee Press, 2007), 93–104.

102 See Jay, "Queer Children and Representative Men," 512; see also Blackford, *Mockingbird Passing*, 228.

103 Blackford, *Mockingbird Passing*, 210. Gavin Butt, *Between You and Me: Queer Disclosures in the New York Art World, 1948–1963* (Durham, NC: Duke University Press, 2005), 26, describes "a culture in which homosexuality was brought into discourse as an object of epistemological *doubt*; in which it was discursively constituted, by turns, as being both everywhere and nowhere."

104 Lee, *Mockingbird*, 61. The screenplay replaces Boo's brother with Boo's father, who in the novel is already dead.

105 Lee, *Mockingbird*, 62.

106 Lee, *Mockingbird*, 143.

107 Donnelly, *Spectre of Sound*, 21.

108 Blackford, *Mockingbird Passing*, 257–59. On monsters and homosexuality, see Harry M. Benshoff, *Monsters in the Closet: Homosexuality and the Horror Film* (Manchester: Manchester University Press, 1997), and Palmer, *Queer Uncanny*, 152–87.

109 Lee, *Mockingbird*, 67.

110 Lee, *Mockingbird*, 278.

111 These are measures 13–19 of "Jem's Discovery" (5D–6A), right after Calpurnia looks at Jem on the porch, and they are nearly identical to measures 1–6 of "Remember Mama" shifted down from D major to D♭ major. This brief scene was later cut, along with the music.

112 Lee, *Mockingbird*, 321: "Autumn again, and Boo's children needed him."

113 Foote, Final Screenplay, 145–46; cf. Lee, *Mockingbird*, 320–23.

114 Lee, *Mockingbird*, 285. In the final version of her voiceover, the Ewells were cut from this group of outcasts, even though Scout had been sympathetic to the motherless Mayella Ewell, noting that she "must have been the loneliest person in the world. She was even lonelier than Boo Radley, who had not been out of the house in twenty-five years" (218).

CODA

1 Stanley Cavell, *The World Viewed: Reflections on the Ontology of Film* (Cambridge, MA: Harvard University Press, 1971), 10.

Index